THE PAINTED SEASONS

A YEAR IN THE LIFE OF THE BRITISH COUNTRYSIDE

DICK TWINNEY

The fauna and flora of the British Isles is vividly brought to life in the original paintings of wildlife artist and illustrator Dick Twinney.

The Painted Seasons is presented as an illustrated diary of week-by-week, month-by-month life in the countryside as time passes through the seasons of the year.

Each evocative painting is complemented by an informative, sometimes anecdotal, commentary: we are encouraged to be aware of the seasonal changes and above all, to respect the vulnerability of the natural environment and the creatures and plants which eke out a tenuous existence within its bounds.

The detailed paintings which comprise *The Painted Seasons* are the creation of an artist whose whole life revolves around the natural world. His home is sanctuary to a menagerie of creatures, some of them maimed through injury, who have inspired many favourite studies. Beyond these boundaries Dick Twinney is blessed with great good fortune, for the variety and beauty of the North Cornwall landscape and its wildlife are this artist's inexhaustible supply of raw material.

This beautiful book is a delightful record of the secret world that exists among the hedgerows, moorland and coastline of Britain. Dick Twinney has combined a great artistic talent with a dedicated affinity for the preservation of nature and its habitats to create something quite special.

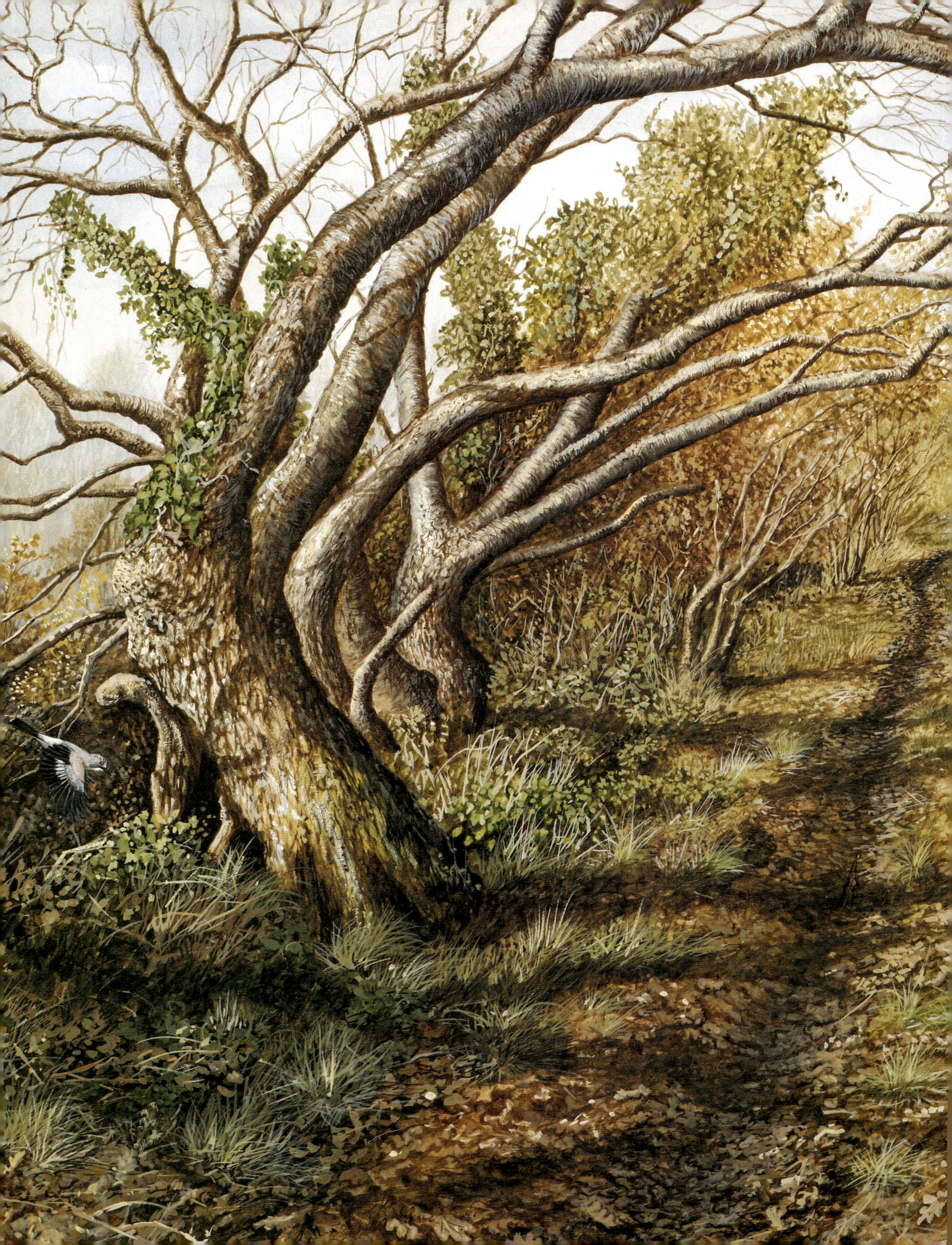

THE PAINTED SEASONS

A YEAR IN THE LIFE OF THE BRITISH COUNTRYSIDE

DICK TWINNEY

For Shaila,
Best Wishes,
DICK TWINNEY

TREVOYAN

For Bryony, who was not around for the first and second editions
but who now shares my wildlife world. Love Grandad.

This edition published by TREVOYAN in 2005.
Trevoyan Farm,
St Merryn, Padstow,
Cornwall, PL28 8PP
Great Britain.

ISBN 0-9549867-0-9

Originally published by Webb & Bower (Publishers) Limited in1990.
Reprinted in 1993.

Designed by Vic Giolitto.

Printed and bound in China.

CONTENTS

INTRODUCTION

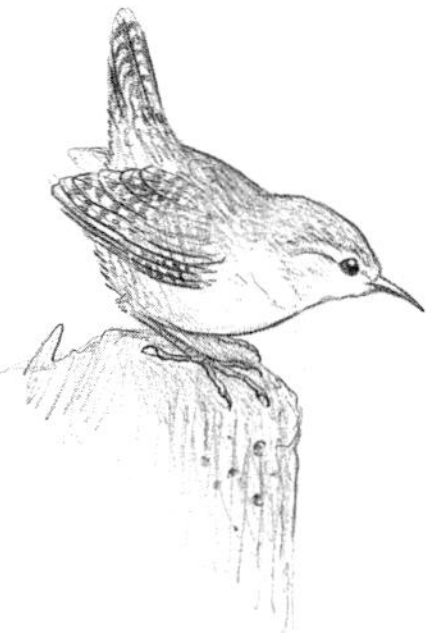

Although the paintings in this book are the culmination of nearly five years' work, they really represent a lifetime's love of wildlife and the countryside.

For as long as I can remember I have been fascinated by animals and the natural world. This is due in some part to spending my formative years in the small Devonshire town of Teignmouth, an area of outstanding natural beauty and variety. The town has a tidal river on one side, green meadows and mixed woodland reaching up to open moors on the other; it faces the open sea, with freshwater lakes within cycling distance and the magic of Dartmoor behind.

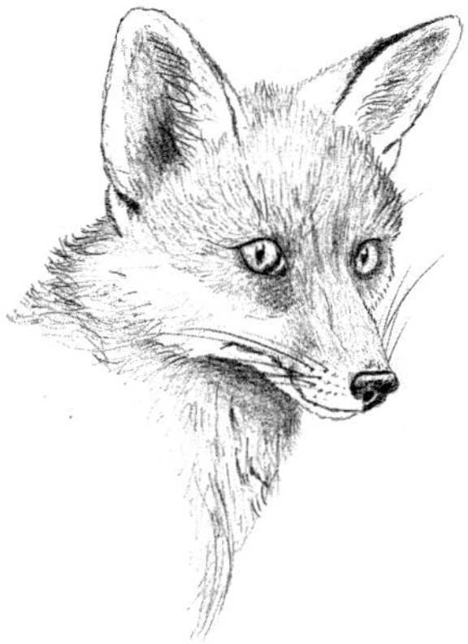

Not being particularly interested in sport I channelled all that youthful enthusiasm into discovering the natural world. While my friends were involved in such after-school activities as football and cricket, I would be crawling through the long grass looking for voles, watching waders on the river, or hunting for emperor moth caterpillars on the moor.

Having inherited a natural ability to draw from my father who was a skilled carpenter of the 'old school', a real craftsman, I was soon combining the two loves of my life, art and nature, no doubt to the detriment of other school subjects in which I had no interest and therefore achieved poor exam results. This lack of academic qualification, with no chance of further education, ruled out a career in the veterinary or zoological professions. I did have the option, however, to attend art college but a career in art then was considered far too risky and not a 'proper job'.

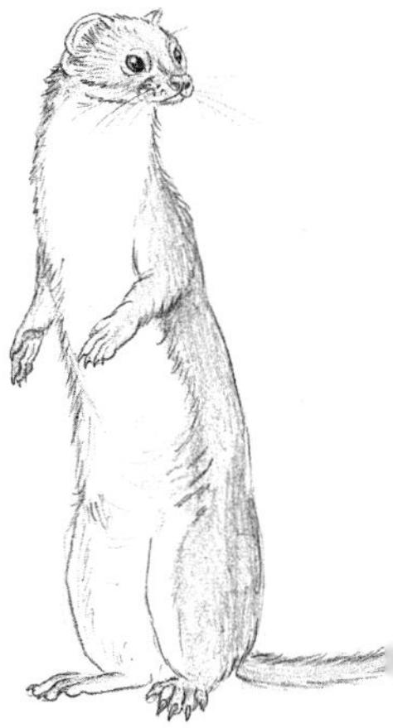

So, at fifteen, I left school and, following in my father's wartime footsteps, joined the Royal Air Force as an aircraft fitter. The next fourteen years I progressed through the service, still drawing and painting for pleasure in a very amateur way, occasionally selling the odd picture for a few pints. I still maintained my keen interest in natural history, particularly when serving in Borneo as a helicoptor crewman where I had the unique opportunity to study the great variety of plants and animals of the rain forest. I even had my own pet monkey!

When I returned from overseas I met my wife Ann, who was brought up in the Welsh countryside and fortunately shared my interest in and love of animals. We married in 1966 and soon acquired our first 'rescued' dog. We spent the next few years in Lincolnshire and eventually came back to the West Country, thanks to a posting to RAF St Mawgan in Cornwall.

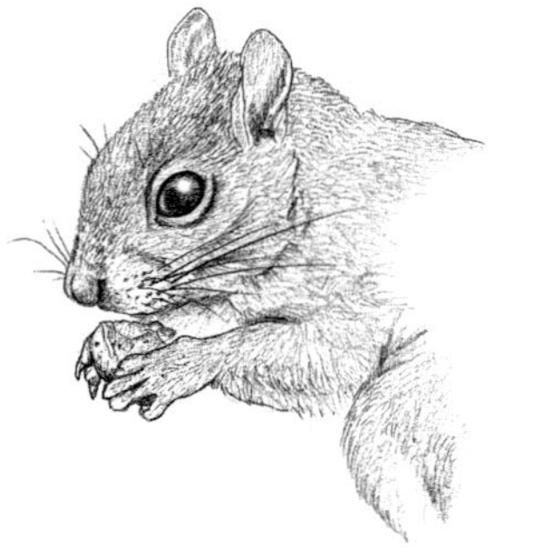

During the period I served at St Mawgan I became interested in, as a part-time hobby, the old Cornish craft of slate engraving. This together with a unique form of engraving on metal which I developed, proved to be very popular. Such was the interest in my work I left the RAF in 1973 and embarked on a career as a professional artist. When I look back on those early years I wonder how we ever survived. A meagre income had to support a mortgage, an ever-growing family of animals, plus our two children, Garrick and Jodene, born in 1974 and 1979 respectively. I was still engraving, selling my work on a market stall in Truro's Pannier Market. By this time I was also painting local scenes, engine houses and Cornish shipwrecks and, of course, wildlife. Gradually the painting took precedence over the engraving. I knew that my future lay in developing my skills as a wildlife artist.

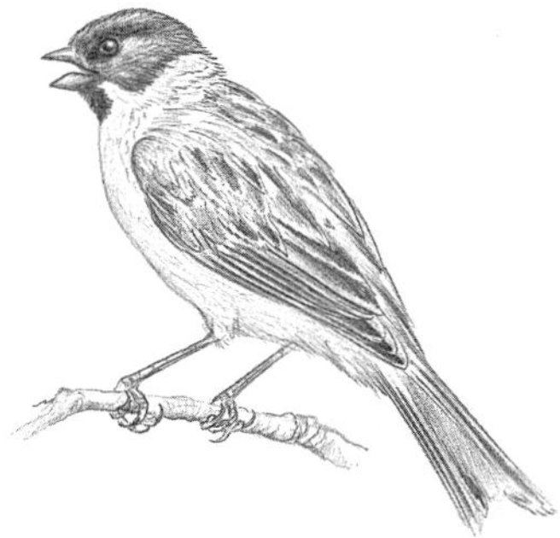

As I concentrated on developing my own technique I studied the paintings of Archibald Thorburn, Robert Bateman and Raymond Ching, the three artists whose work I most admired. Being completely self-taught, I had no preconceived ideas of either style or technique. But I recognized the amazing detail in Ching's work, the composition and imagination of Bateman and Thorburn's brilliant use of light. I always try to emulate the specific skills of these three great artists in my paintings.

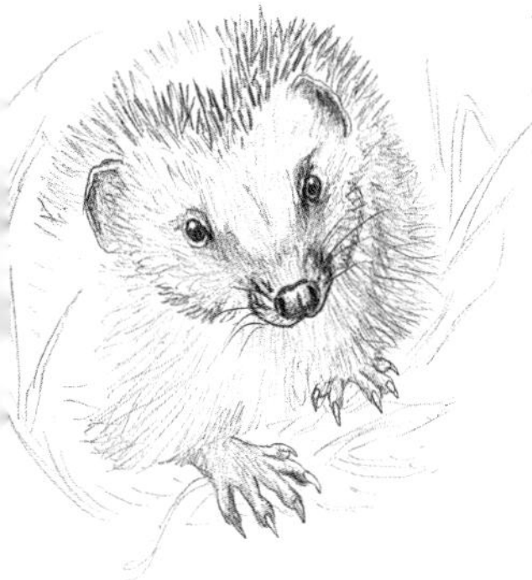

When I paint I try to use every possible form of reference. This might include dead specimens, video film, photographs, field sketches and, of course, live models when possible. Foliage and plants are all painted from life in my studio, where I often reconstruct hedgerow scenes. I realize that my highly detailed style is somewhat frowned upon by many of today's art critics, but I really enjoy my work and have gained immense personal pleasure from every stamen, whisker, feather and spider's web I have painted in the sixty-eight paintings that comprise this book.

The Painted Seasons has been a labour of love, shared closely with my family, including our dogs and other animals, who have all been involved in one way or another. Ann with her typing skills, the sorting out of my terrible spelling and the constant supply of cups of coffee, Garrick and Jodene helping me collect specimens and accompanying me on walks, together with our dogs. Our other animals played their part as models and provided much needed inspiration, many of them appearing in the forthcoming pages.

This is not a serious natural history book as such – I leave that task to those better qualified – but the main message I hope to impart through my work is most definitely serious. My aim is to stress the tremendous importance of habitat. Even the smallest field corner supports a great variety of life, very often the start of the food chain. There is no point in the captive breeding of otters and barn owls if they have nowhere to go when released. We are all acutely aware of the decline of many species of mammals and birds; but it is essential that we also realize that every new housing development, industrial estate and bypass, while helping in the so-called progress of mankind, is also hastening the decline of the animal world through loss of habitat.

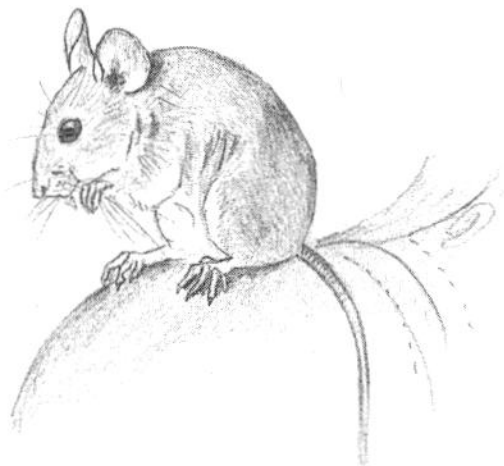

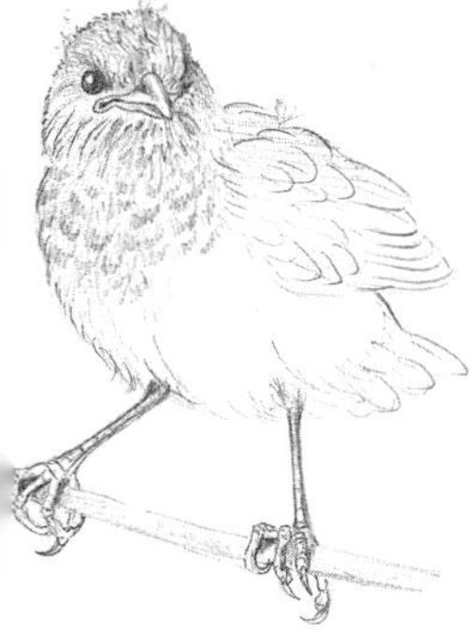

DICK TWINNEY
ST COLUMB 1989

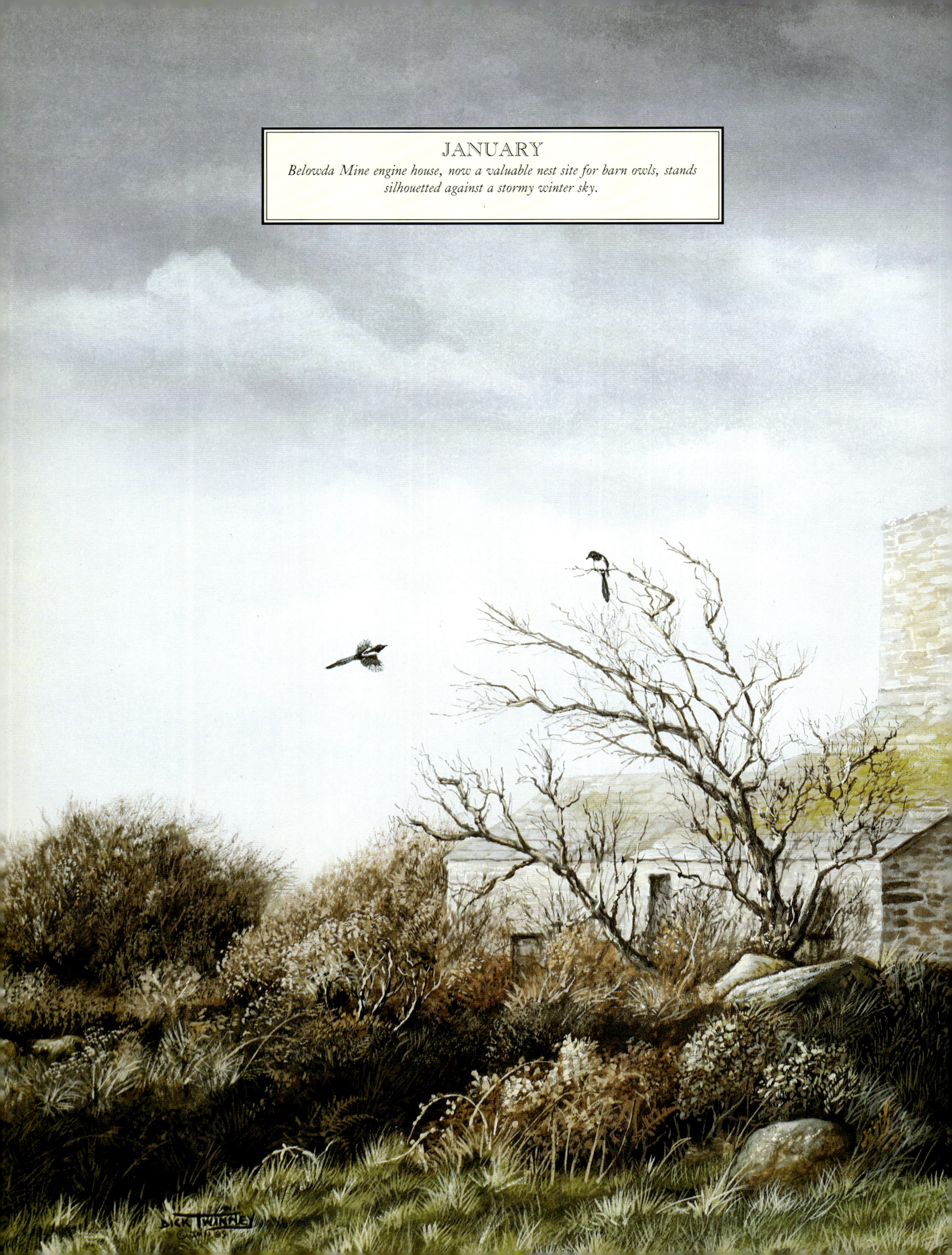

JANUARY

Belowda Mine engine house, now a valuable nest site for barn owls, stands silhouetted against a stormy winter sky.

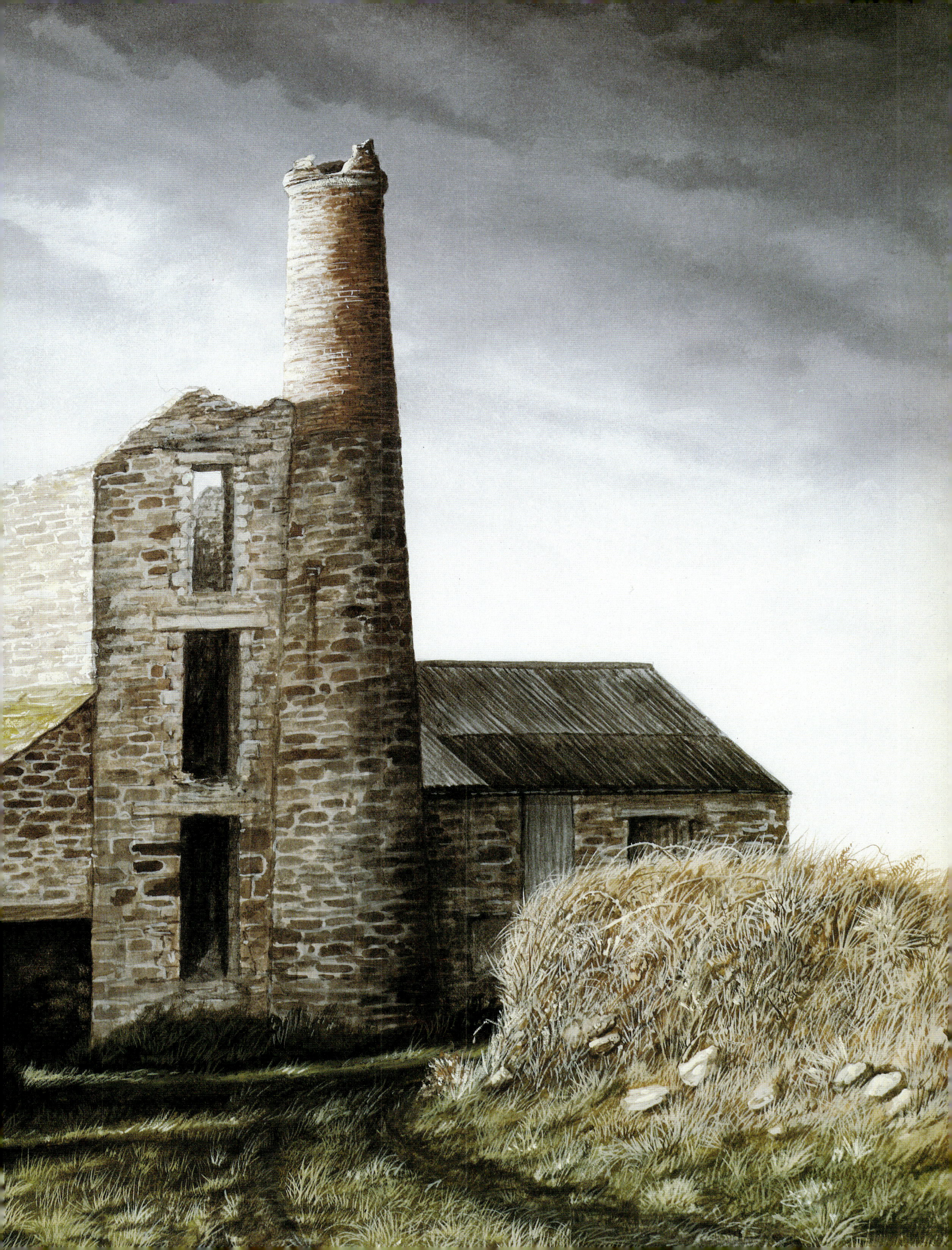

FIRST WEEK

LITTLE OWL

Although not common where I live in North Cornwall, the little owl can sometimes be seen sitting motionless on a telegraph pole or fence post, surveying the surrounding countryside with fierce yellow eyes. It is not a bird which draws attention to itself, being of small size with greyish-brown speckled plumage. It is easily missed as it sits immobile.

They often have a favourite perch to which they will return time and time again, as in the case of the bird I have portrayed for January. We saw this particular owl on several occasions on our winter trips to one of the local beaches, its regular observation post being a stone jutting out of a roadside hedge. It was a good vantage point, giving the owl unrestricted views across the surrounding fields and scrubland.

Little owls are often seen during the day, their main hunting period being dawn or dusk. Dor-beetles and cockchafers form an important part of the owl's diet during spring and summer but at this time of the year they will eat worms, slugs and mice.

The little owl is not a true native of Britain. It was introduced around a hundred years ago to Kent, where it soon settled. From there it has spread over most of the British Isles, including recently throughout Cornwall and parts of Scotland.

After an initial honeymoon period in this country the little owl soon became the target of gamekeepers who claimed they were killing game-bird chicks. A great many little owls were killed before an inquiry into their feeding habits discovered that although they did occasionally take chicks, their main food source of slugs, snails and other pests makes the little owl beneficial to man.

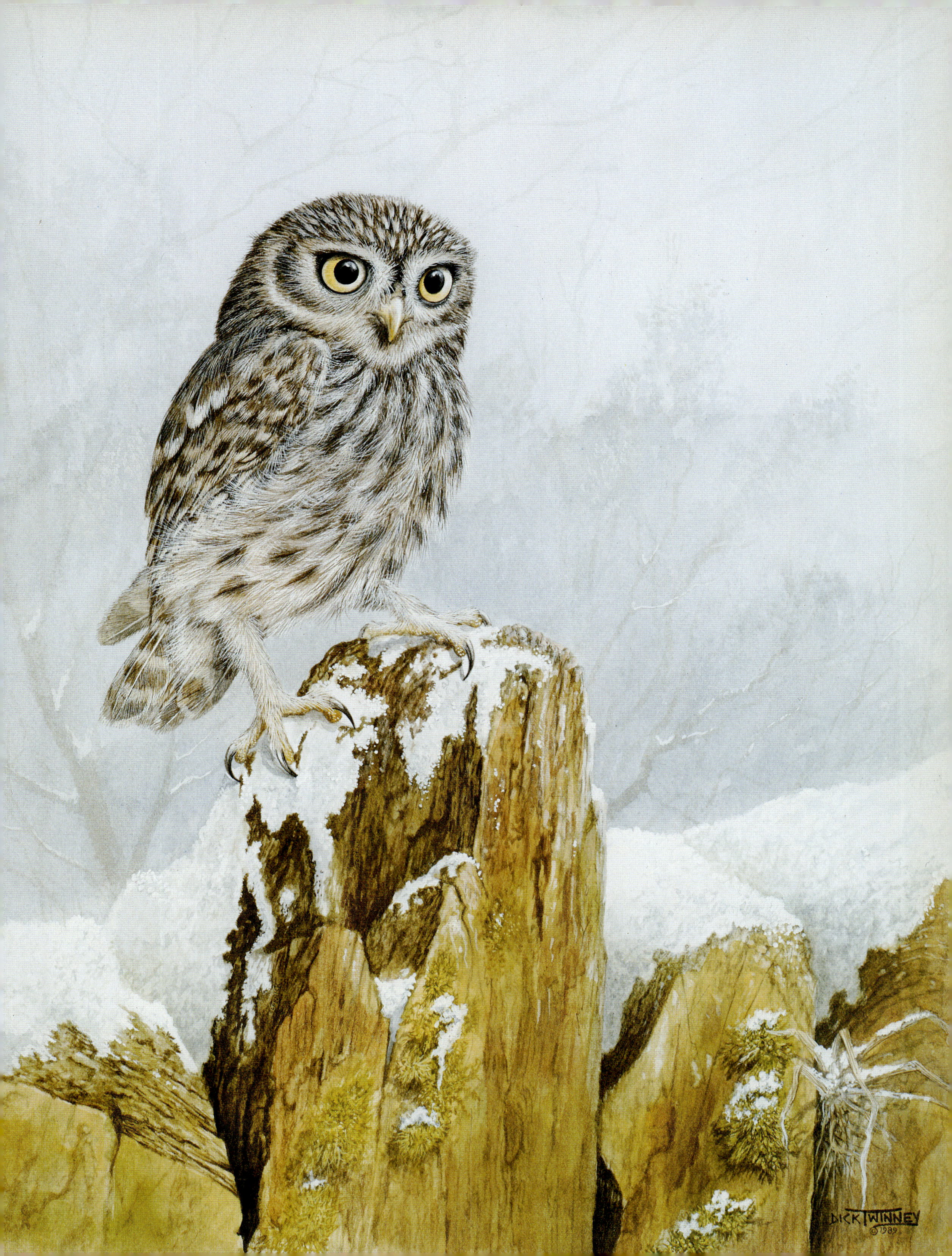
DICK TWINNEY
© 1989

SECOND WEEK

BULLFINCH

Outside my studio window is a rather overgrown cotoneaster shrub, intertwined with a mass of honeysuckle whose berries, along with those of the cotoneaster, provide valuable food supplies for the birds in harsh weather.

Every year we are visited by a pair of bullfinches (possibly not the same pair, but I like to think so). They always seem to arrive in January, usually when the weather is at its wintery worst and always after the cotoneaster, and most of the honeysuckle, has long been stripped by the thrushes.

This year the first of the winter's snow was with us, the sky dark with the promise of more to come, as the small soft flakes drifted downwards gradually covering the garden with a blanket of white. The bullfinches arrived with a flourish, scattering the powdered snow from the branches, their beautiful plumage standing out crisply against the white and grey background.

The honeysuckle berries had dried up so it was the seeds within that the bullfinches were after. They fed energetically for around half an hour, giving me plenty of time to observe them closely and draw some preliminary sketches. In fact they came every day at various times for a week, until every last seed had gone.

Given their meticulous feeding methods it is easy to see how destructive these birds can be to farmers and gardeners. But for the artist they make a truly beautiful subject, particularly the male with his more striking plumage. Long may they continue to return!

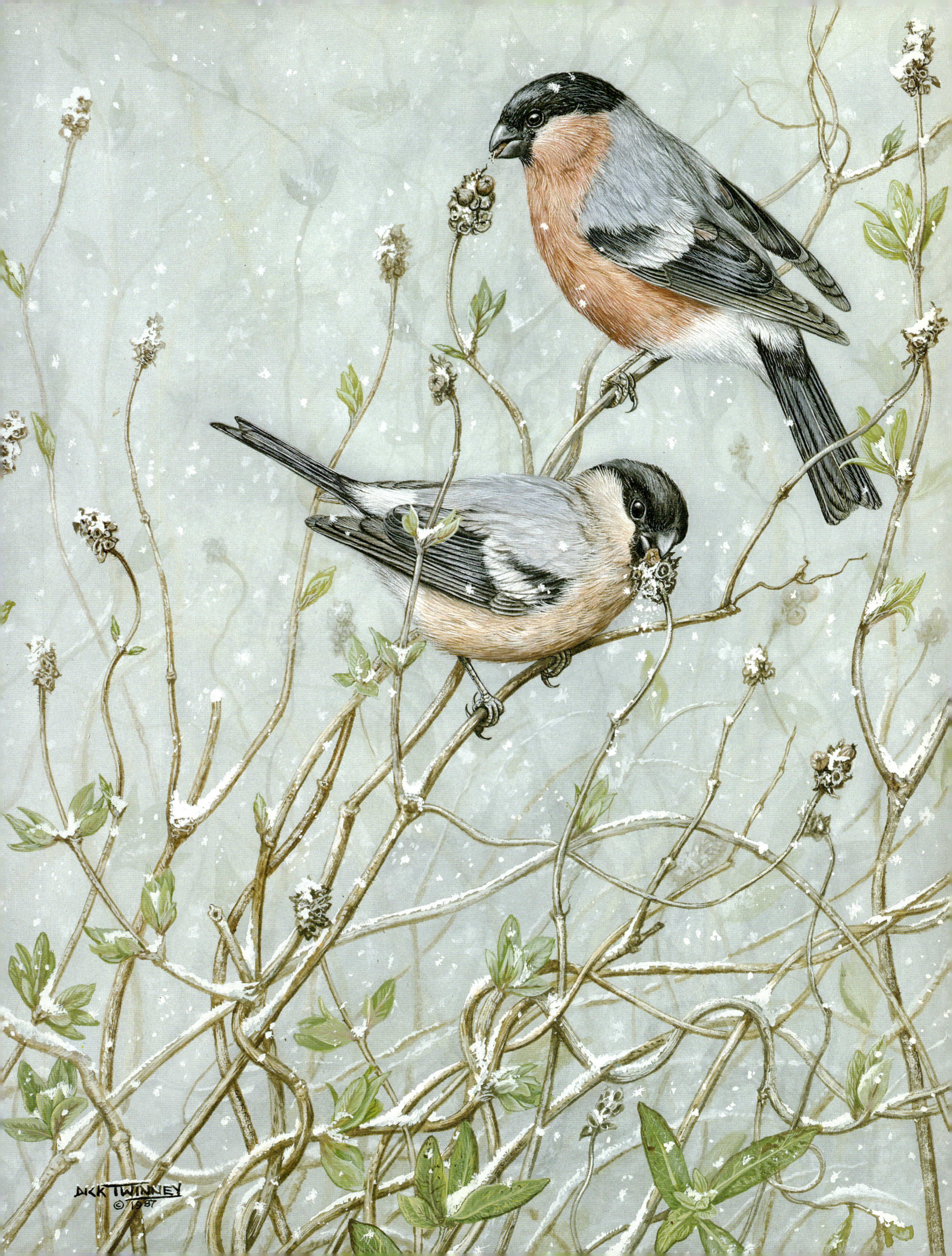
DICK TWINNEY
© 1987

Third Week

RABBITS IN THE DUNES

Rocky peninsulas and towering awe-inspiring cliffs usually spring to mind when first thinking of the north coast of Cornwall. However, there are also many miles of marram-grass covered sand-dunes. These provide a completely different habitat for many specialist plants such as the sea rocket, sea sandwort, spurges and sea bindweeds.

The dunes are also the favoured haunt of many mammals and birds, the most ubiquitous of these being the rabbit. In near optimum conditions the rabbit has flourished: burrows are easily excavated in the sandy soil; there is a plentiful supply of grasses as a food source; and limited persecution by man as most dunes are on National Trust property so shooting is generally prohibited.

Although rabbits can be a great pest to farmers, foresters and gardeners, there are few more charming and amusing sights than rabbits at their evening feeding and play sessions. They are forever on the go, chasing each other, sometimes fighting. Unlike many other wild animals, providing you keep still, they will tolerate the close proximity of humans, particularly rabbits which have made their homes in the dunes behind popular and busy beaches and have become used to people.

For the subject of this painting I have chosen a most familiar sight on winter's evening walks across the dunes. The rabbits have been disturbed by our dogs and have shot back to the safety of their burrows, where they will assess the extent of the danger, disappearing underground should the threat be real.

At this time of year the vegetation lies dormant, the thick mat of mosses and grasses, together with a network of fine roots, holding the loose sandy soil in position. The contrasting colours of various shades of green will, as the weeks advance, be interspersed with early spring flowers such as primroses and violets.

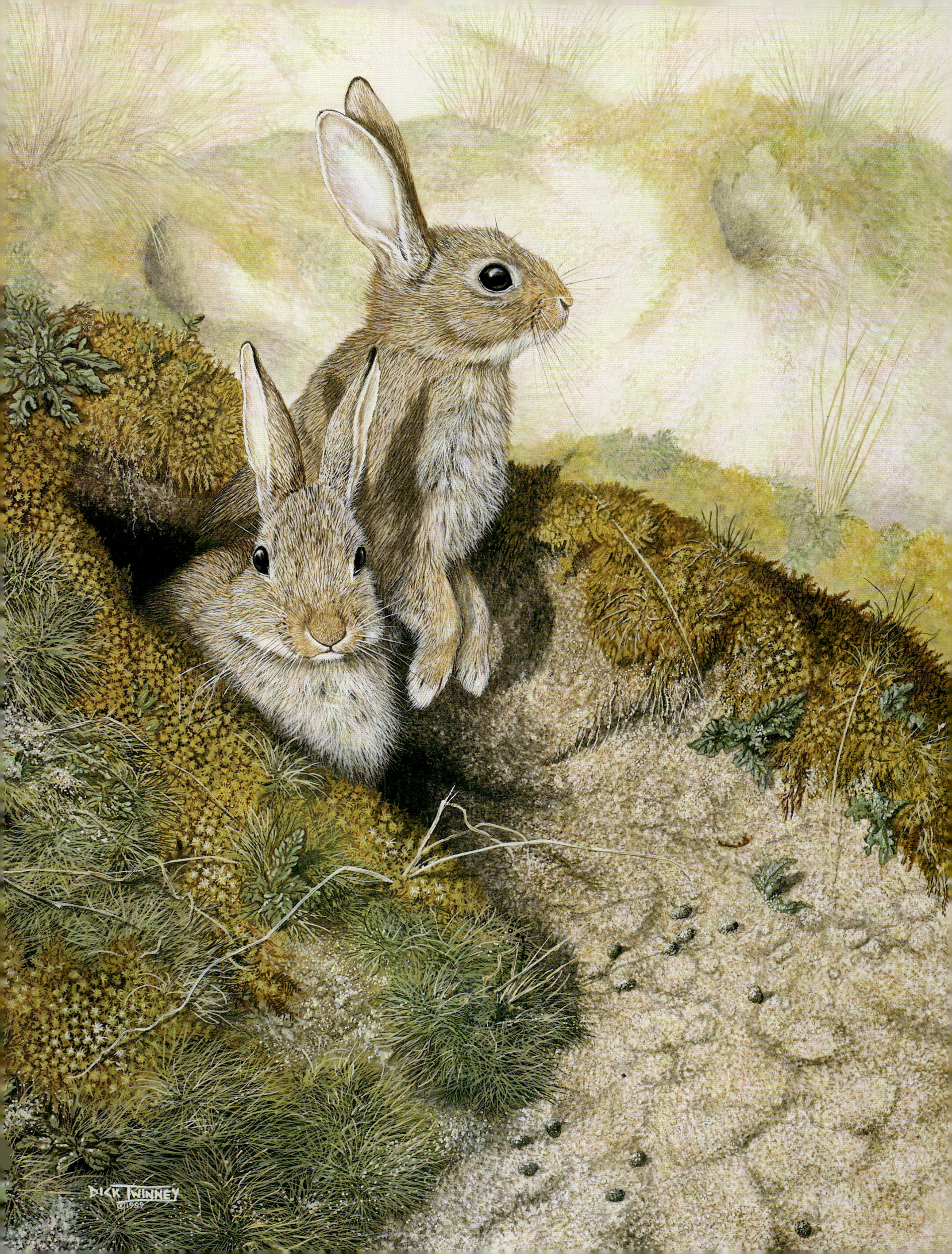
DICK TWINNEY
©1989

FOURTH WEEK

LONG-TAILED TITS

One day in mid-January I set out to collect material for a painting of yellowhammers in and around the early flowering gorse. The light was superb, as it often is at this time of the year, the sun being so low in the sky it provides a whole new perspective on familiar scenes. On rounding a corner in one of my regular fields, I was gradually alerted to the chirping and piping calls of a family of long-tailed tits coming from the scrubby hedgerow. Moving quietly I approached the stunted oak where most of the activity was taking place and there spent a delightful half-hour with this family group of some eight or nine long-tailed tits.

They were quite unconcerned by my presence and that of my dogs who were pottering nearby. At times the birds came within a metre or so, allowing me to observe at close quarters their delicate pinkish white plumage and neat black markings.

Due to the lie of the land the light from the winter sun seemed to come from below the horizon, which had the effect of spotlighting the busy little birds who were seeking out small insects from the lichen-encrusted branches of the oak.

As so often seems to happen in nature, the whole scene of animal, foliage and winter-sky colouration was in perfect unison, thus creating an overall picture of delicate pinks, whites and greys. Even the soft grey-green of the lichen blended to perfection. The yellowhammer painting would have to wait, this scene was to be my next subject!

In late January long-tailed tits are frequently seen in the company of blue and great tits forming quite large flocks, although these are often widely scattered. They feed on insects, spiders and buds and, when feeding, seem to take over a hedgerow or small copse, flitting from tree to tree constantly changing their position. They are truly among the most acrobatic of birds.

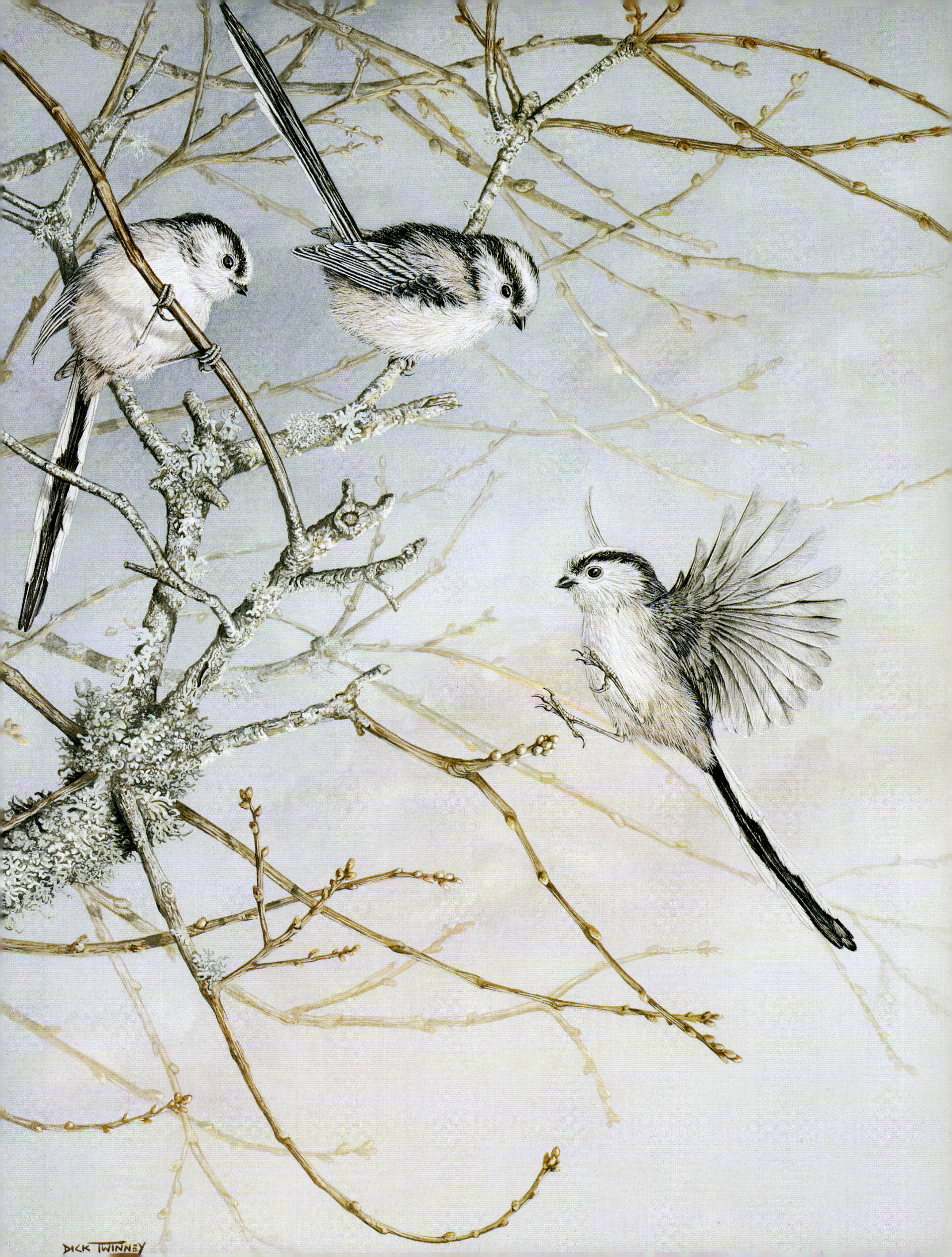
DICK TWINNEY

FIFTH WEEK

HUNTING SHREW

A rustling of dead leaves and a high-pitched squeak will usually betray the presence of the common shrew – but you will still be very lucky to spot it. The common shrew is a creature so tiny that even in little cover it is able to remain hidden, despite a very active life-style.

A ferocious hunter, it is a beast of amazing vitality, completely at home among the old tree branches, ferns and mosses of hedgerows and woods. It will eat almost anything it comes across, including worms, beetles, slugs and snails.

For this painting I have taken an interesting piece of old wood, which has been gathering dust in my studio for some time, waiting to be included in a painting once a suitable animal came along. I am totally fascinated by the complex and abstract shapes that old branches and roots form and get great pleasure from drawing and painting them. This particular piece, being quite large, is appropriate for this painting as it illustrates the shrew's diminutive size. It also has many nooks and crannies which would hide spiders and slugs shortly to be detected by the shrew's sensitive pointed snout. Continually twitching, it moves from side to side as the animal travels over the wood in fast, jerky movements, searching each crevice for creatures that might make a meal.

Shrews have to eat almost continuously to survive, so during harsh winters when most invertebrates are inactive or hibernating, a great many shrews die. Those that live on to reproduce do so at a prodigious rate, having several litters of up to seven young, thus ensuring that this small hunter of the hedgerow 'jungle' remains one of our most common and widely distributed small mammals.

As well as being predatory in their own small world, shrews are also preyed upon, their most common enemy being owls. They are one of the main prey species of the barn owl.

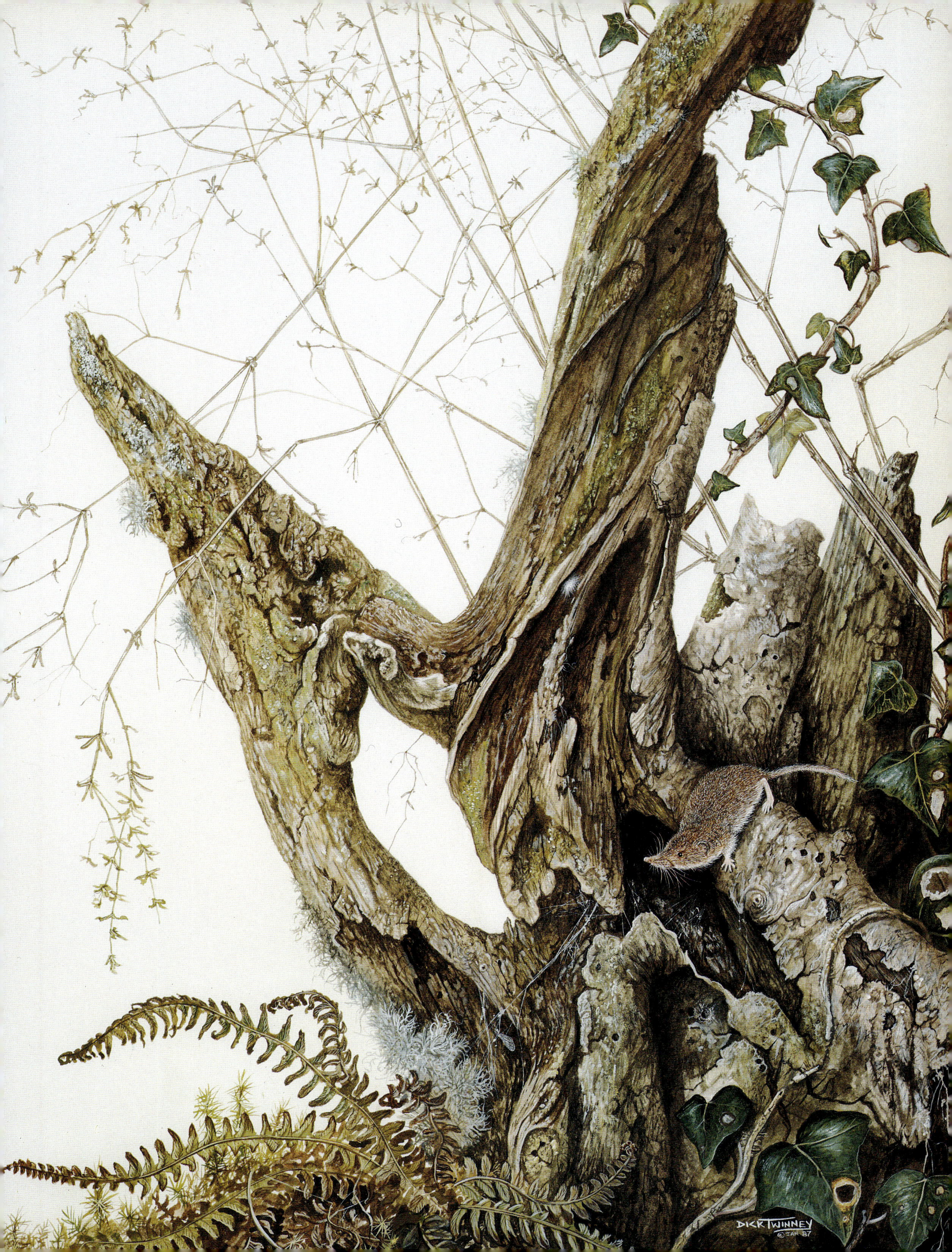
DICK TWINNEY
© JAN 87

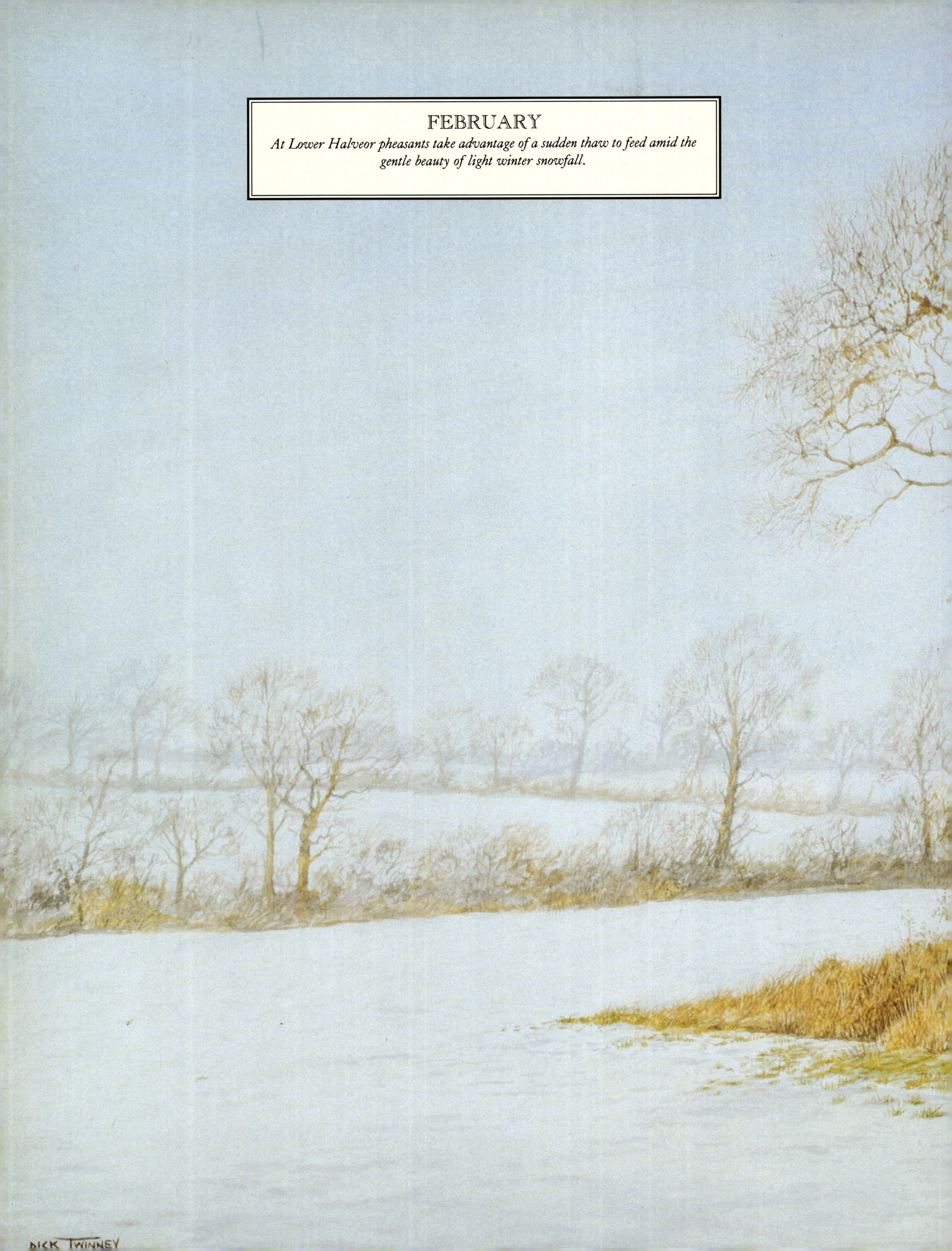

FEBRUARY

At Lower Halveor pheasants take advantage of a sudden thaw to feed amid the gentle beauty of light winter snowfall.

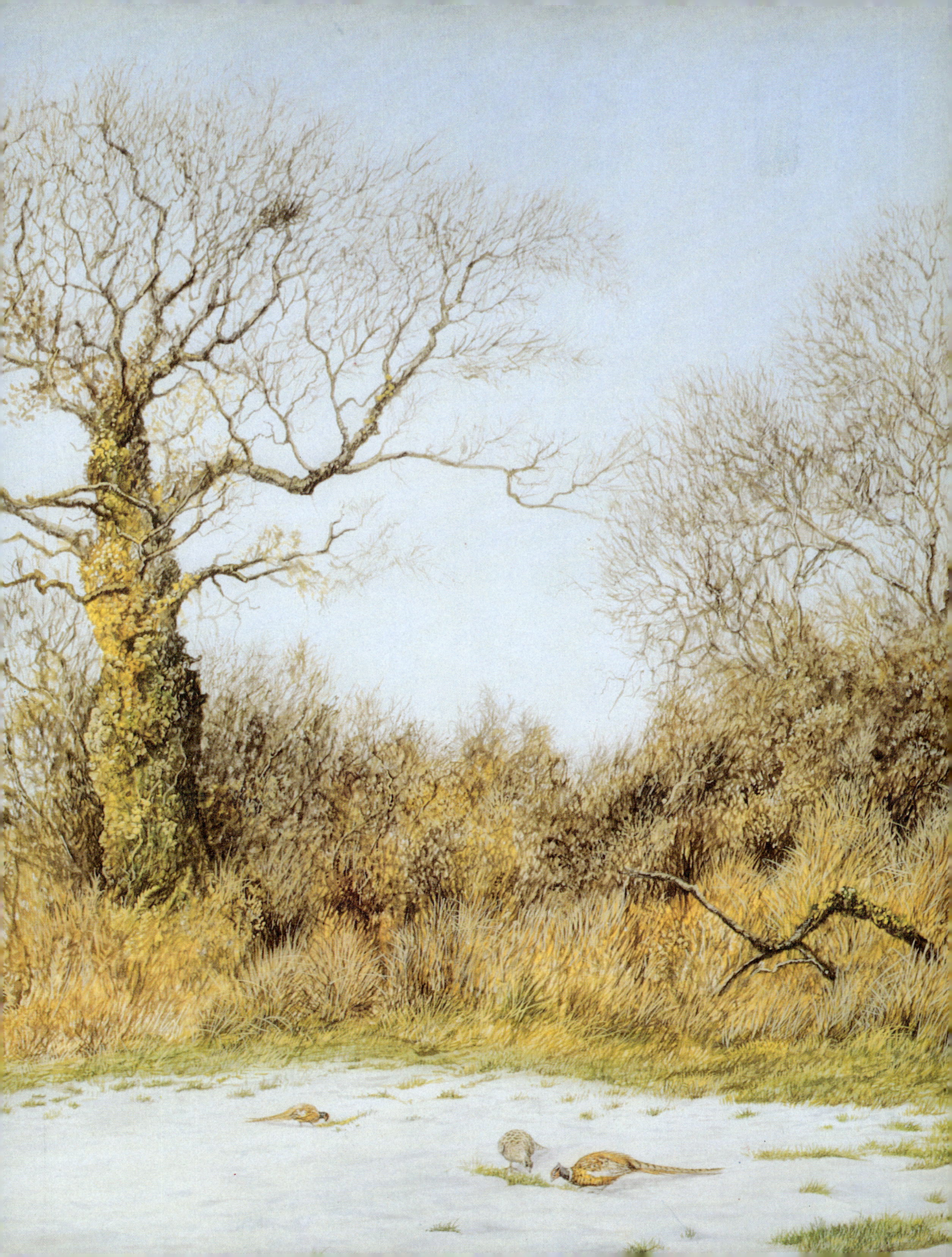

FIRST WEEK

DIPPER

February is arguably the most inactive month in nature's calendar. As an artist, it represents for me a time of greys and browns, unless, of course, we have a snow fall which can change the overall picture within a very short time.

It can be a month of hardship for many animals; most winter berries and seeds have long been eaten or hidden from sight among the fallen leaves or soil. The new growth lies patiently awaiting the warming earth; often frozen in hard ground it remains inaccessible to most creatures. Insects stay hidden deep in the cracks and crevices of the trees and stone walls. However, rivers and streams are constantly alive, flashing and glistening with light as the swirling waters bounce and tumble over rocks and exposed roots. Even in areas where the rivers are slow moving there invariably seems to be an abundance of life in the river itself and along its banks.

The little river portrayed in the painting is very near my home and is a typical 'Cornish stream', with a stony bottom and overhung by trees and bushes. On its journey from moorland source to the sea, it is crossed by many attractive stone bridges which make delightful subjects for the artist and also provide nesting sites for many water-loving birds, such as the dipper. An amazing little bird, the dipper has many fascinating attributes, including the ability to walk on the bottom of streams, completely immersed in the water. It is an efficient swimmer despite lacking webbed feet. The dipper's versatility in the water has allowed it to develop a taste for many water insects, including the larvae of dragonflies, mayflies and caddis flies, all hunted underwater.

The dipper is a small inconspicuous bird. Its remarkable colouring blends well with the background which I have deliberately kept muted to give a 'February feeling' to the painting.

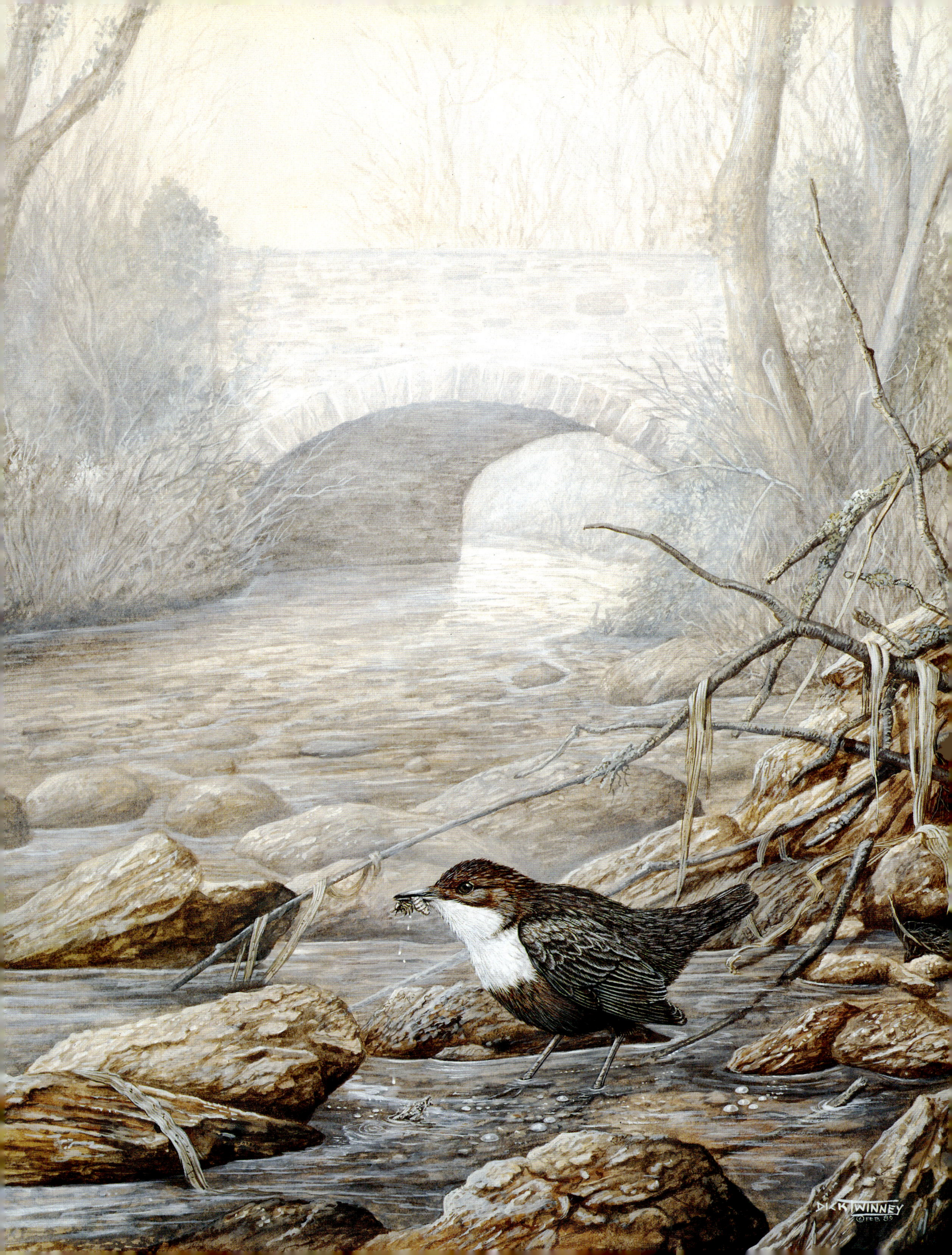
DICK TWINNEY
©FEB 89

SECOND WEEK

WRENS AND SNOWDROPS

This painting is rather special to me as it typifies the direction my work is taking. I now try to put my chosen subject (in this case wrens) in interesting but technically correct situations. This is also the first painting I have worked on completely in the public eye, an ordeal I should not like to repeat too often, preferring the security of my own studio without distraction. However, I am quite happy with the end result.

The wrens were observed from my studio window, where barely a day goes by when I do not see one or two scurrying mouse-like underneath the cotoneaster in search of small spiders and insects. They are such self-important little birds with their perky upturned tails and a loud piercing song, seemingly far too loud for Britain's second smallest bird (the goldcrest is the smallest).

Severe weather at this time of the year can play havoc with the wren population. They will find tree holes, cracks and crevices or even nesting-boxes in which they gather in large numbers, huddled together in feathery bundles to contain body heat.

As you progress through this book you will realize that one of my favourite subjects is old wood and the magical and interesting forms it takes. This piece provided a perfect dark backdrop for the newly emerged snowdrops, giving great emphasis to the purity of white.

The snowdrop is always a very welcome sight, pushing up from the hard winter-chilled ground with its sword-like leaves and adding sparkling droplets of colour to the greens and browns of the winter hedgerow bottom, giving promise of better weather to come.

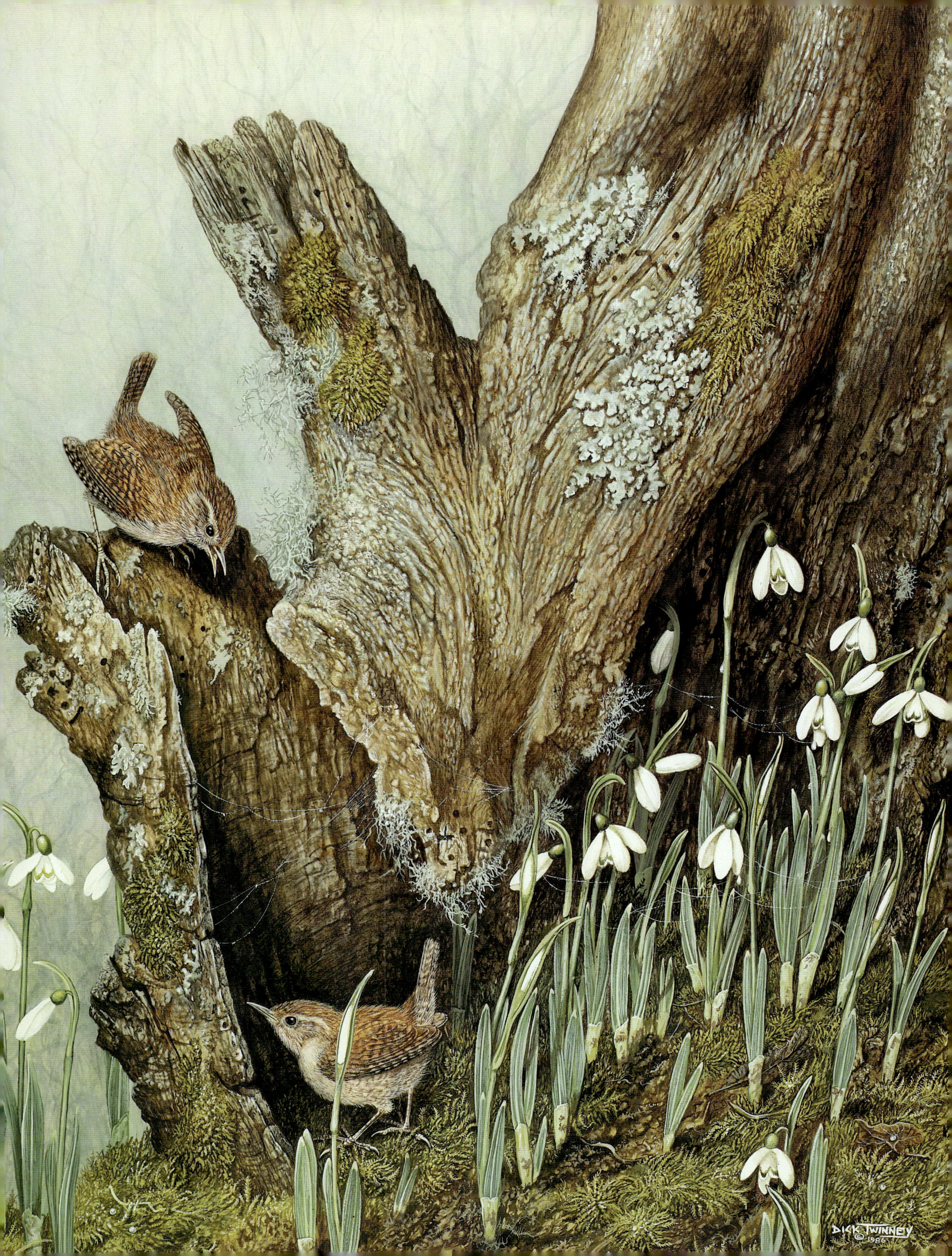
DICK TWINNEY
© 1986

THIRD WEEK

YELLOWHAMMER

At this time of year yellowhammers, along with other finches and seed-eating birds, gather in large flocks and can be seen feeding in the open stubble fields, although they quickly return to the nearest cover on being disturbed. They seem to feel secure once they have reached the hedgerow and will often allow you to approach quite close before taking to the wing and moving a little further down the hedge.

One day in late February, perhaps due to the inclement weather and the electric atmosphere that heralded an impending storm, I was able to get very close indeed to a beautiful cock bird, who was perched on a dead gorse branch. He was silhouetted against a particularly dark patch of cloud which further enhanced his magnificent yellow plumage. Combining this scene with a clump of living gorse from nearby makes a very suitable subject for February.

While painting this picture I noticed that the yellowhammer's basic colouring is identical to the gorse that it so often frequents. Although they are found in all types of habitat, they seem to favour small copses, hedgerows and rough areas with an abundance of blackthorn, gorse and willow.

Yellowhammers are a favourite bird of the whole family; not only do they have striking plumage, I particularly like their funny little song which I brought to the attention of my children when they were very young. They were thrilled when I pointed out that the bird was saying 'Little bit of bread and no cheese'.

For this painting I have used masking fluid to mask off the bird and the gorse flowers. This allowed me free rein to work on the dark sky, without the worry of not obtaining a crisp clear yellow for my principal subjects.

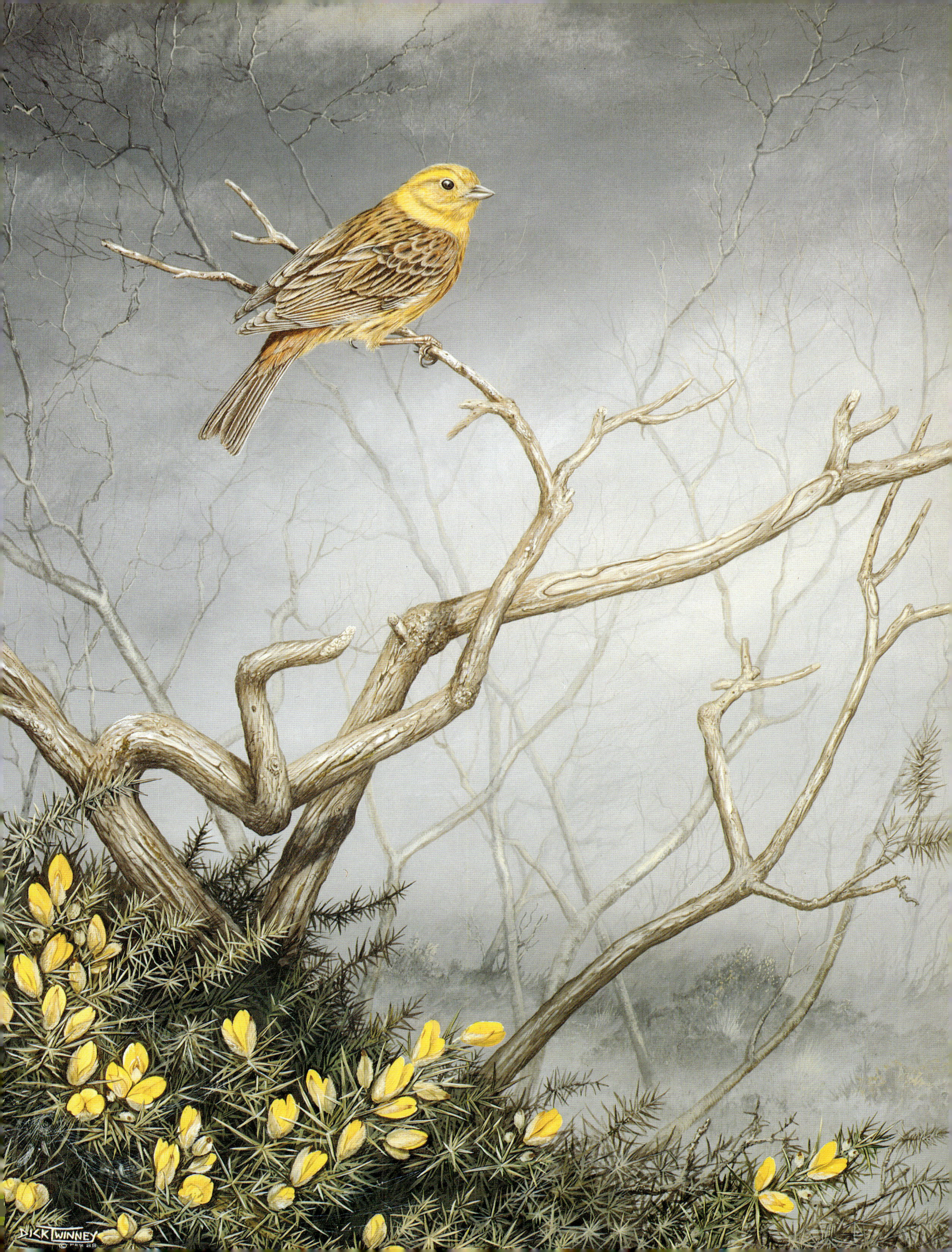
DICK TWINNEY

FOURTH WEEK

WOODCOCK

The base of an overgrown hedge makes good hunting territory for the woodcock, particularly where the ground is moist. The woodcock is normally an extremely shy bird, keeping to deep cover in woods and scrub, but in February 1986 extremely harsh conditions forced a change in normal bird behaviour. Thousands of ground-feeding birds such as plovers, snipe and woodcock, driven down into the West Country by the bad weather to seek refuge in a normally milder climate, found the ice-hard ground impossible to penetrate for their diet of small worms and insect larvae so they ventured into gardens and on to roadsides in their endless quest for food. Many thousands perished through lack of food or became road casualties. Others, in a half-starved state, were taken by cats and other predators. Everywhere there seemed to be birds with their feathers fluffed out, desperately trying to contain body heat, in the face of the bitter north-easterly winds.

The particular bird illustrated here was fluffed up in the lee of the hedge and I was able to observe it for some time, taking note of its stance and the beautiful mottled brown plumage which normally would act as camouflage, but in these snowy conditions made it stand out against the white background. This was the only time I have ever seen a woodcock on the ground. Usually they are airborne, startled by one of my dogs while we are out walking. They rise vertically on powerful clattering wings, dodging and swerving among the trees which, unfortunately for some, makes them an attractive sporting target for the man with the shotgun.

For this painting I obtained a dead specimen from a shooting friend as I wanted to reproduce accurately the unique and complicated feather patterns. It also gave me the chance to study the incredible bill which has a highly developed flexible tip which enables the bird to grasp its prey underground without opening the entire bill.

Although resident in Britain, woodcock are winter visitors to the West Country arriving with the first of the frost and departing north in early spring to breed.

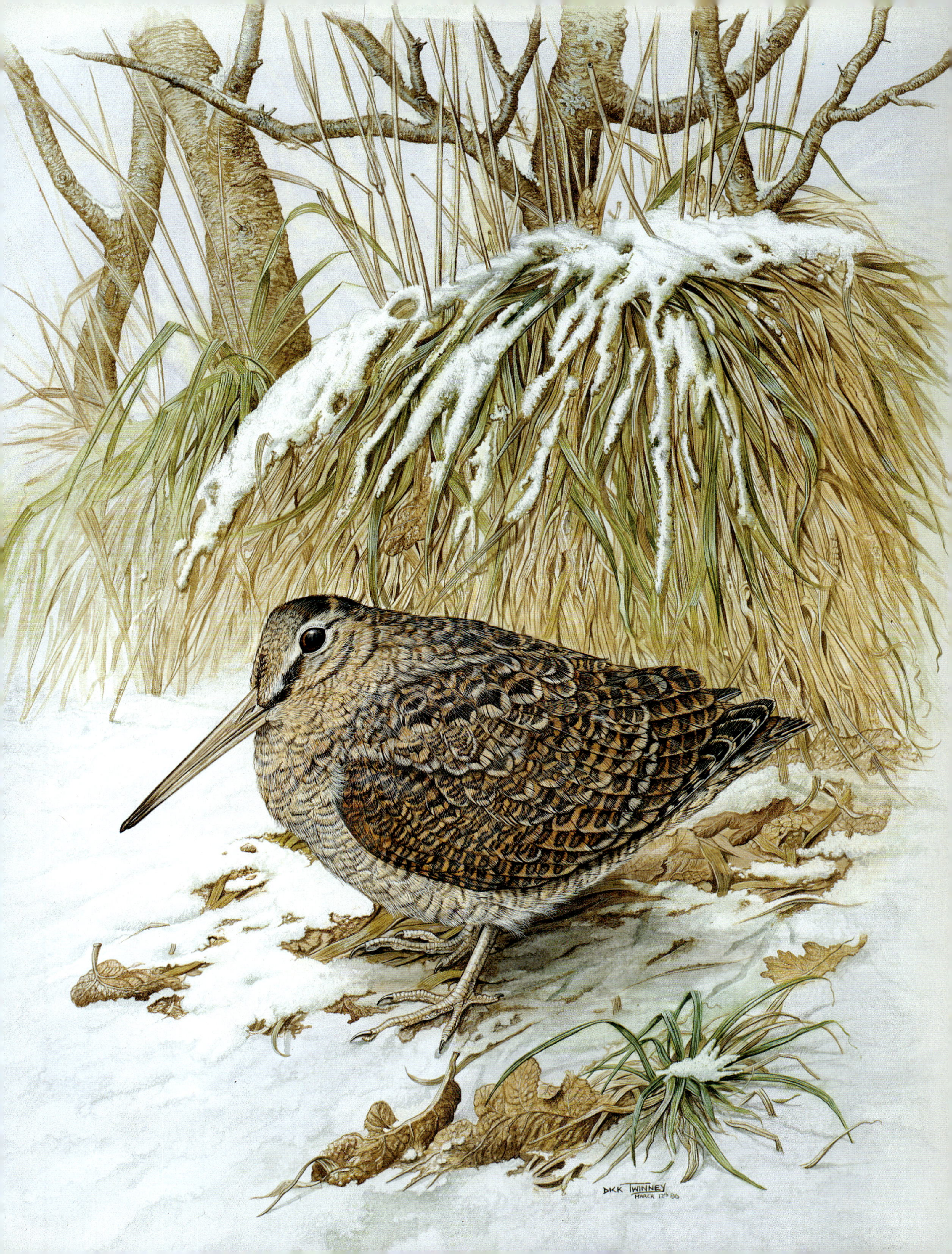
DICK TWINNEY
MARCH 12th 86

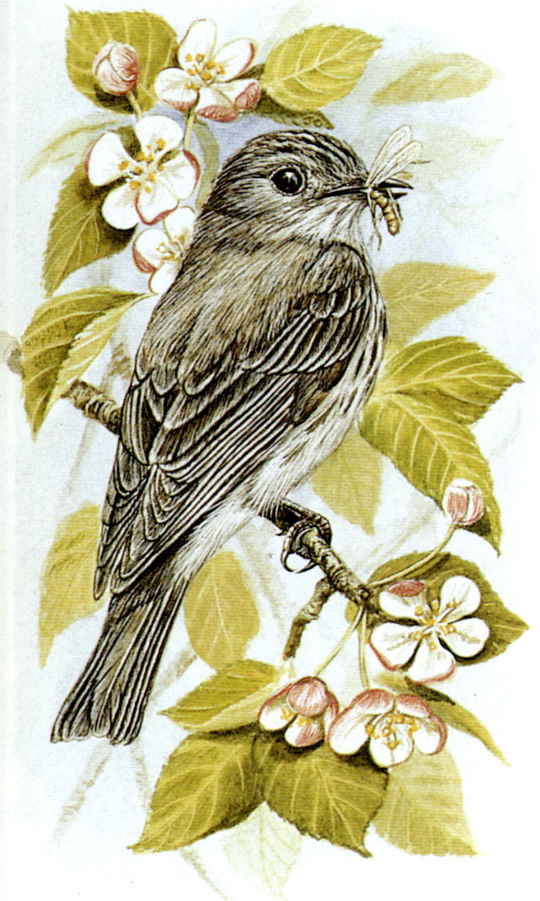

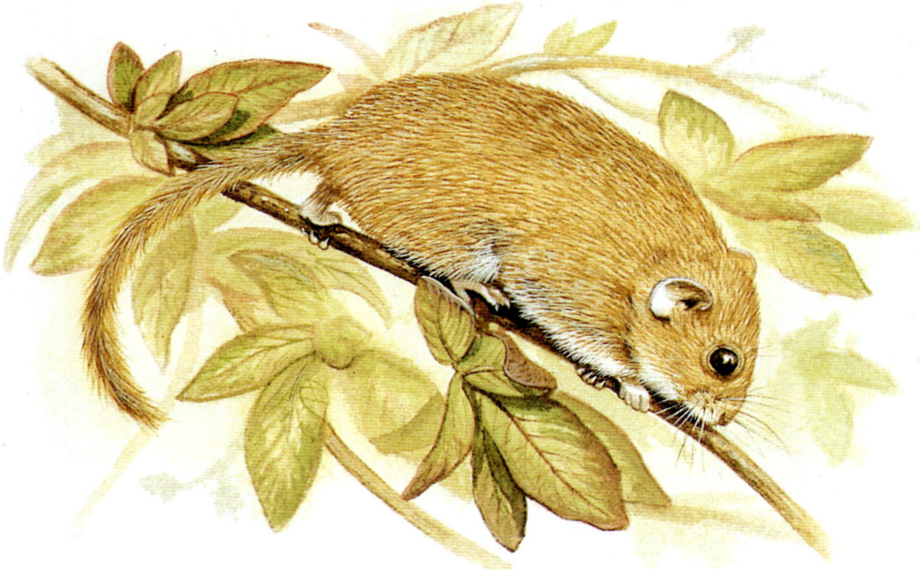

SPRING

Spring in the countryside, a time of rebirth, nature's calendar continuing onwards, sometimes early, sometimes late, depending on our fickle weather. A few hot days in early April are sufficient to activate the rich carpet of life in our hedgerows and fields. Celandines are the first to show, followed by primroses, violets and bluebells. As the spring flowers become more abundant insects take to the wing, ground invertebrates leave their winter quarters and the first butterflies are seen – the brimstone followed by speckled wood, orange tip and the miracle of migration announced by the arrival of the red admiral.

The dormouse and hedgehog leave their snug winter nests in the hedgerow bottoms; while bats flicker and dive in pursuit of the numerous moths and cockchafer beetles that have crept out from their various winter homes. Then, with a dramatic sense of timing, the magnificent emperor moth emerges from its cocoon.

As the spring sunshine penetrates the stony ground of our moors, hedgerows and cliff-tops, snakes and lizards start to appear, at

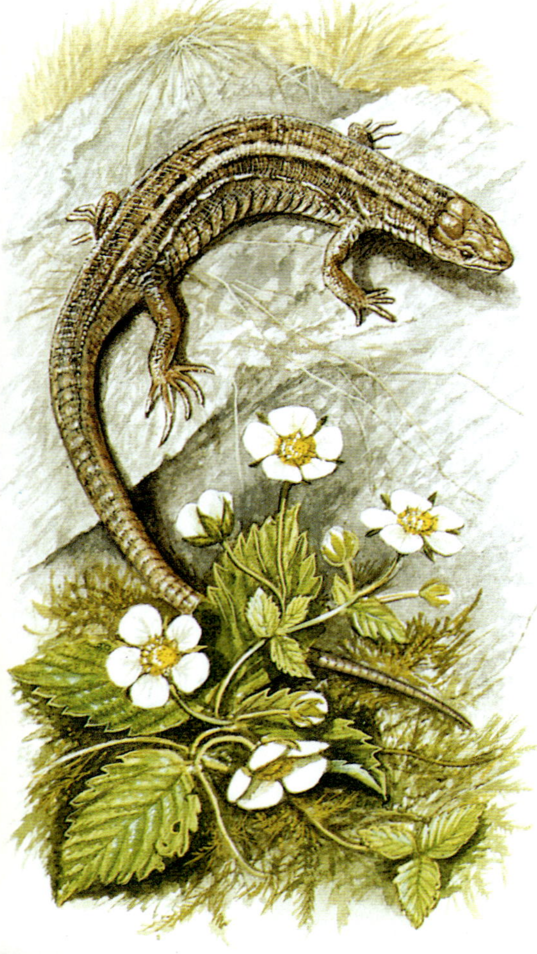

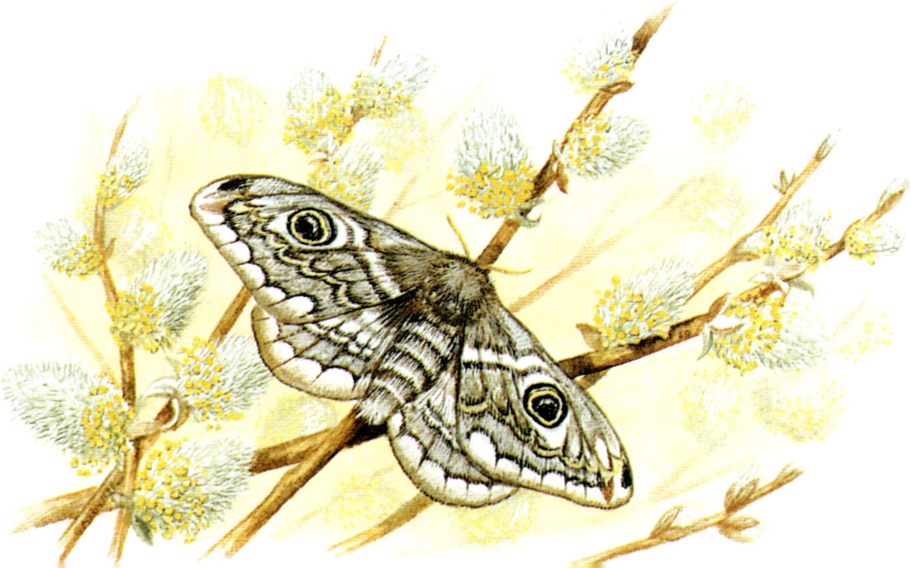

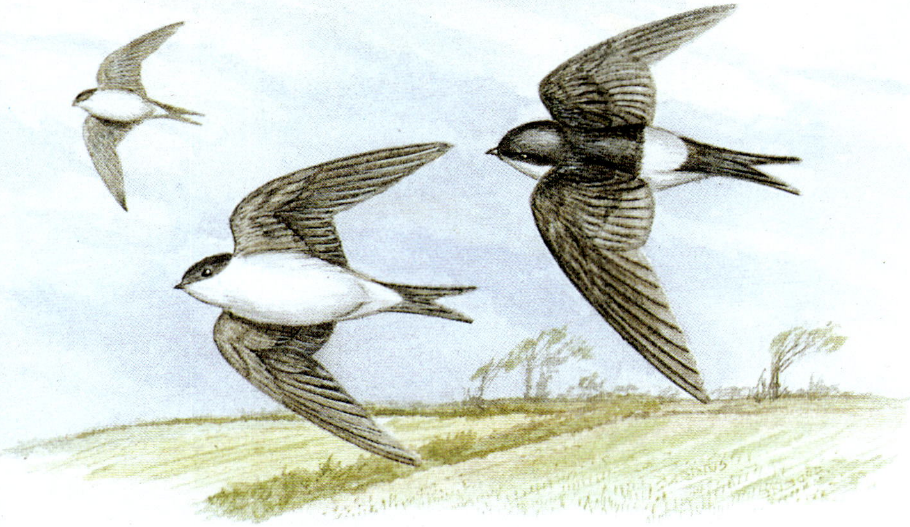

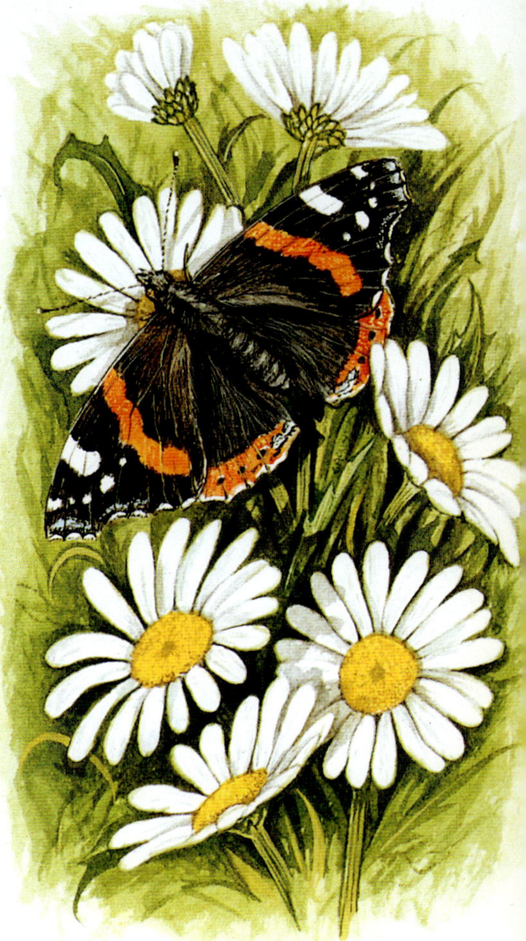

first rather sleepily, but gradually becoming more active as the warming rays heat their blood.

Trees and bushes becomes clothed with an ever-thickening mantle of leaves; the familiar flowers of the hazel and sallow are much in evidence. Fruit trees burst into flower, both in our gardens and the countryside, attracting the flying insects much loved by the ever increasing number of birds arriving on our shores – spotted flycatchers, swallows, martins and warblers. The well-known call of the cuckoo echoes over the landscape, as does the gentle crooning of the turtle dove. The bird-song of the dawn chorus reaches its peak as cock birds establish their breeding territories. Nests are being constructed everywhere, including the neat mud cups of the house martin, who chooses its man-made sites under the eaves.

Wild strawberry flowers, germander speedwell and stitchwort appear star-like among the fresh green of the hedgerows. In the open fields the brilliant white and yellow ox-eye daisies join forces with meadow orchid, dandelion and charlock, providing the delightful and varied colours so typical of this first season of the year.

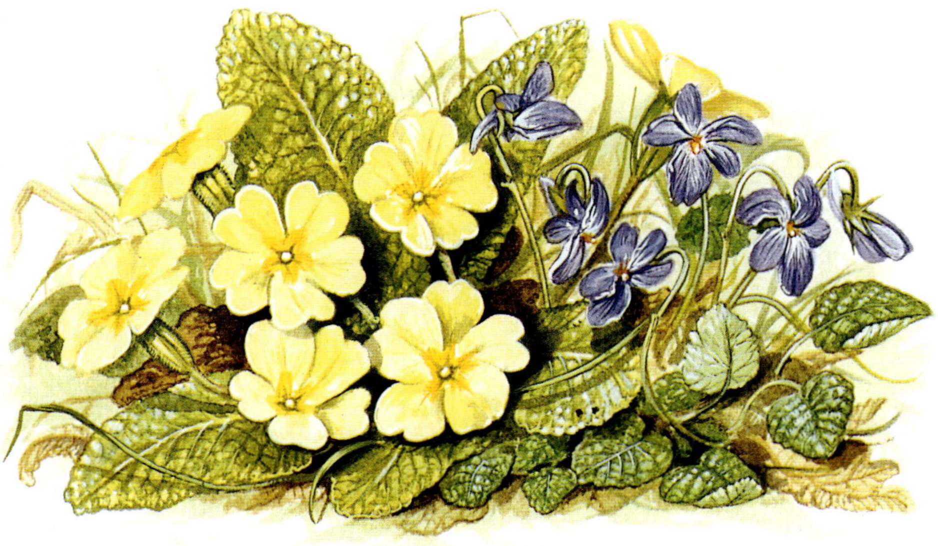

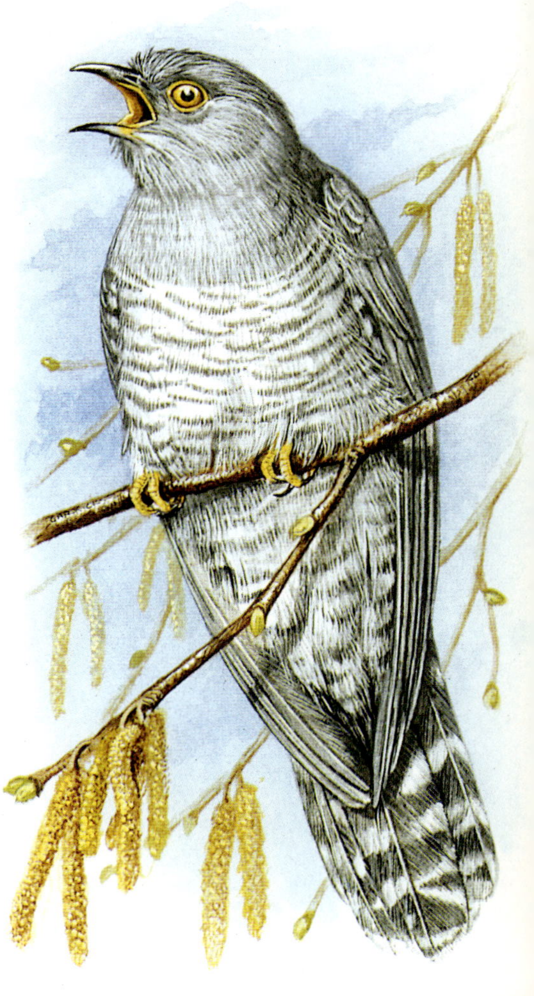

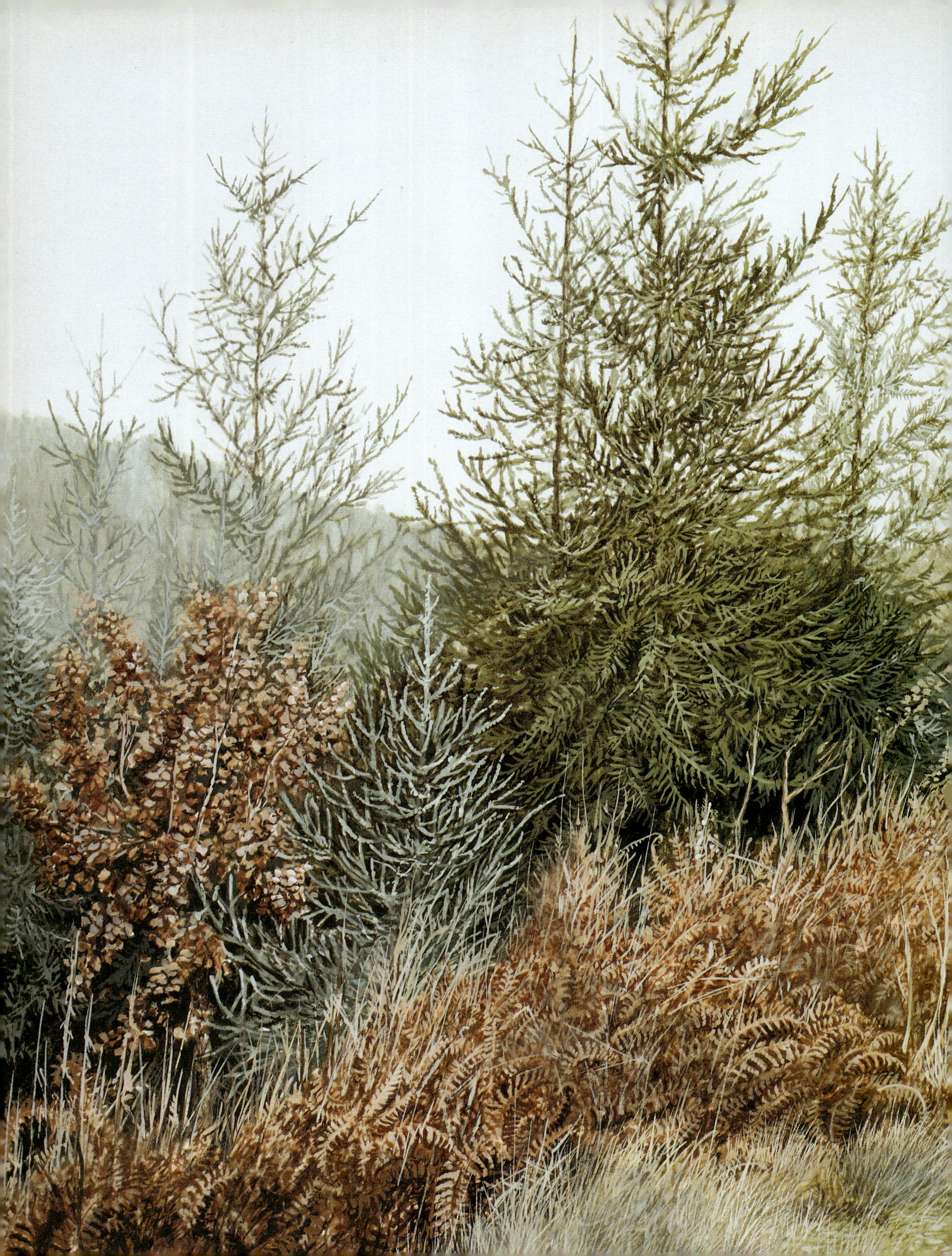

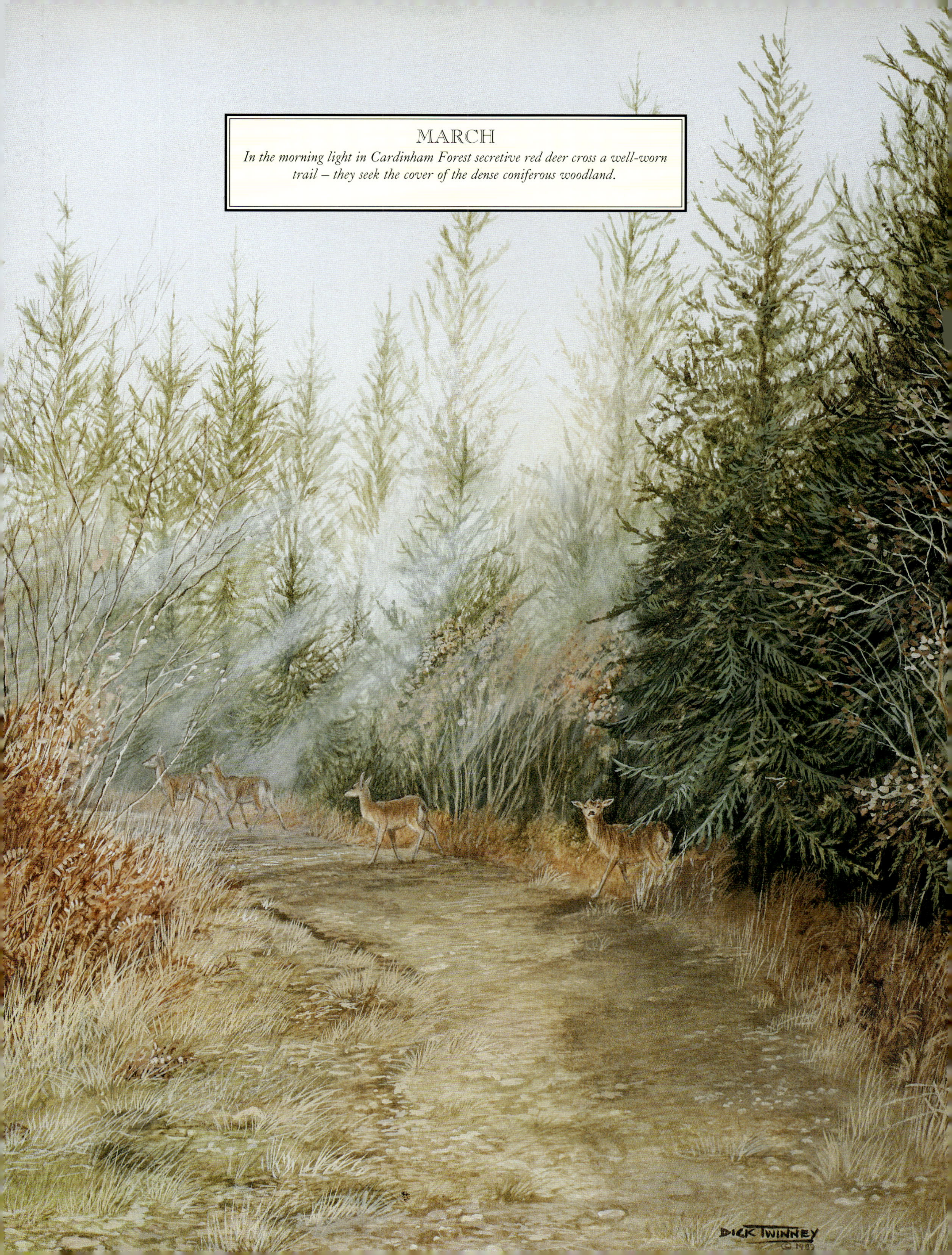

MARCH

In the morning light in Cardinham Forest secretive red deer cross a well-worn trail – they seek the cover of the dense coniferous woodland.

First Week

COMMON TOAD

In late February and early March the first toads emerge from their secluded winter quarters. Hedgerow bottoms, stone walls, wood piles and the garden compost heap may all have provided snug homes for the toad during the cold weather. In our garden the pile of old elm logs has been used frequently for many generations of hibernating toads. On carefully lifting the logs, toads of various sizes can always be found. Toads can live to a good age (up to forty years has been recorded) and they take five or six years to reach maturity.

The toad is not everyone's favourite creature but I admit to having a soft spot for 'Mr Toad'. Perhaps it comes from personal affection for Kenneth Grahame's character portrayed in *The Wind in the Willows*. The toad is a true gardener's friend, feeding on many pests such as snails, various beetles and woodlice. In fact the toad will eat almost anything of appropriate size that may come his way. Small snails are swallowed whole, while large ones are broken up in the mouth into more manageable pieces. Toads tend to feed mainly at night when their prey is at its most active. They shelter during the day under foliage or return to their winter quarters. However, a shower of rain heralding the appearance of snails and worms will also tempt a hungry toad out into the open at any time of the day or night.

The toad's rather grotesque appearance, with his dry, warty body, rather unathletic build and dull, brownish colouring only helps to highlight his beautiful eyes. These golden-orange jewels, provide a marvellous focal point for this painting. The beauty of the eyes is also enhanced by keeping the background very subtle; our ivy-covered wood pile provides the perfect natural setting. An old wood pile is an important asset in a wildlife garden, providing home and shelter for a host of other garden residents as well as for our friend 'Mr Toad'.

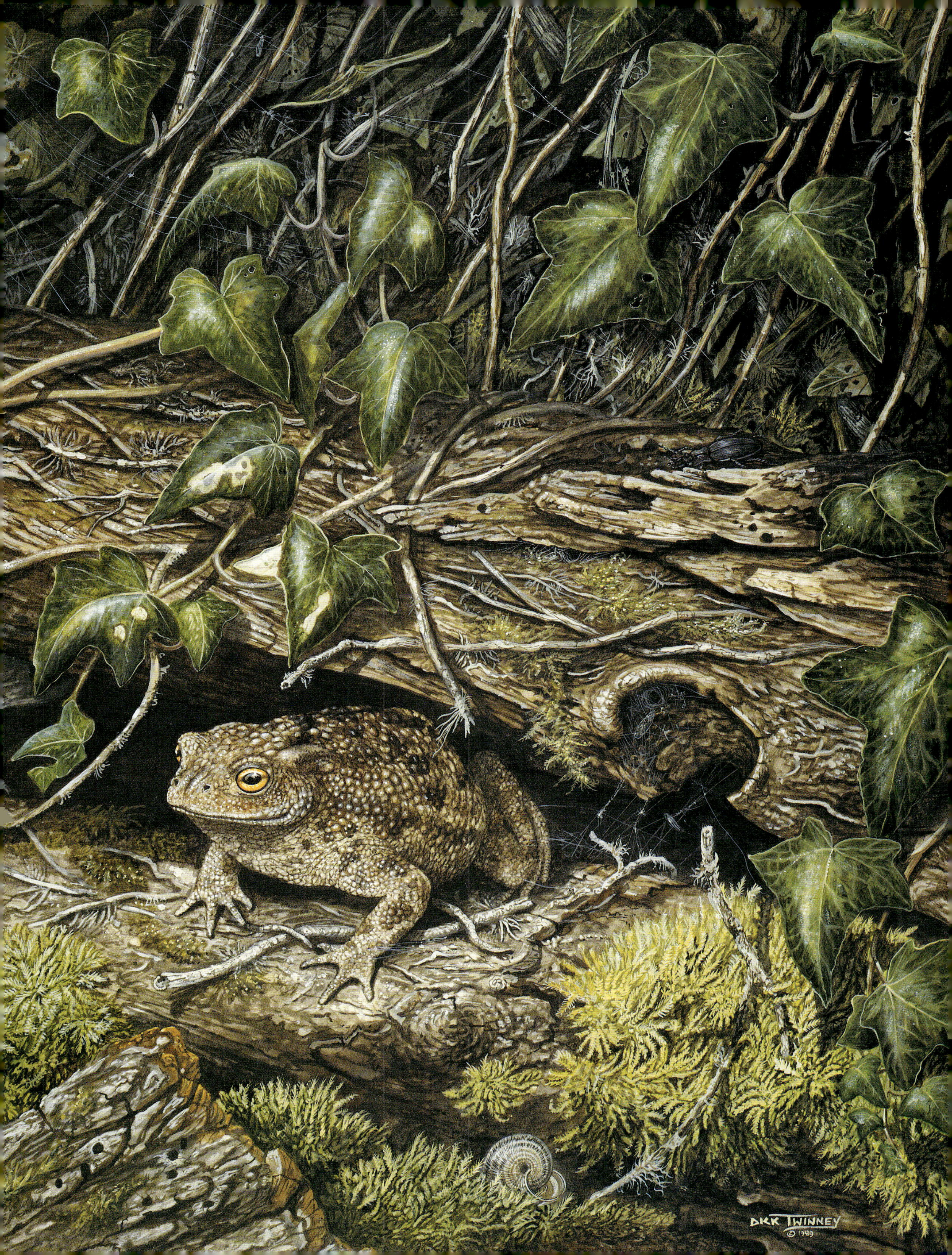
DICK TWINNEY
© 1989

SECOND WEEK

HOUSE SPARROWS

It is mid-March and a week of fine weather has given many birds that 'spring' feeling. They are singing more and busy claiming territorial rights. The early nesters are starting to build, one of the most enthusiastic of these being the cheeky house sparrow. Their continual chirping and cheeping, together with the cock bird's courtship displays, are a sure sign that spring is on the way. Their nest is an untidy affair of hay, straw and grasses lined with feathers which are collected by the beak-load from the local hen-houses and farms.

Here, at my home, our local sparrows collect the moulted feathers of our resident gulls – one cock sparrow kept us amused on many occasions by doggedly attempting to carry just one feather too many. He would gather together a great clump of feathers, some almost as big as himself, try to pick up just one more and then drop the one he was already carrying, which on a breezy day would then blow across the garden. Hopping in pursuit and dropping others on the way, he would end up with just one feather and be forced to start all over again. We often wondered if he ever managed to complete his nest.

Sparrows build their nests in farm buildings, roof spaces, gutters and occasionally in thick hedges. The particular nest under construction in my painting is one of many in and around the old farm buildings down our back lane. I love these old buildings with their weathered beams, lichen-encrusted stonework, rusty ornate hinges, nails and door fastenings, and still the odd bit of real 'binder twine', all toning together naturally – how out of place are the new, bright coloured twines used today.

Sparrows are often taken for granted, being so plentiful, but they really are delightful little birds, and so full of character. Many people overlook the fact that a typical 'country' sparrow in full breeding plumage is a fine sight.

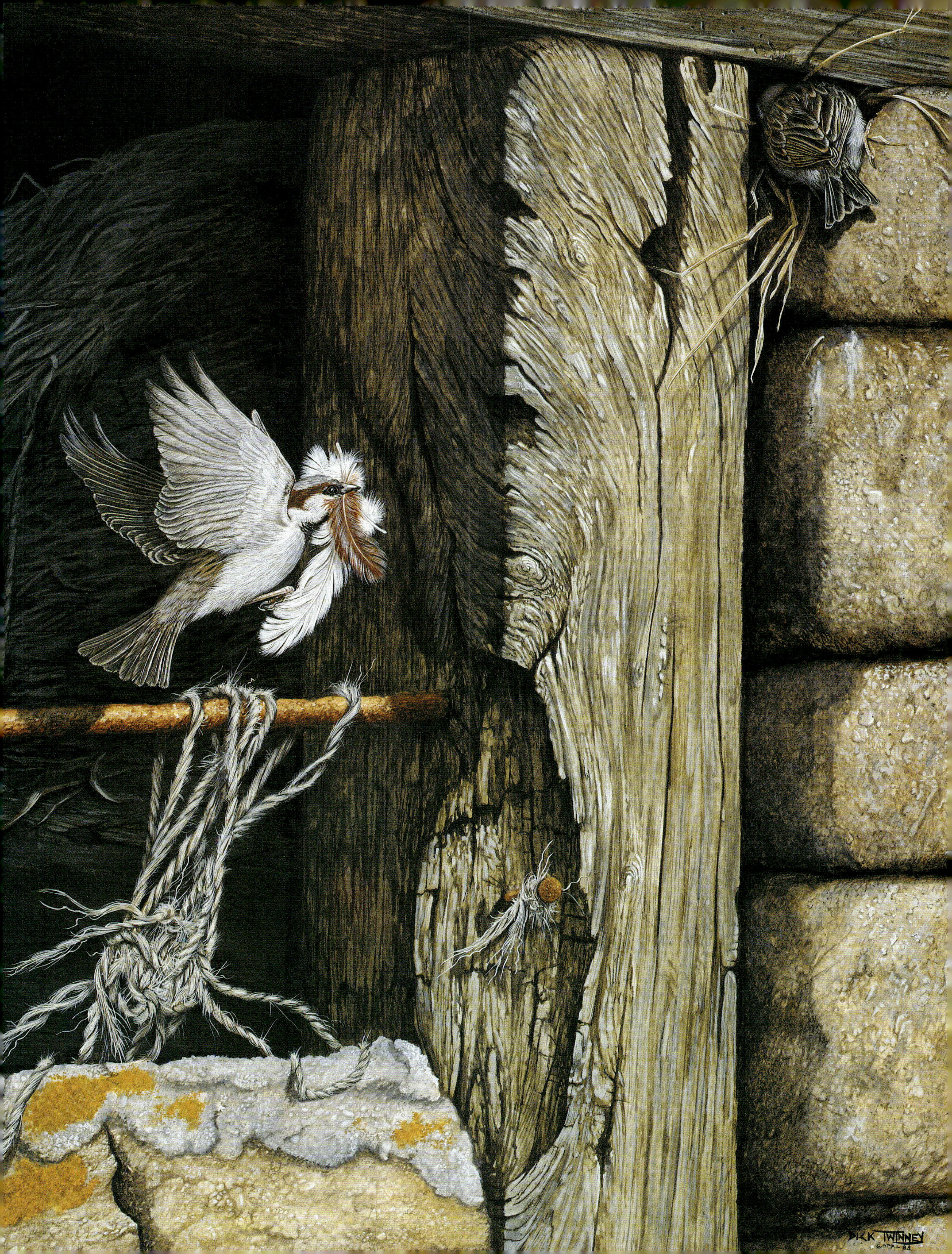
DICK TWINNEY
©APRIL 88

Third Week

HEDGEHOG

The burst of warmer weather which is the sign for many birds to start nest-building is also a time for some creatures to emerge from their winter quarters. In this painting we have one such animal. With a great deal of grunting and snorting the 'hedgepig', 'urchin' or 'hedgehog', as it is now called, blinks to remove four months' sleep from his bright, button-like eyes. As the evening sunlight penetrates his snug winter home in the base of the stone wall, he pushes his black sensitive nose outside his nest, sniffing and testing the still evening air. He has one thought in mind: food. All fat reserves have been used up during the winter months so now he must turn his undivided attention to the task of seeking out some juicy slugs, snails or other ground invertebrates to build up his strength for the coming mating season.

While he has been hibernating, the red dead-nettle in front of his nest has burst into flower. This particular common weed will continue to flower right through until October. A tiny zebra spider has been attracted outside by the warming stones and the stonecrop is beginning to grow at the tips.

It is a time of awakening, but a cold snap will soon send the hedgehog back to his nest for a few days. We have had many hedgehog families in our garden over the years and welcome them with enthusiasm, providing meaty scraps to supplement their diet. Hedgehogs have few enemies in the natural world, although the occasional badger or hungry fox may take a young or sickly animal. The principal enemies of the hedgehog are road traffic and slug pellets. Road casualties are sufficient cause for concern but there are few more distressing sights than a hedgehog stumbling around in daylight with obvious brain damage caused by the build-up of toxins from eating contaminated slugs and snails.

Hedgehogs are most welcome residents of the garden, not only for their role as 'pest controllers' but simply for being such delightful characters. Avoid using toxic poison to eliminate garden pests. There are other methods freely available – just as effective but 'hedgehog-friendly'.

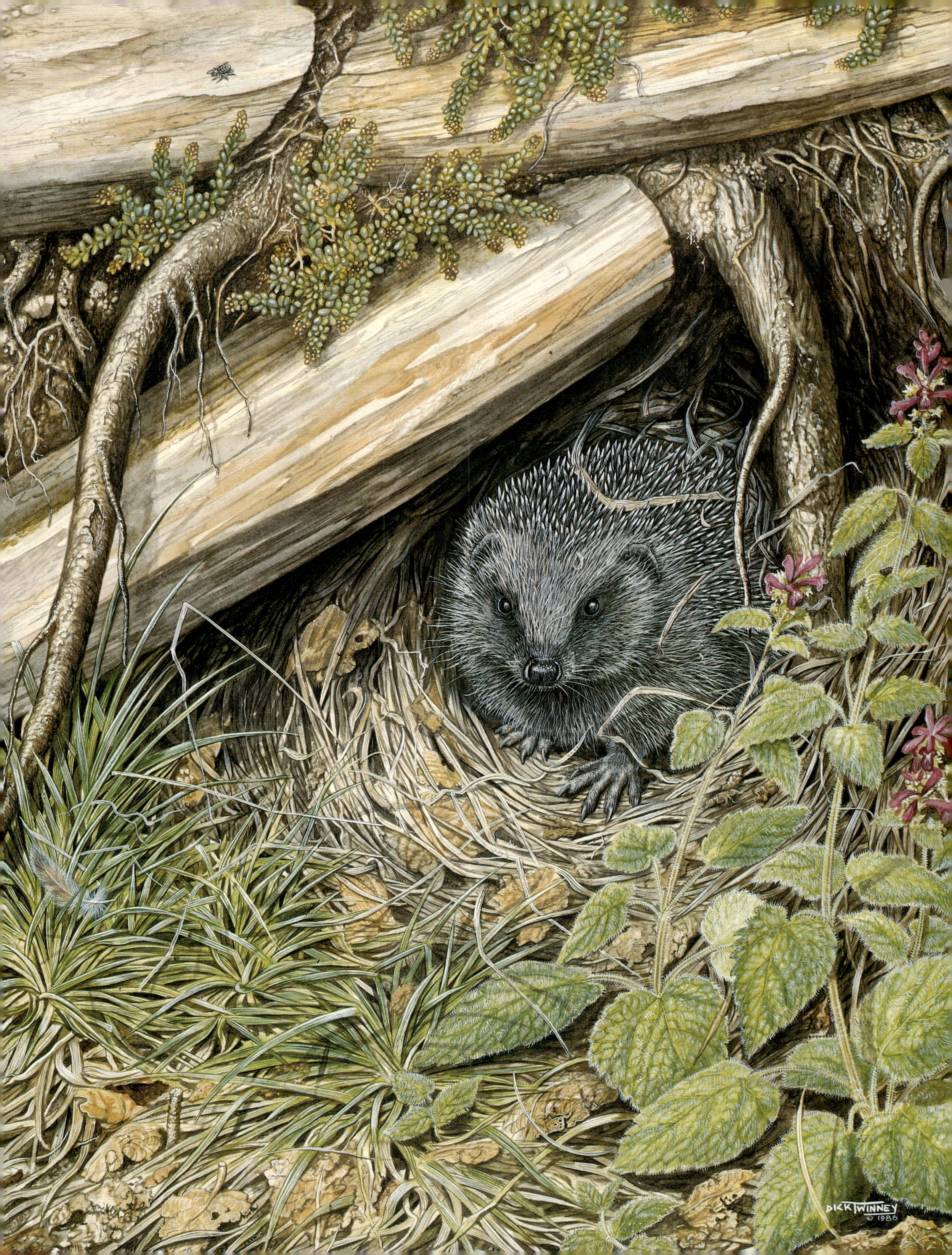
DICK TWINNEY
© 1986

Fourth Week

BUZZARD AT NEST

The buzzard is a truly magnificent bird of prey. Fortunately it is now a common sight in a variety of habitats, ranging from moor and farmland to the coast.

Buzzards vary considerably in colouring, from a dark, blackish brown to almost white. The bird illustrated here is in its most typical plumage. They are large, powerful birds and look at their impressive best when soaring and gliding on outstretched wings, or perched motionless, surveying the countryside with fierce, alert eyes. With radar-like precision they will scan the ground for the slightest movement that would betray the presence of suitable prey.

Recently, however, I observed a buzzard acting in a quite different manner. The bird was hopping about in a field hunting insects – probably grasshoppers. For a fleeting second it would stand motionless, then suddenly dash through the long grass, displaying an ungainly, clownish gait, to pounce on its intended victim. The would-be meal frequently escaped, leaving the buzzard peering at the ground with a bemused and unpreditory expression.

Buzzards build large, untidy nests of twigs and branches and will often use the same nest year after year. These nests can grow to an impressive size as fresh twigs are added each year. There are usually several suitable nests in any given territory, each one built to the required specification before the bird finally decides upon a home in which to lay its eggs.

The nest featured in this painting is built high in a maritime pine. This tree is indigenous to the western Mediterranean, but is a welcome resident to this country because it provides fine nest sites for many species of birds. Artistically, these pines provide an added delight to the scenery as they have been bent and twisted to many fascinating shapes by the prevailing salt-laden winds.

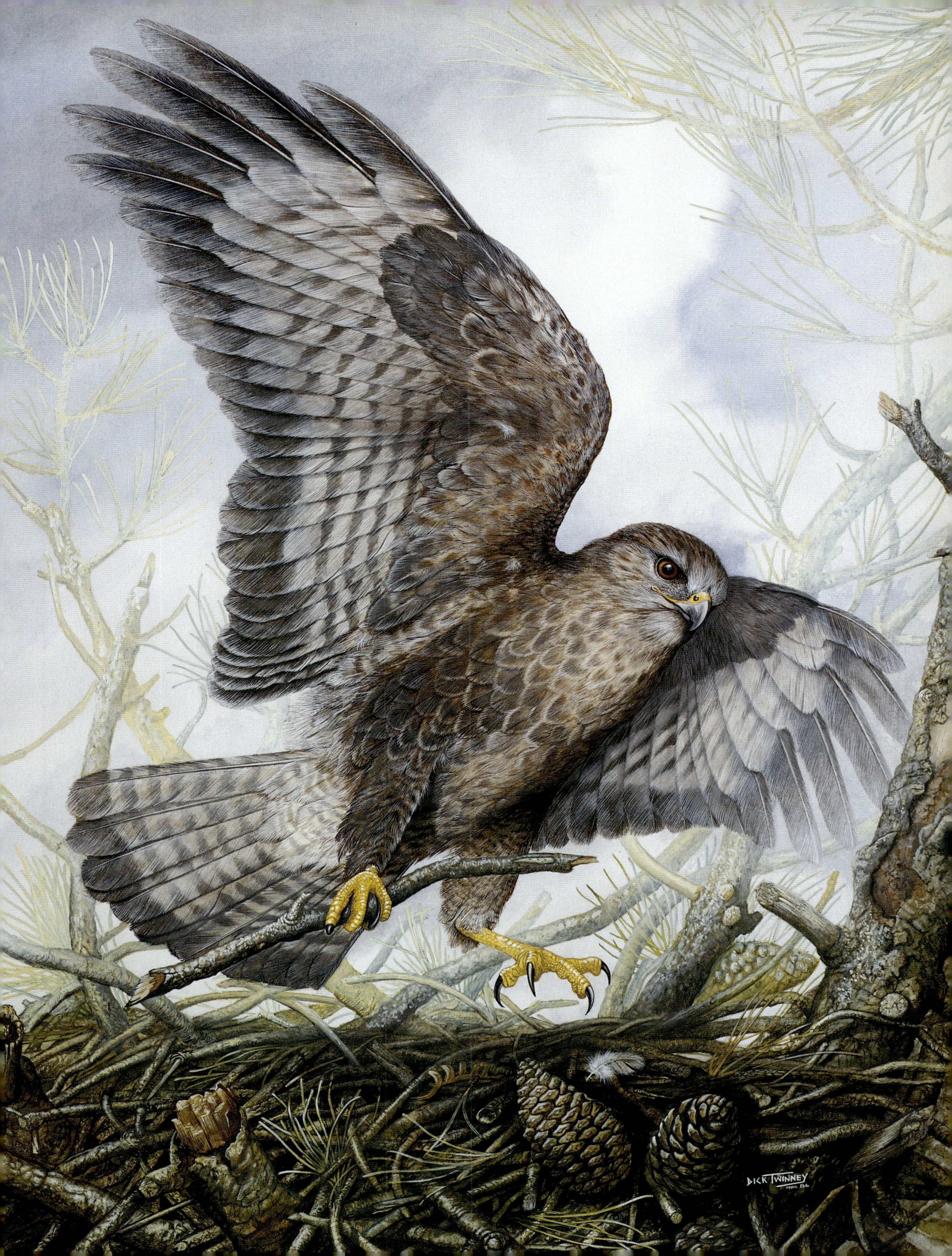
DICK TWINNEY
APRIL 86

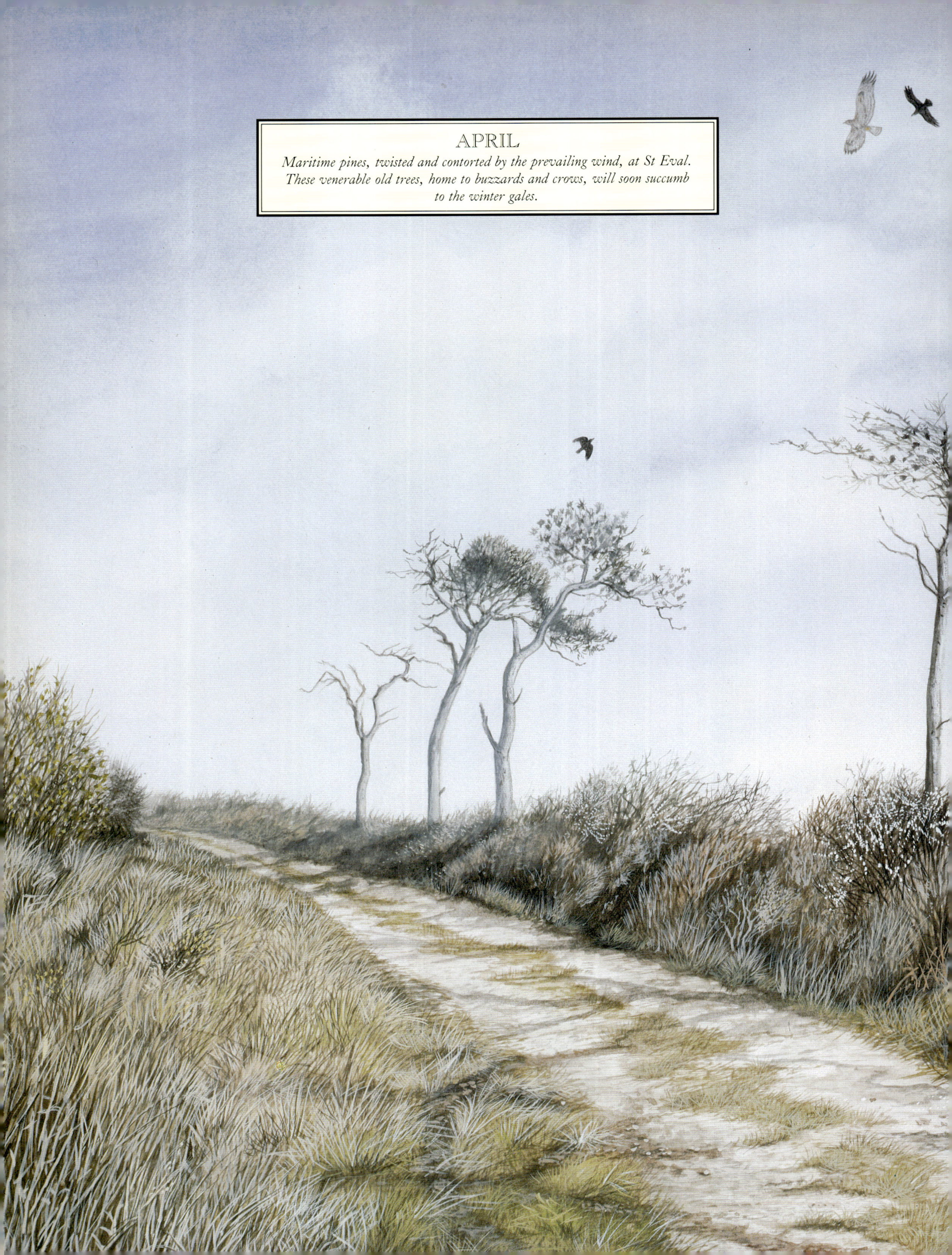

APRIL

Maritime pines, twisted and contorted by the prevailing wind, at St Eval. These venerable old trees, home to buzzards and crows, will soon succumb to the winter gales.

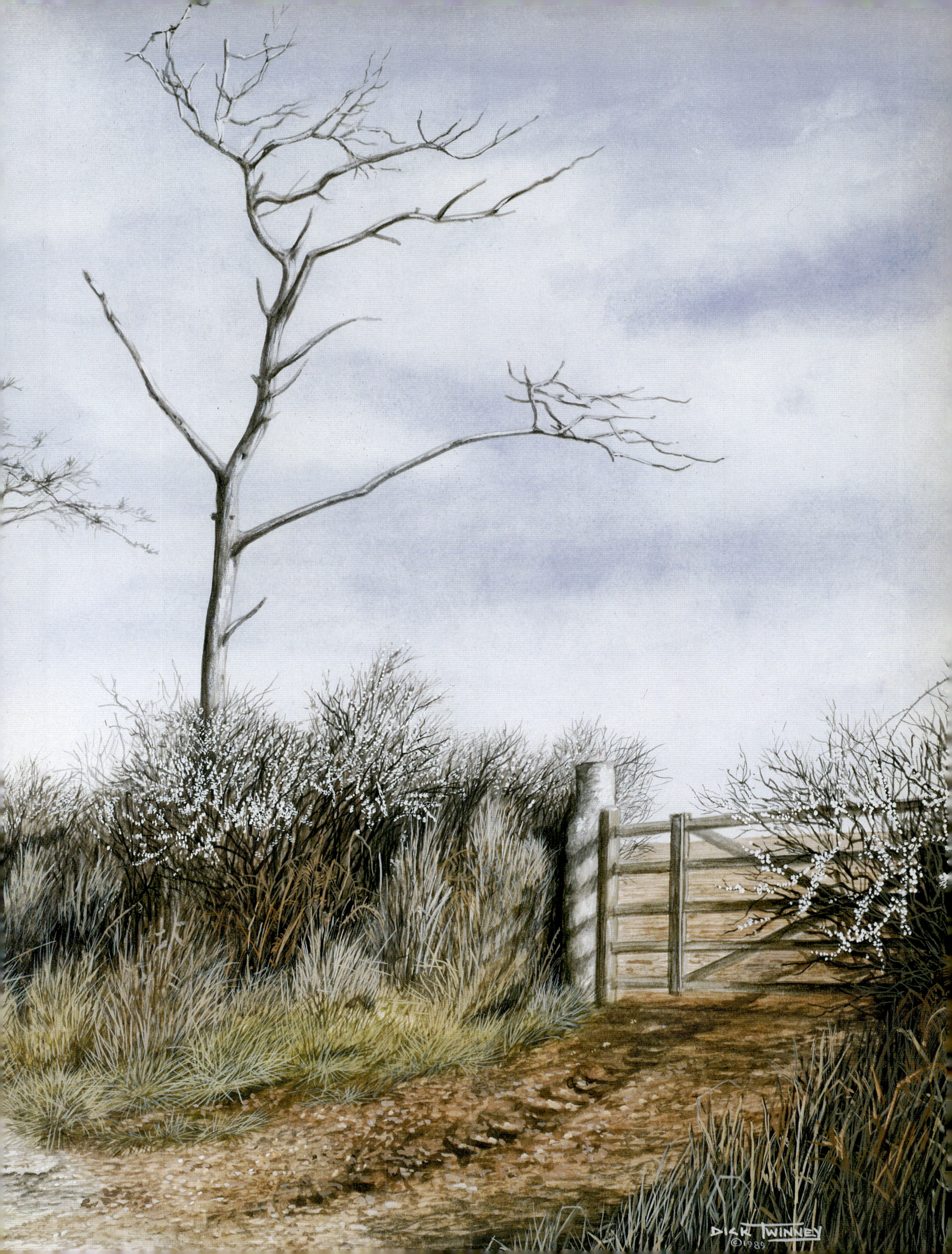
DICK TWINNEY
©1989

FIRST WEEK

DAFFODILS

This painting was taken from the hedge below the old barn in Halveor Lane, close to my home. The hedge was a mass of golden yellow patches of wild daffodils growing up in magnificent profusion out of the hedgerow-top covering of moist green mosses and ferns. It was a very wet day, which gave the foliage an incredible richness which seemed to magnify the colours.

The blackberry still had some old leaves, though the edges were burned and discoloured attractively by the winter frosts and winds. These contrasted sharply with the fresh green leaves just breaking out. The polypody fern, shown here, is very common in the warm, damp English climate and in the area depicted it gave an almost jungle-like feel, especially with the continuous drip, drip of the rain from the backcloth of old gnarled oak trees. These trees had covered the area in fallen leaves and acorns some months previously. Now all that remained of the acorns were the holders. The actual acorns had long since been eaten or carried away by such hedgerow inhabitants as woodmice, squirrels and jays.

The moist undergrowth had brought several banded snails from their holes in the hedge. The specimen illustrated here is the white-lipped form but the colours on this species of snail vary greatly and can be any combination of brown, yellow or white with thin or thick bands. I had great difficulty painting this particular snail, which I had brought back to my studio, as it was extremely active and kept moving off the fern upon which it was placed. I greatly enjoy painting these tiny creatures; it is always a challenge to try to capture every minute detail in watercolour.

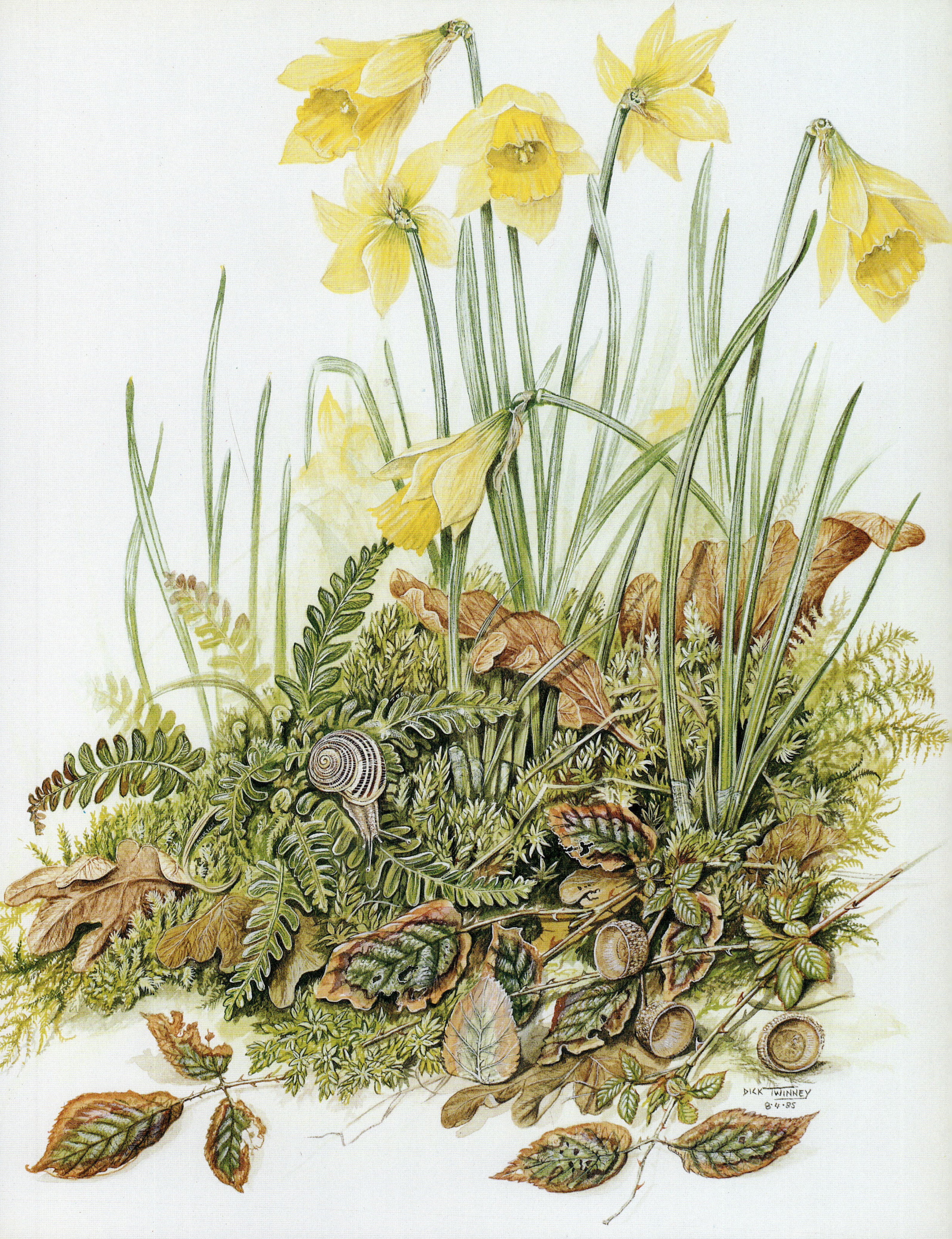
DICK TWINNEY
8·4·85

Second Week

WOODMICE

Some time ago, during one of my favourite walks down Lower Halveor, I found a super old boot lodged in the hedge. It had obviously been used as a food store for woodmice as it was bursting with old sloe stores, hawthorn stones and ash keys, all with the kernels and seeds neatly removed. There was also some old nesting material in the toe area.

The only flowering plants at the scene were some celandines, their bright yellow waxy flower heads standing out brightly against their dark green foliage. Growing behind the boot was a hart's-tongue fern which still showed the effects of bitter cold February winds. The hawthorn was yet to leaf, although some of the buds were just starting to open. In the time it took to complete this painting (about two weeks) the hawthorn in my studio vase had burst into a mass of fresh green leaves.

The woodmouse, or long-tailed fieldmouse as it is sometimes known, is a great personal favourite and I have often kept them as pets to allow for closer observation. They are a neat, alert little creature, extremely active and, although mainly nocturnal, are occasionally about for short periods during the day, giving their presence away by a rustle of dead leaves as they nip through the grass or hedge bottom. Large inquisitive eyes, large ears and a continual watchful attitude are essential as they are preyed upon by many animals including weasels, foxes, owls, kestrels and the domestic cat.

During the autumn their main source of food is seeds and nuts, but at this time of the year they turn to buds, snails and centipedes. They will, when living near man, make full use of garden fare, particularly peas for which they have a great liking. They will also readily make their homes in our outhouses and sheds. One family has moved in under one of our outdoor aviaries where they take full advantage of the regular supply of bird seed.

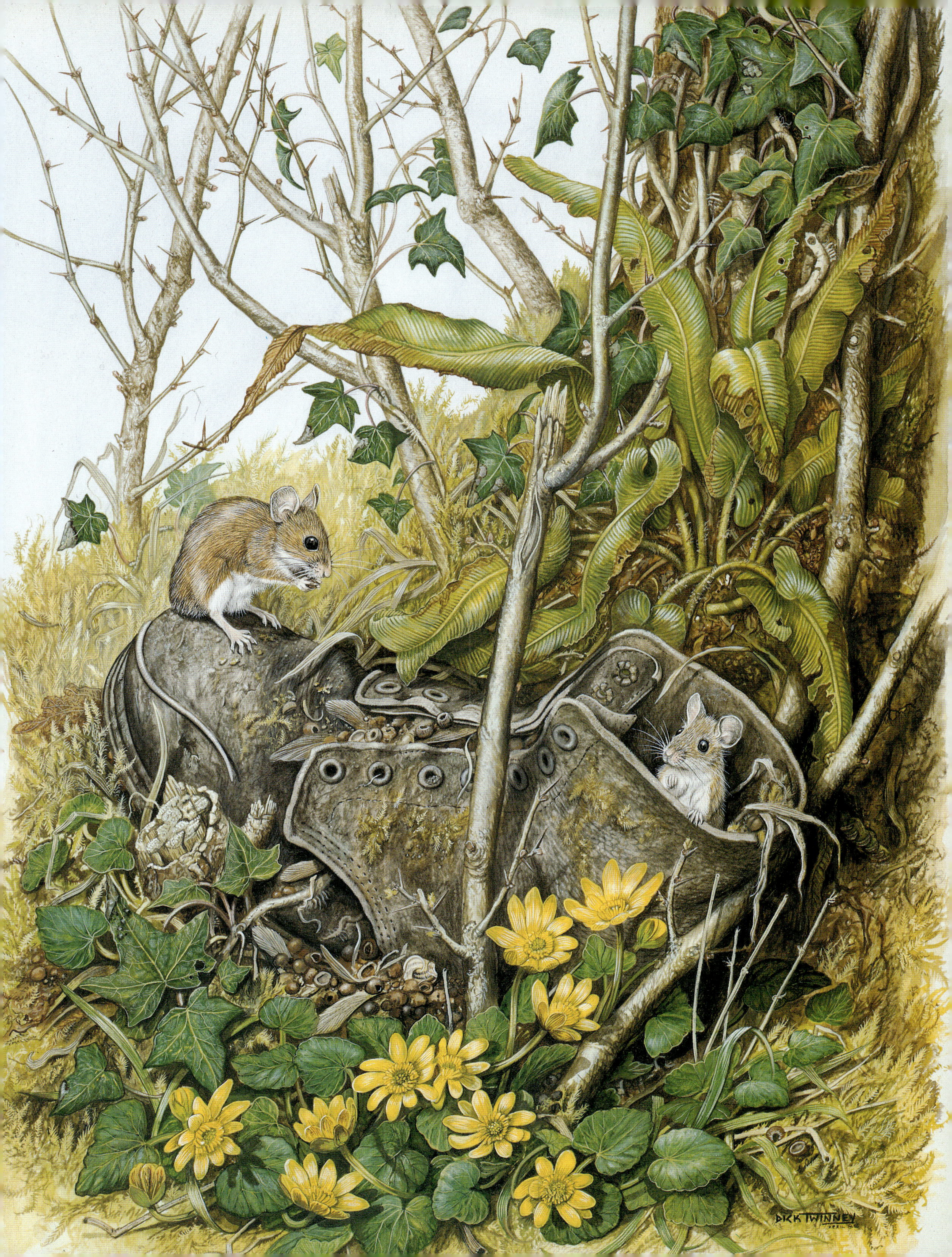
DICK TWINNEY
APRIL 06

THIRD WEEK

REED BUNTING

On a clear bright day down a small lane on the top of a high, barren moor, a male reed bunting was bursting with song from a favourite perch on a stunted oak tree.

The hedge here is made of granite blocks and stones, infilled with moorland peat. The oak had claimed a foothold on the edge of the hedge, where its twisted form leant away from the prevailing wind. The foliage on the hedge consisted of bracken, various heathers and moorland grasses. Everywhere was covered in mosses and lichens.

The male reed bunting was immaculate in full breeding plumage, his black head showing clearly silhouetted against the pale blue sky. His song consisted of three notes, followed by a whistle, which it repeated over and over again. Although loud and far carrying it sounded very monotonous, especially if compared with a nearby skylark's rich and varied song.

As I drew nearer the male bunting took flight, giving a loud whistle of alarm. It was then that he was joined by a female bunting, who must have been lower in the hedge or on the ground and, due to her inconspicuous plumage, had remained unobserved. She was probably gathering nesting material, usually this would consist of various grasses.

Reed buntings, as their name implies, were once birds of wetland habitats, but as these areas have been drained for agricultural purposes they have demonstrated their adaptability by moving on to drier areas such as the moors.

They nest low to the ground in a rush or grass tussock and usually lay five eggs which are pale green or buff in colour with heavy black spots and streaks. In common with other ground-nesting birds, but unlike perching birds, the bunting, if disturbed at the nest, will divert attention by feigning injury. The bird will shuffle along the ground with wings outspread as if broken.

The reed bunting is an attractive little bird which is well worth closer study. Since expanding its habitat some have been observed at bird tables, feeding with chaffinches and greenfinches.

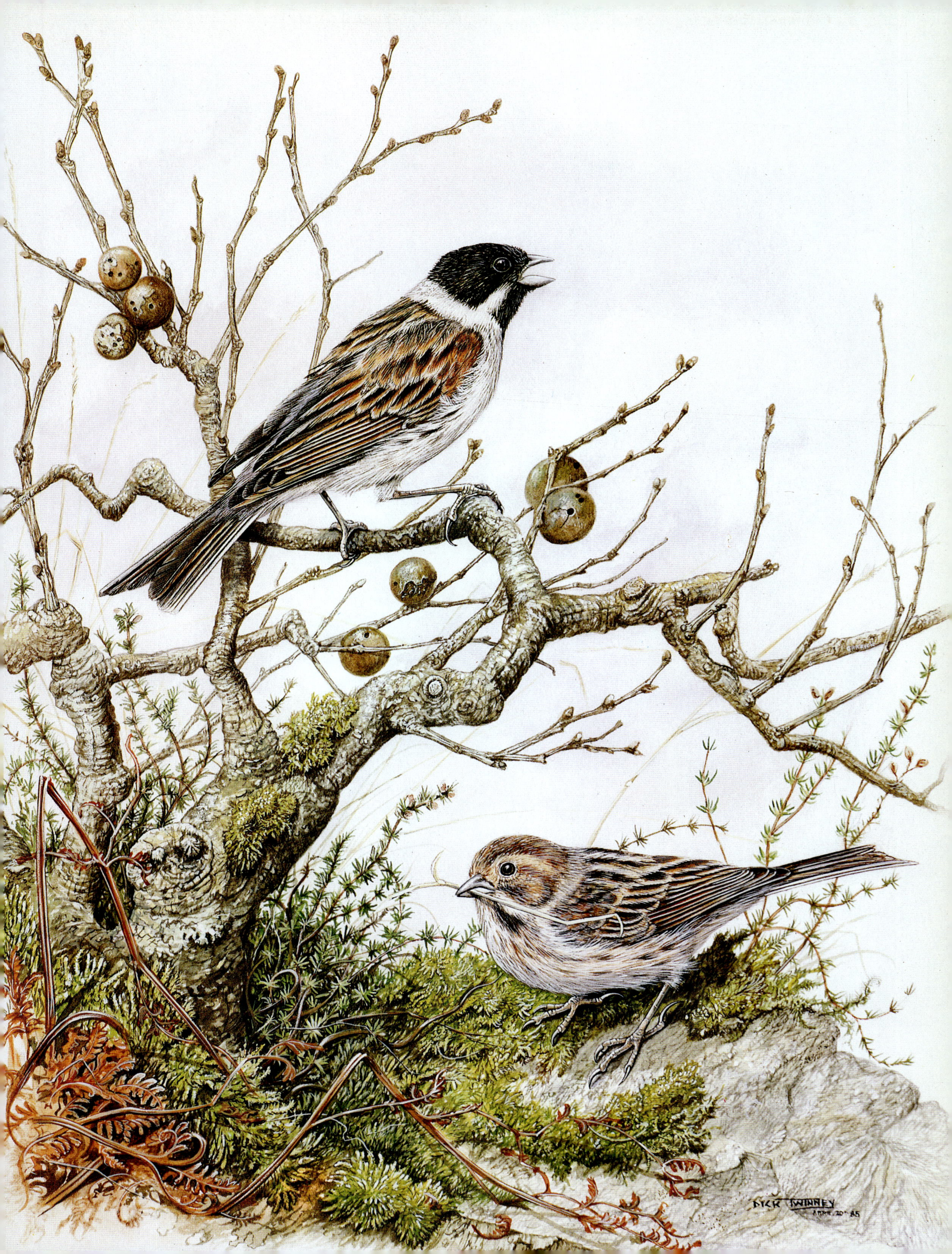
DICK TWINNEY

Fourth Week

TAWNY OWL AND STARLINGS

This painting has been in my imagination for some time. The composition took shape after I saw a tawny owl inadvertently try to land in a tree full of roosting starlings.

It was dusk and the starlings had obviously just settled down for the night. They were fairly quiet apart from the odd local dispute over a particular branch, when suddenly the whole tree erupted with whirring wings and shrieking calls. I did not realize what had happened at first, then I saw the harassed tawny owl beating a hasty retreat, pursued by the indignant starlings who soon gave up the chase to return to their chosen tree to chatter and call to each other about the disturbance. This incident took place in the autumn of 1986; during April 1987 I discovered a starling's nest site in an old woodpecker-holed tree. They were constructing their nest, fliting busily to and fro. I suddenly thought why not combine the two incidents in a painting. It would give me the opportunity to capture the aggressiveness of the angry starlings (this time in summer plumage) along with the surprised agitation of the owl, feathers puffed out, eyes staring and beak clacking. Having had to care for many injured tawny owls I have often observed this defensive behaviour and always treat it with respect.

For this painting I have worked from dead specimens as it was essential to re-create accurately the complex plumage of these two very different species of bird. This type of painting is a real challenge – here I had to show the owl's plumage as soft and gentle with a velvety matt finish, whereas the starlings' iridescent feathering is much harder. I was very pleased with the end result; I could never have achieved the detail by working exclusively from photographs.

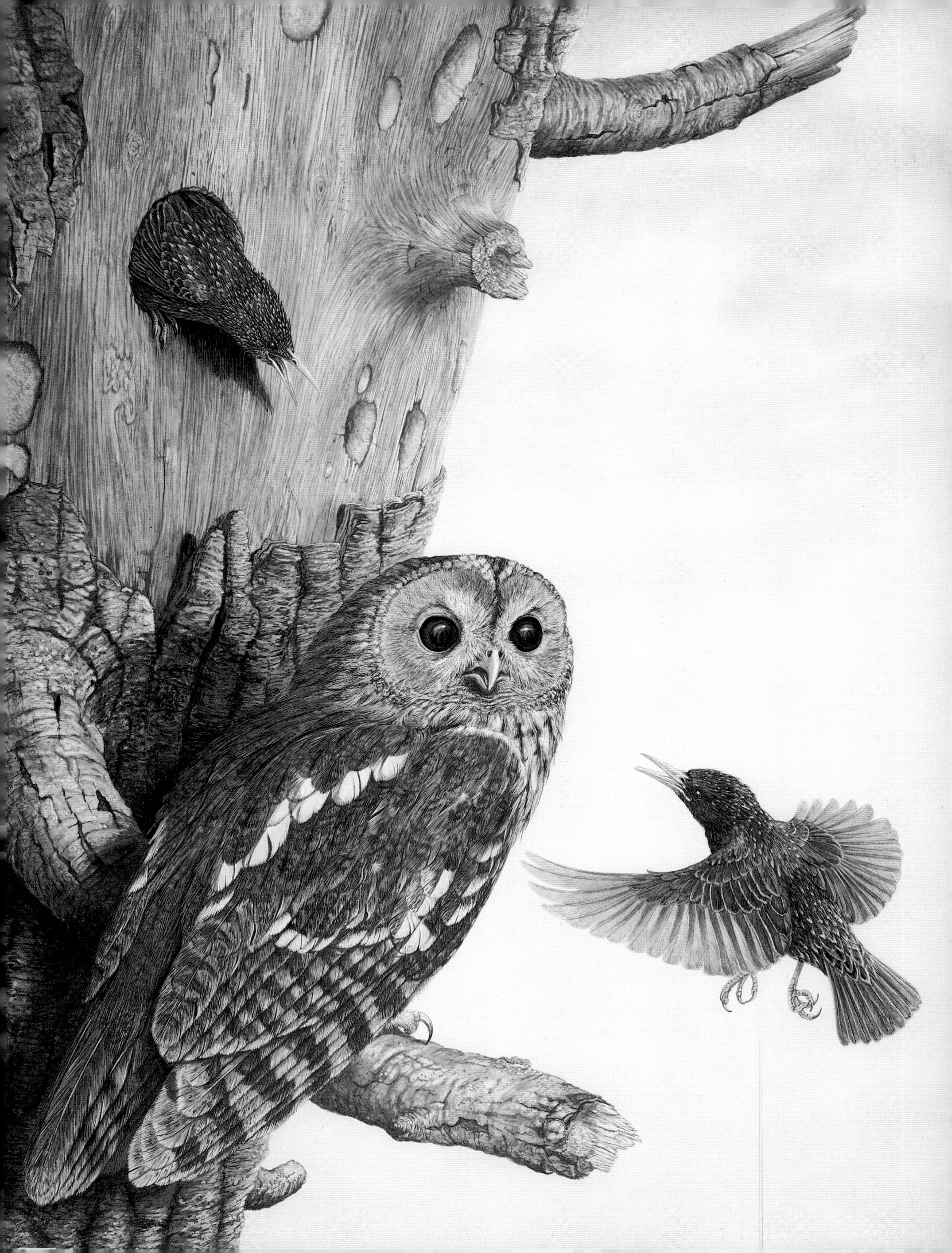

Fifth Week

BRIMSTONE AND PRIMROSE

I always look forward to seeing the brimstone as it usually coincides with the first warm weather of the year, emerging from hibernation as early as March should the temperature rise sufficiently.

It is one of my favourite butterflies, being unique among British species with its interesting wing shape and rich butter-yellow colouring. It is also thought to be the origin of the word 'butterfly', which is derived from its early name of 'butter-coloured fly'.

Brimstones make a fine sight on a sunny spring day, fluttering through the filtered sunlight of the tree-lined hedge, their beautiful colouring standing out against the fresh green of the emerging foliage and new grasses.

For this painting I have shown two males in pursuit of a female as a prelude to courtship. I have included primroses in the picture as they complement the brimstones colouring to perfection, the delicate flower heads silhouetted against the broad fleshy leaves. The primrose is one of the most abundant and widespread of our spring flowers and can be found throughout the British Isles, wherever there are woods, hedgerows and grassy places. Its name comes from *prima rosa* and means first rose, a suitable companion to the brimstone, which is usually our first butterfly.

The brimstone is one of the few British butterflies which hibernate in the adult stage, usually choosing thick evergreen foliage in which to spend the winter months. A particular favourite is ivy, in which the resting butterfly is superbly camouflaged, its closed wings closely resembling the ivy leaves.

Brimstones lay their eggs during May on buckthorn bushes, the larvae emerging in June. These, too, are extremely well camouflaged, being of a similar green to the food-plant.

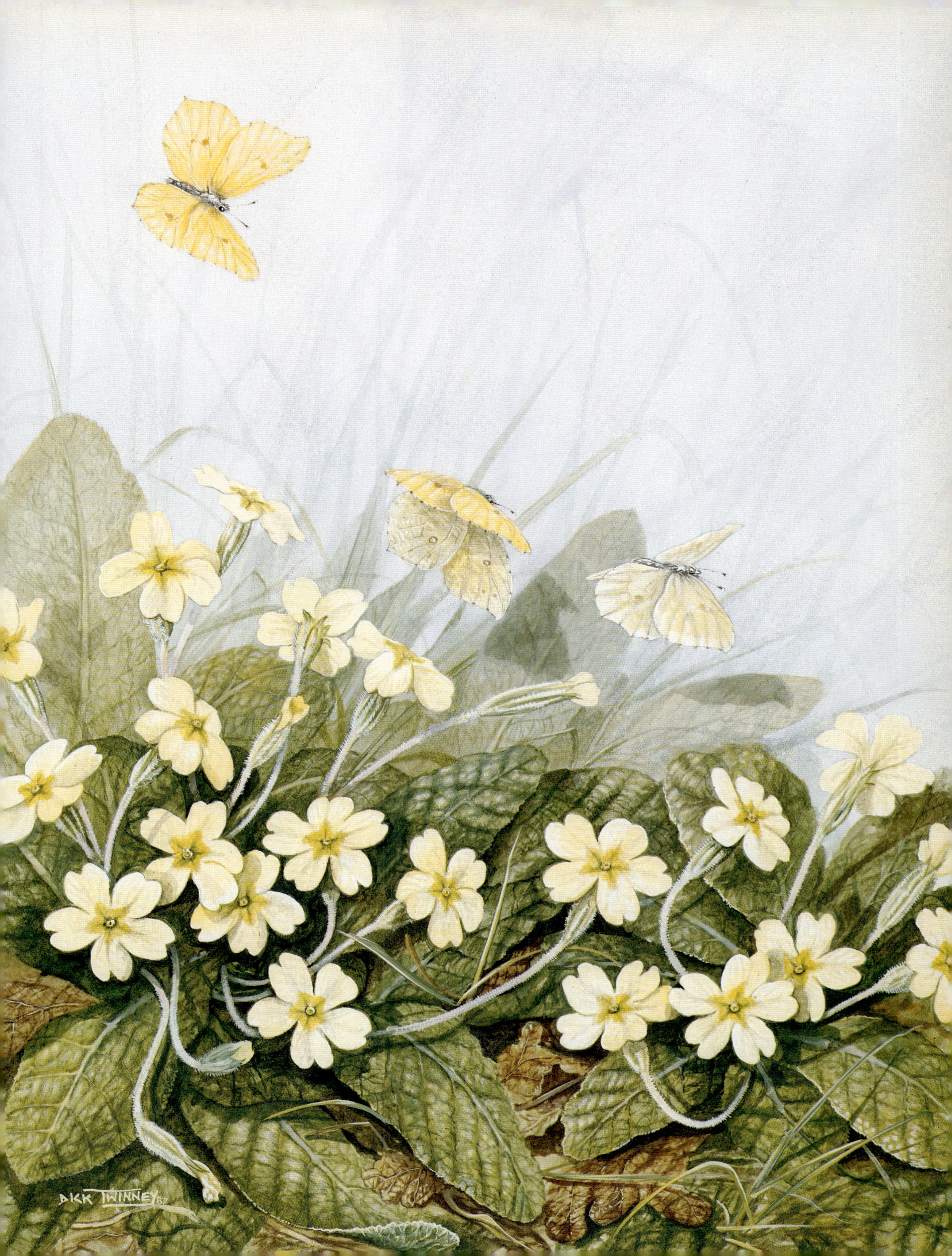
DICK TWINNEY 87

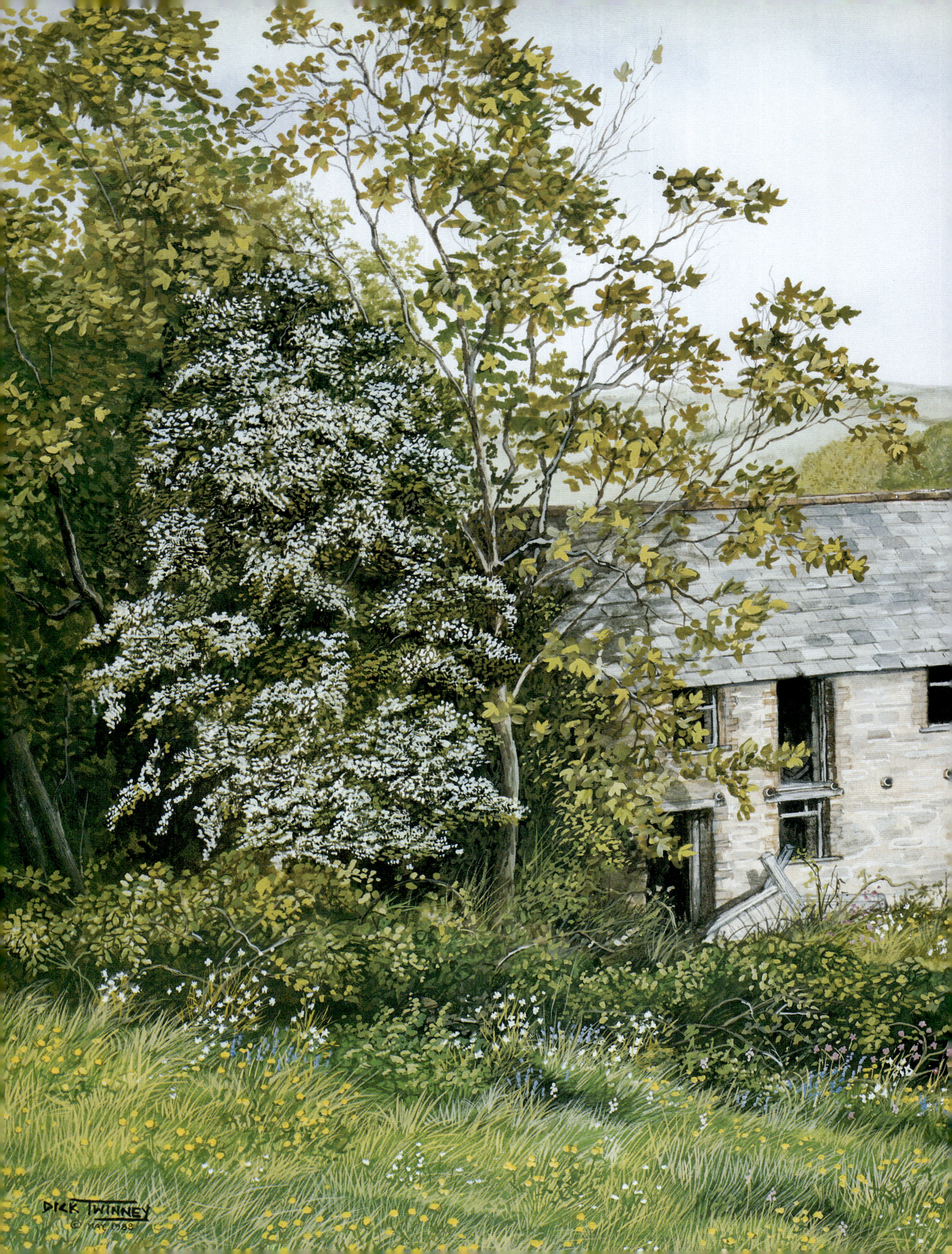
DICK TWINNEY
© MAY 1988

MAY

The old barn in Halveor Lane is sanctuary for a variety of wildlife and plants. Will it too fall victim to the builder's avarice?

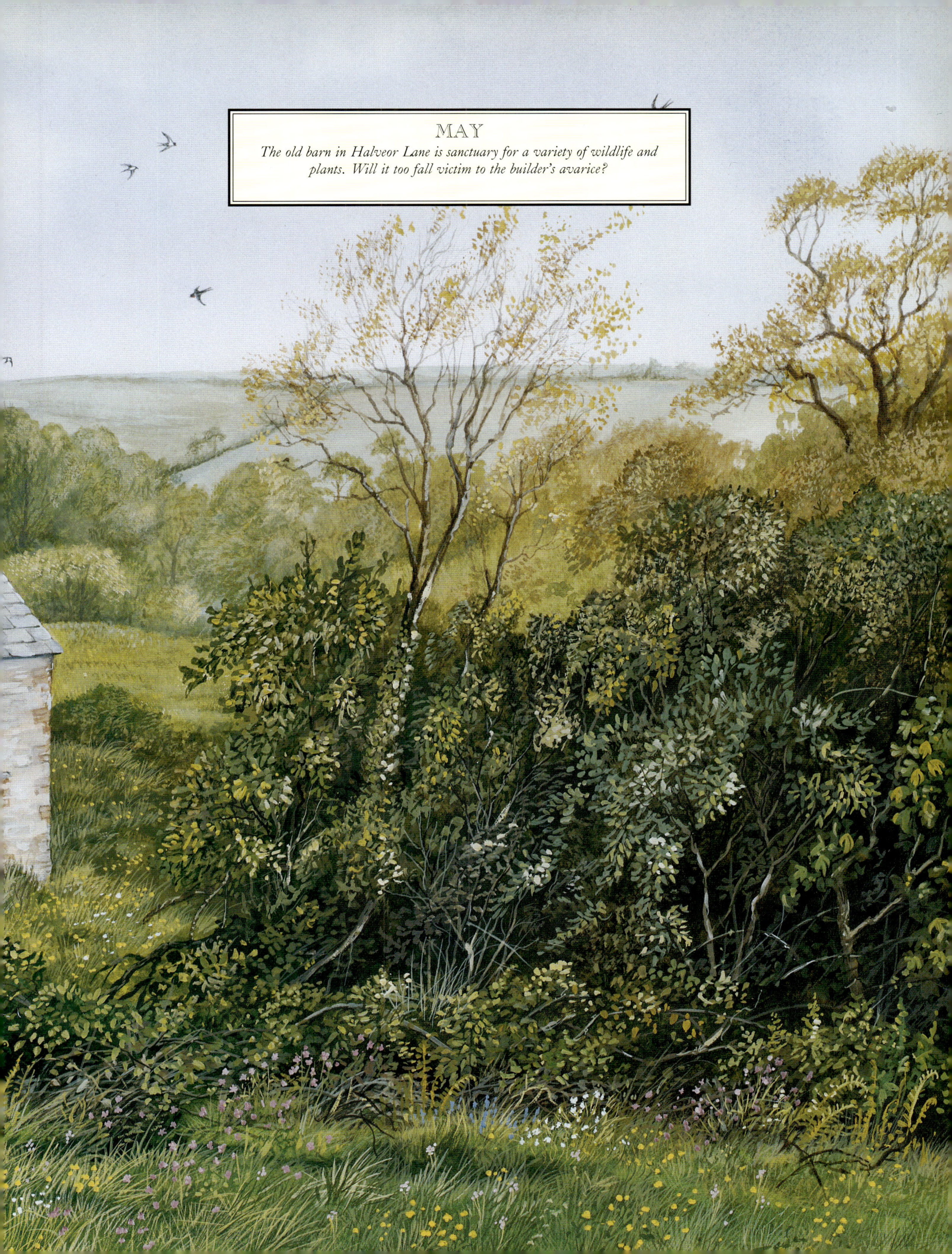

First Week

BLACKBIRD AT NEST

May is the time of prolific nesting. In no other month are so many nests being constructed and eggs laid. Early nest-builders like sparrows, thrushes and the blackbird already have hungry youngsters ever clamouring for constant sustenance. The parent birds are back and forth, searching the hedge bottoms, gardens and lawns for ground invertebrates.

Resident blackbirds, which have nested in our garden for many years, are no exception. Enormous beak-loads of wriggling worms are constantly in transit from source to ever-open gapes. The family scene I have painted here was actually happening in a rose bush but I have situated it in an ash tree, a previous nesting site, which allowed me to bring the old nest into my studio for reference.

Baby birds have always fascinated me and I love watching them, particularly at feeding time. In the painting the male blackbird has arrived with a fine meal of juicy worms. Three of the nestlings are straining for attention while one has not quite realized what is going on. This is the first brood of the year; the young birds will take flight after about two weeks. They are still fed for some time after leaving the nest and it is at this time that they are at their most vulnerable to predation, and many are lost. However, the parent birds may have another two or even three broods which helps maintain the blackbird's position as Britain's most common breeding bird.

Blackbirds are a delightful addition to any garden, the male's most melodious song awakening the day and taking the lead in the dawn chorus. They are a bird of great character and charm. Blackbirds are also one of the first birds to detect danger – a prowling cat or patrolling sparrow hawk is brought to the attention of all garden dwellers by a loud, scolding chatter. They are also very territorial during the breeding season and woe betide any intruding rival male – he is soon given short shrift, accompanied by much tail cocking and scolding.

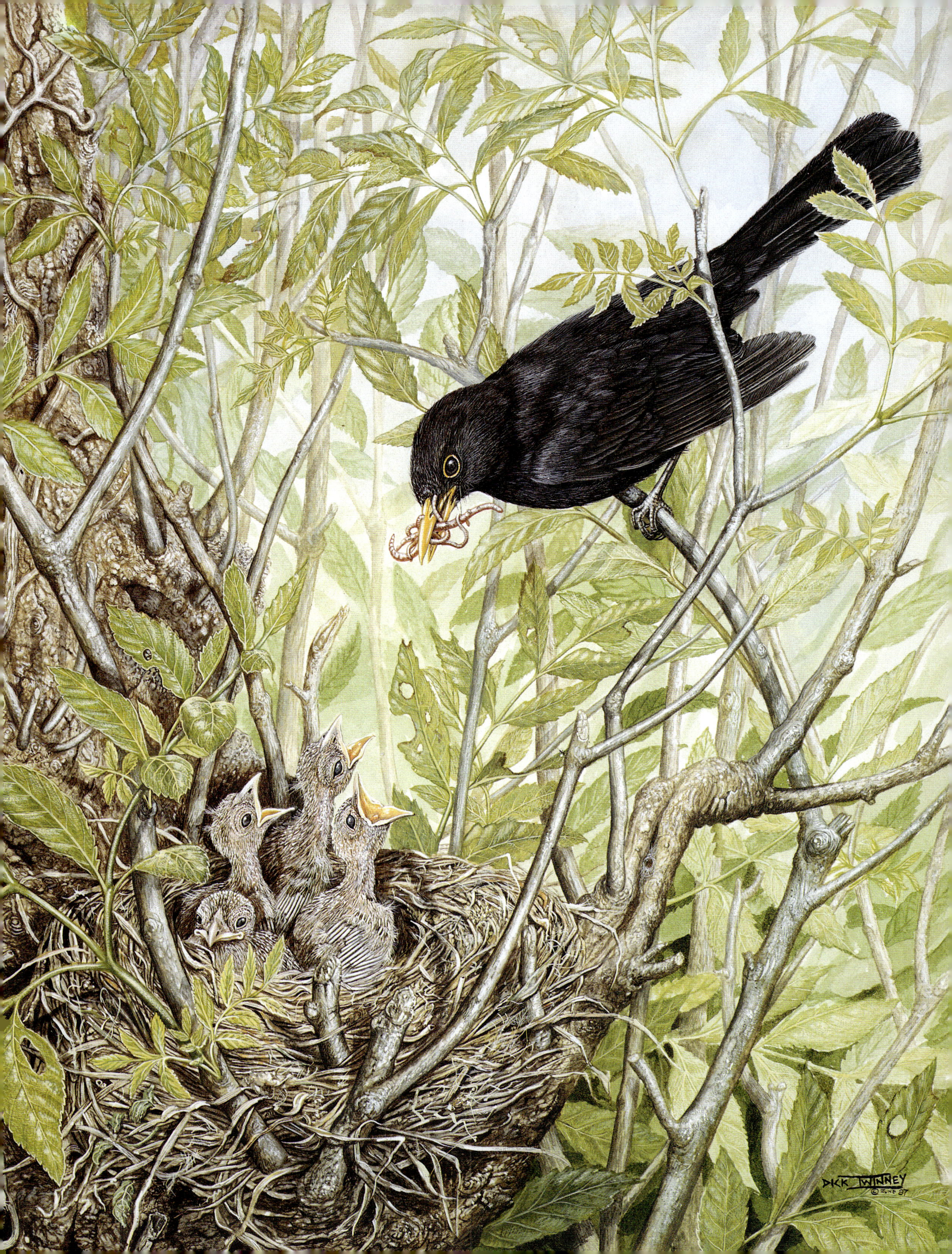
DICK TWINNEY
© JUNE 87

Second Week

WEASEL

In the summer of 1985 we kept a young weasel for a few weeks. It was found in a farmhouse kitchen where it had taken refuge in a wellington boot. It had been around for some time and to survive had been feasting on the dog's dinner.

When it was first brought to us it was little bigger than my thumb, but it grew rapidly. We kept it in a large aquarium where it gave us hours of entertainment, particularly at feeding time, when it would emerge from the hay provided for cover and would stand bolt upright on its hind legs, exactly like a miniature otter. It was very playful and would roll around in the hay, diving with real enthusiasm into the hollow logs which were in its temporary home.

Under normal circumstances the only time you are likely to see the weasel is when it crosses the road. They are generally very secretive and spend their time in thick cover, where they make use of vole runs and mouse tunnels, slipping through the grass and scrub in a fast, fluid-like motion. They are extremely efficient hunters and prey mostly on small mammals and ground-nesting birds. They, in turn, are preyed upon by owls, birds of prey and larger carnivores.

For this painting I have chosen an area of hedge which was thick with bluebells and greater stitchwort. At this time of year hedges are a mass of colour and one is spoilt for choice when deciding which flowering plant to include in any particular painting.

I have chosen bluebells, mainly because they tower above the weasel, therefore giving greater emphasis to its diminutive size. Bluebells, also known as wild hyacinth, give off a wonderfully rich scent which lingered in my studio while I worked on this painting.

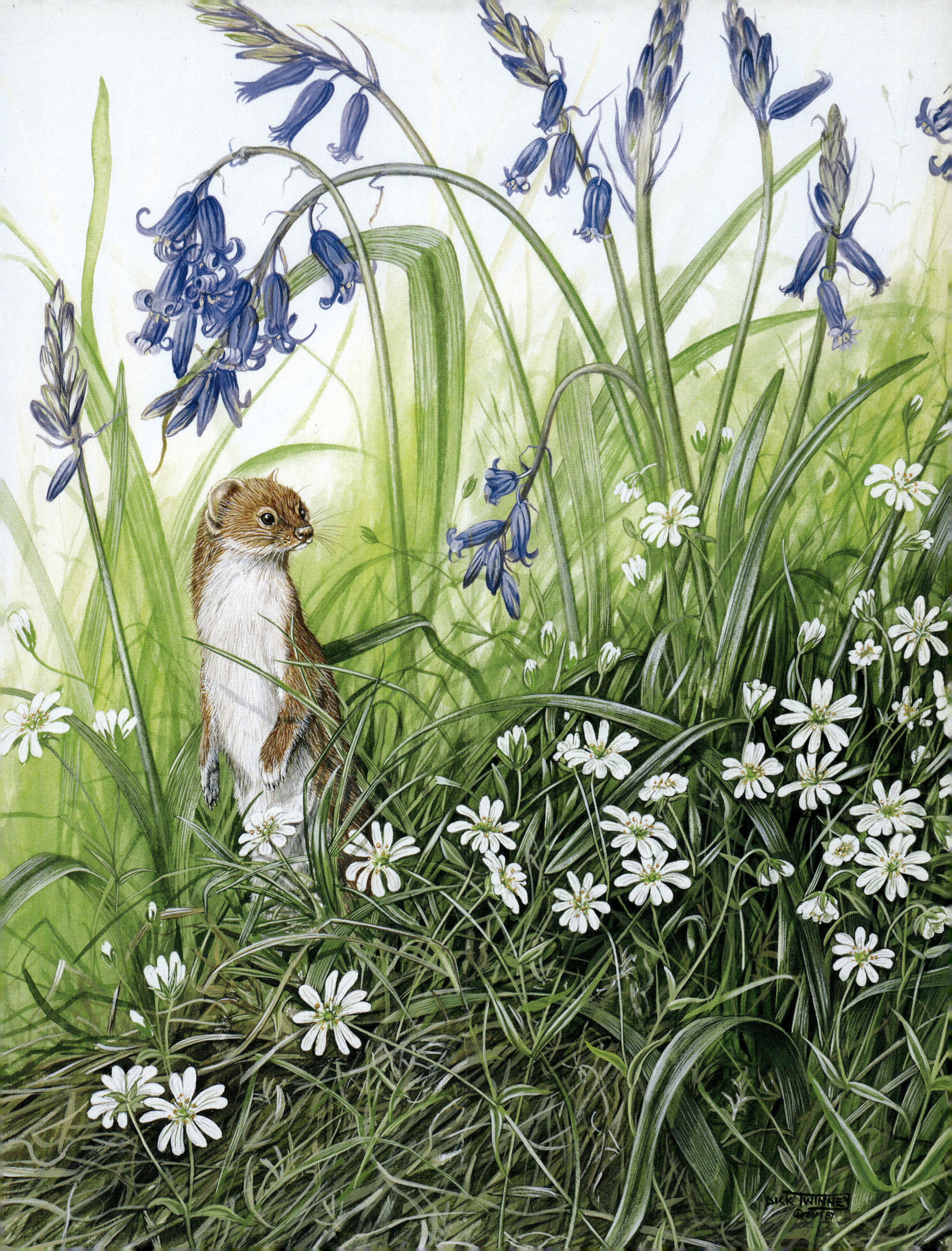
DICK TWINNEY

Third Week

THRIFT, KIDNEY VETCH AND STONECROP

It is sometimes difficult to comprehend the tremendous changes that take place along the cliff-tops during the spring months. While walking the rocky coastline during the winter it is easy to think that the massive black cliffs are devoid of any real flora other than a crouching carpet of brown grasses and small salt-resisting, fat-leaved plants. These cling tenuously to the cracks and crevices of the rock faces and the cliff-top stone walls, battered by winter winds and soaked by the salt-laden spray pushed into the updraughts by the relentless Atlantic rollers. How they survive this sort of punishment is yet another aspect of nature's great ability to adapt to the changing seasons, and change they do.

Suddenly, it seems, the greeny-brown foliage of the winter wind-scorched thrift bursts forth into masses of pink flowers, carpeting the stone walls and cliffs, spreading out in great clusters of colour, enhanced further by other May flowering plants such as kidney vetch and sea campion.

The various pale pink to magenta tones of the much-loved thrift or sea pink (it was featured on George VI brass threepenny pieces) is complemented by the contrasting and much varied colour combinations of the kidney vetch or lady's fingers. The flower heads of this plant can be yellow, red through to purple, or any combination in between, often on the same plant. I have shown the most common yellow form in my painting, which also features the ever present stonecrop with its tight pink buds soon to open out into small star-like flowers in the coming weeks.

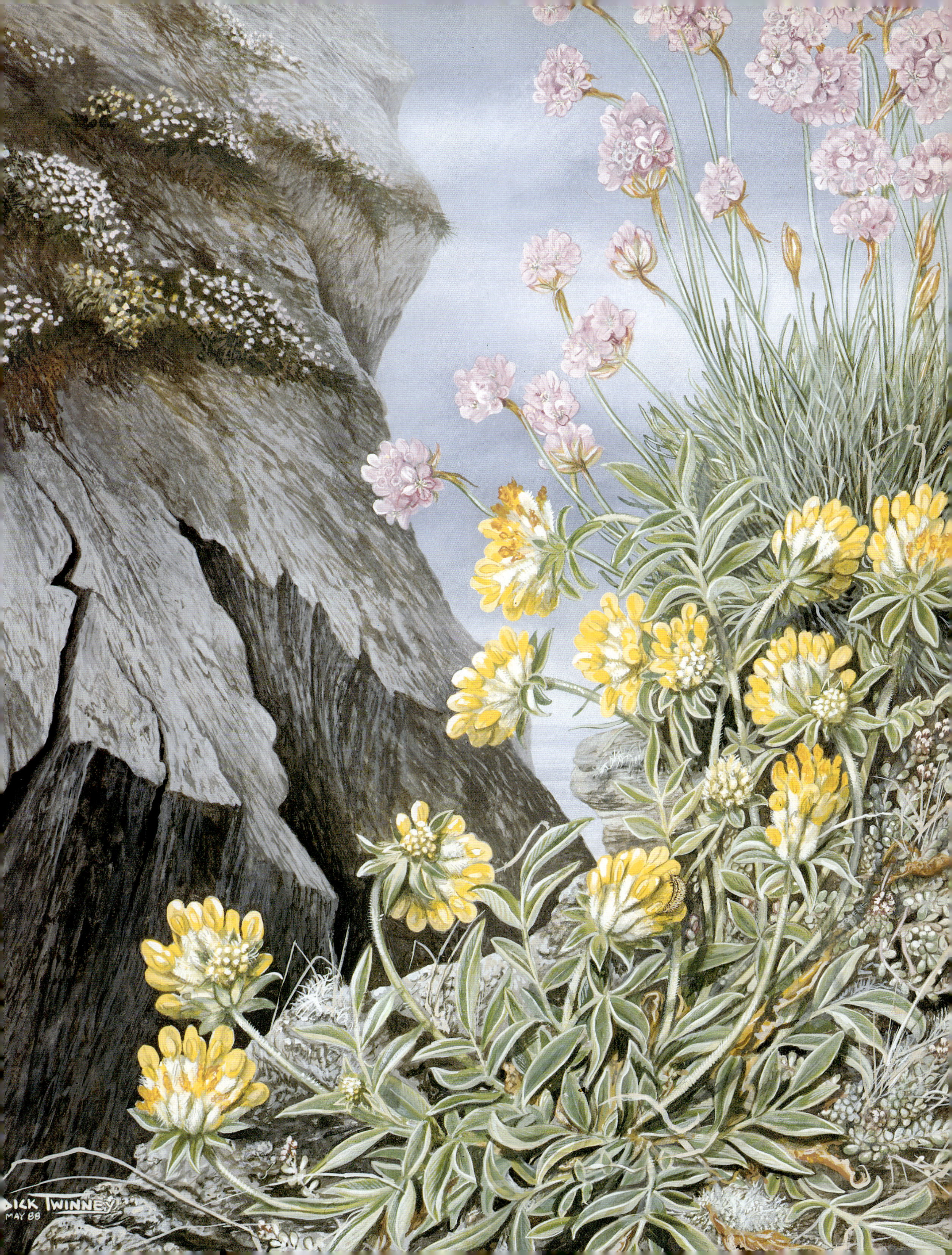
DICK TWINNEY
MAY 89

Fourth Week

SLOW-WORM AND FORGET-ME-NOTS

As the weeks move towards summer and the sun climbs even higher in the sky, the warmth it generates brings out our cold-blooded animals, and lizards and snakes become active in the hedgerows and on the cliff-top. In the West Country there is an abundance of reptiles, the warmer climate and rough terrain being eminently suited to their needs.

Soaking up the energy-giving rays of the spring sunshine, the copper-bronze coloured slow-worm is typically found curled up, almost hidden, among the grasses and foliage of the bankside. The slow-worm is an interesting creature of many contradictions. Firstly its name is totally incorrect, it being neither slow nor a worm. In the past it has also been called 'blind worm' and 'deaf adder' which are equally unsuitable titles. It is also confusing that the slow-worm is not, as it appears, a snake, but a lizard that has evolved into a swift gliding reptile, having no need of legs unlike most lizards. It is a hunter of the leaf-litter, soft earth and hedgebottom, its main food source being small invertebrates, particularly slugs, which makes the slow-worm the gardener's friend and therefore should be much encouraged.

For this painting I have used a fine female specimen for a 'model'. She differs from the more uniformly bronze male by having dark stripes along the back and sides. The area from where we collected this slow-worm is a rough overgrown bank which was gradually coming alive with spring flowers, including the forget-me-nots which I have included in the painting. They have sprung up between the ferns and old gorse stumps in a brilliant array of blue, adding a contrasting touch of colour to this sunny mid-May composition.

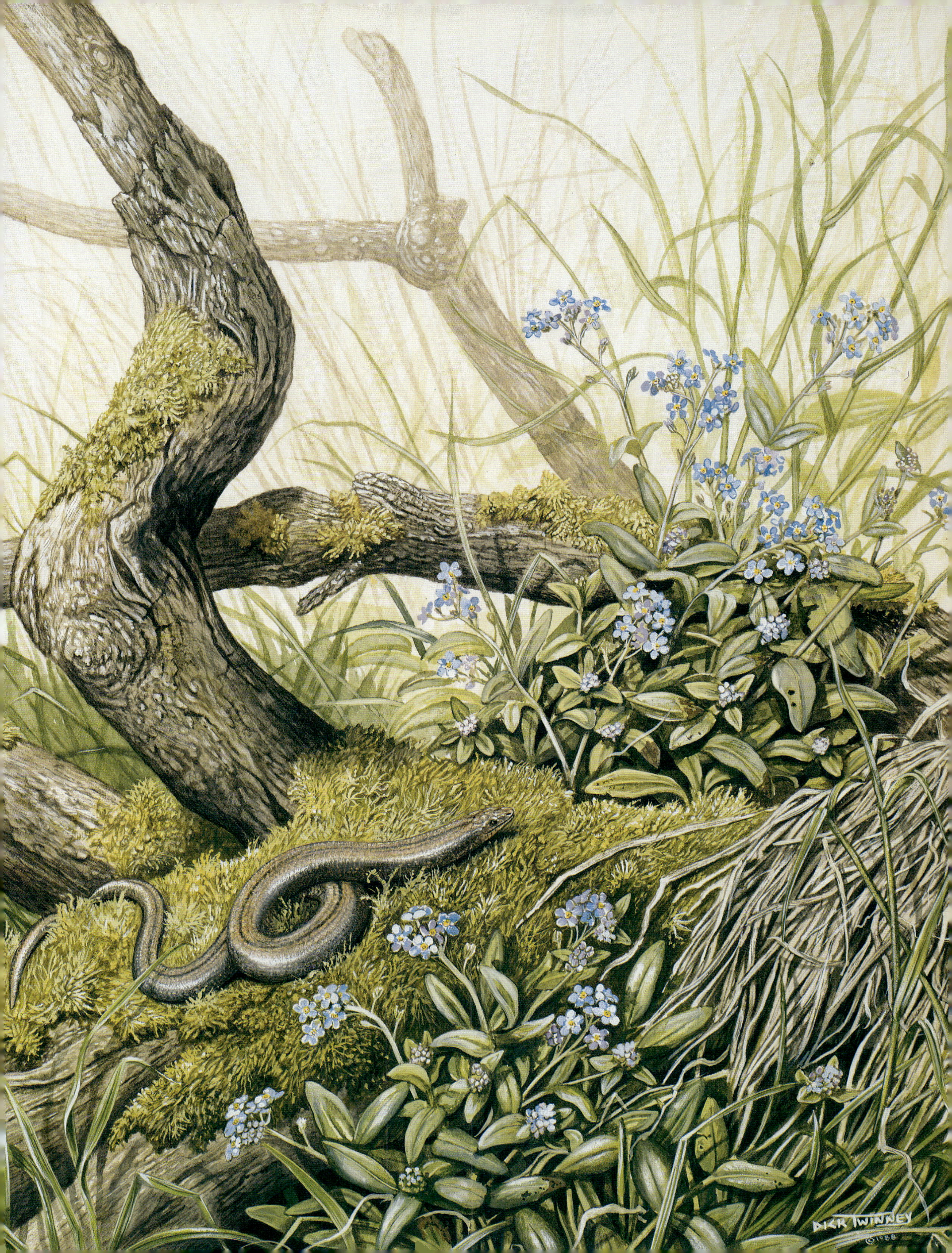
DICK TWINNEY
©1988

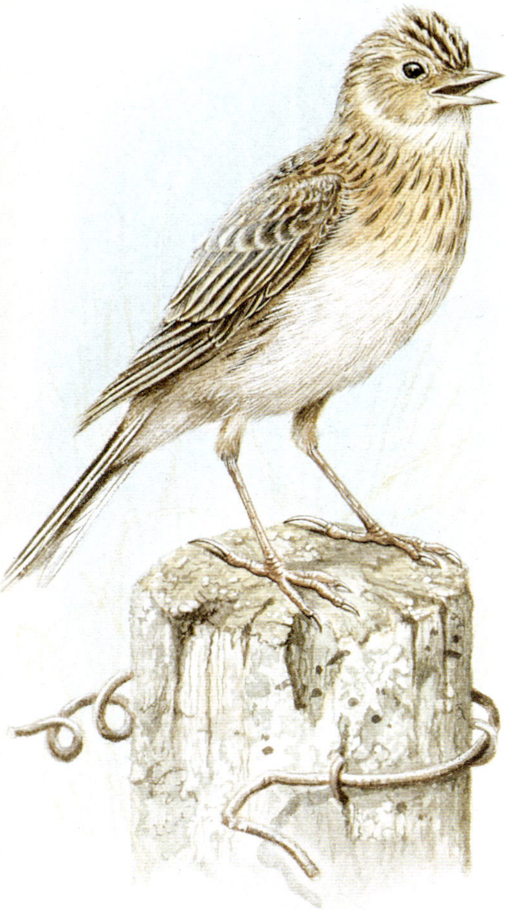

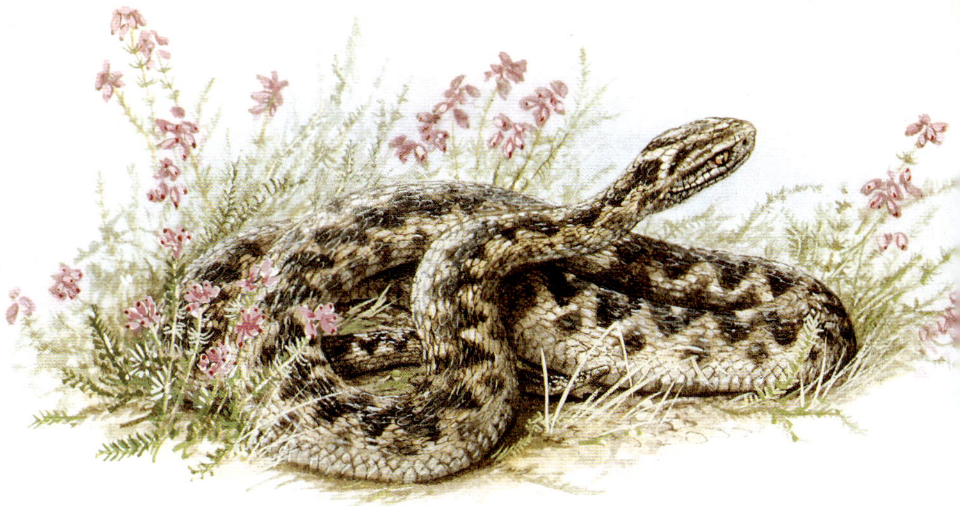

SUMMER

Summer is the middle age of nature's calendar with much of the burst of spring growth slowing down and fruits of the autumn gradually forming. Bird-song can still be heard but not with the full-throated enthusiasm of spring. Summer bird-song tends to be gentler, as in the soft cooing of the turtle dove or the melodious warbling of the sky lark.

Many young mammals are out and about, going through a period of exploration and education, a time when they are most vulnerable. These include hedgehogs, dormice and harvest mice. Red deer hinds give birth to their calves. Young bats are also in evidence, while the adults can be seen on still summer's evenings swooping and diving along regular flight paths in pursuit of flying insects.

For most reptiles summer is a time of birth and growth; it is when we are most likely to see lizards and snakes. One to be aware of is Britain's only poisonous species, the adder or viper, which likes to

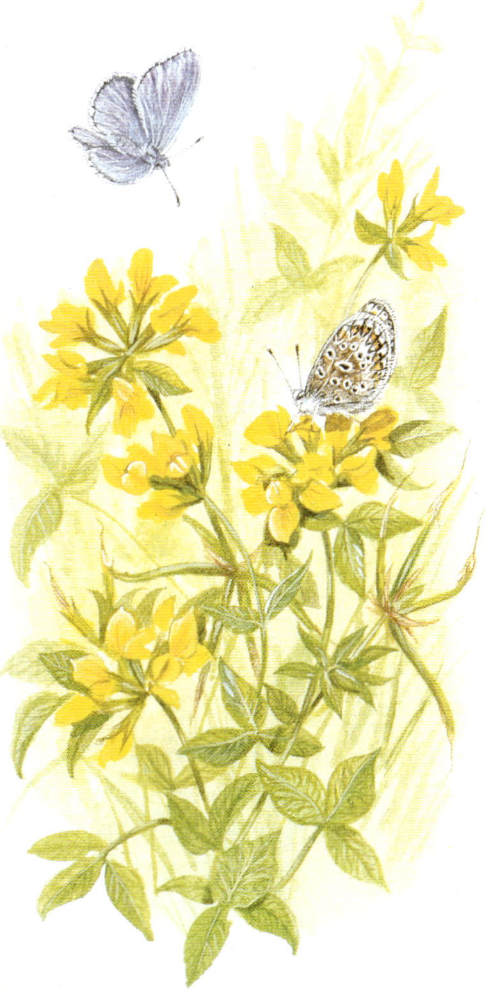

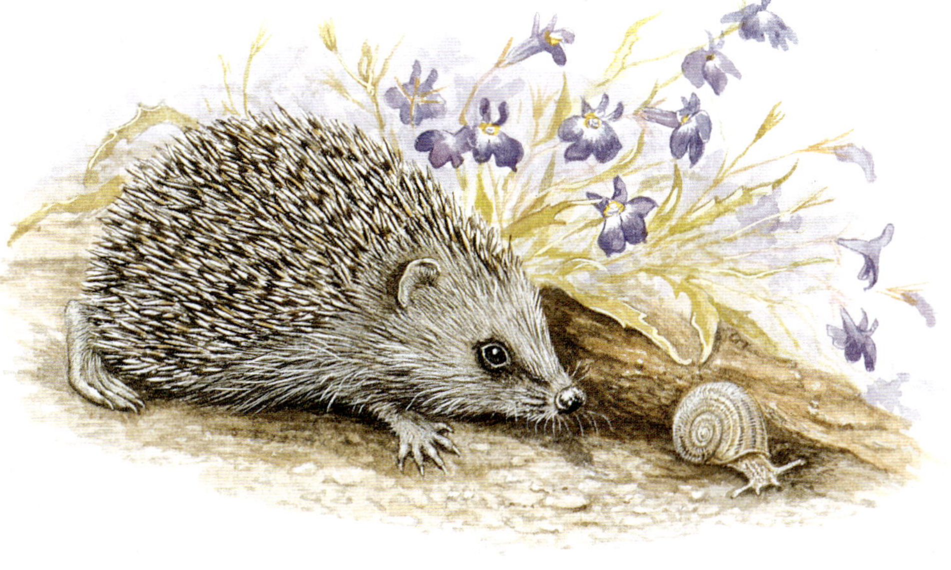

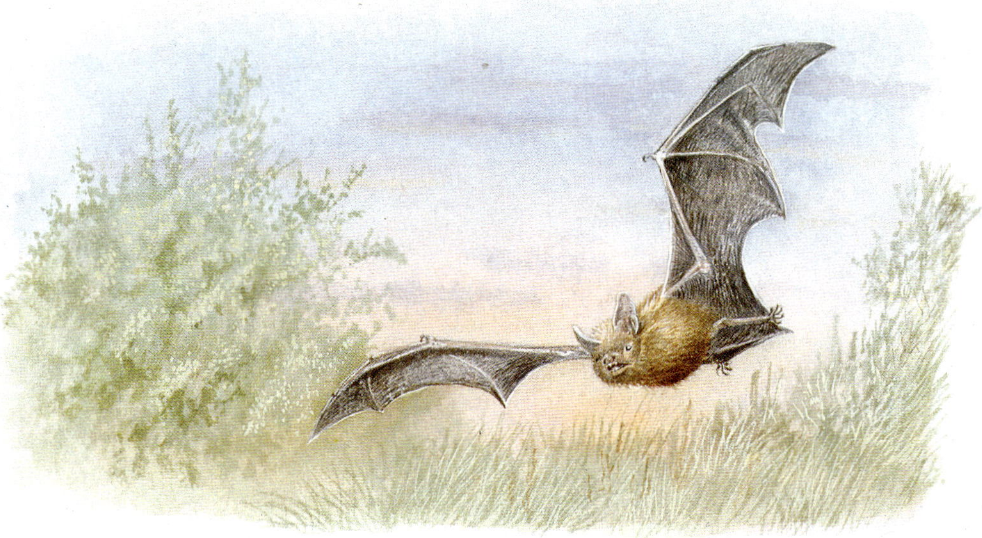

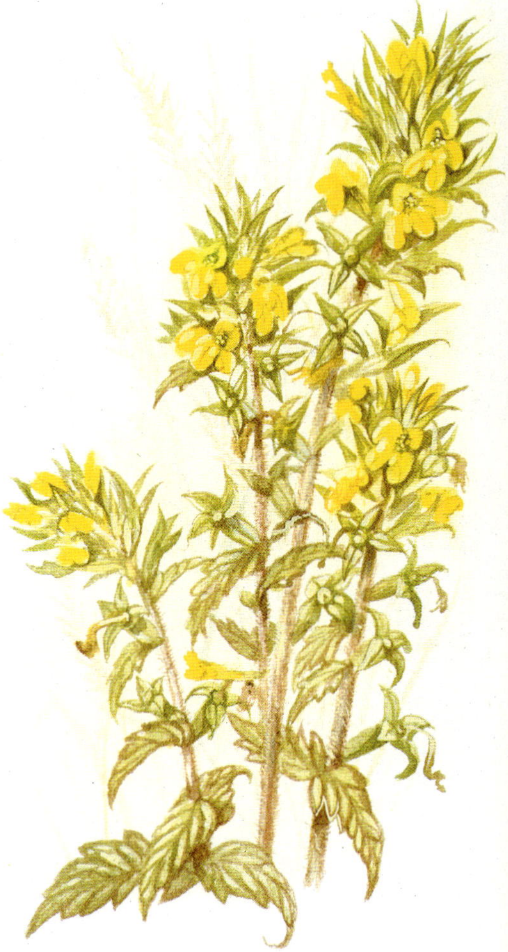

sunbathe on moors and cliff-tops. It will always move away if disturbed.

Most butterfly species are on the wing during the summer months. Look out for small tortoiseshells, red admirals and peacocks. These generally bring a dash of colour to our gardens, while out in the countryside common blues, coppers and skippers are all busy visiting the large array of summer flowers.

In the damper meadows the prominent yellows of the flag, yellow bartsia and bird's-foot trefoil create a bright diversion, while the hedgerows and roadsides play host to pink and white roses, red campions and knapweed. On the higher ground of cliff-tops and moors the pinks of thrift and the various tones of purple heathers are predominant.

One of the most noticeable features of the summer months in the countryside is the way the landscape changes from fresh green to yellow-gold in colour in just a few weeks, as the cornfields ripen off ready for the harvest.

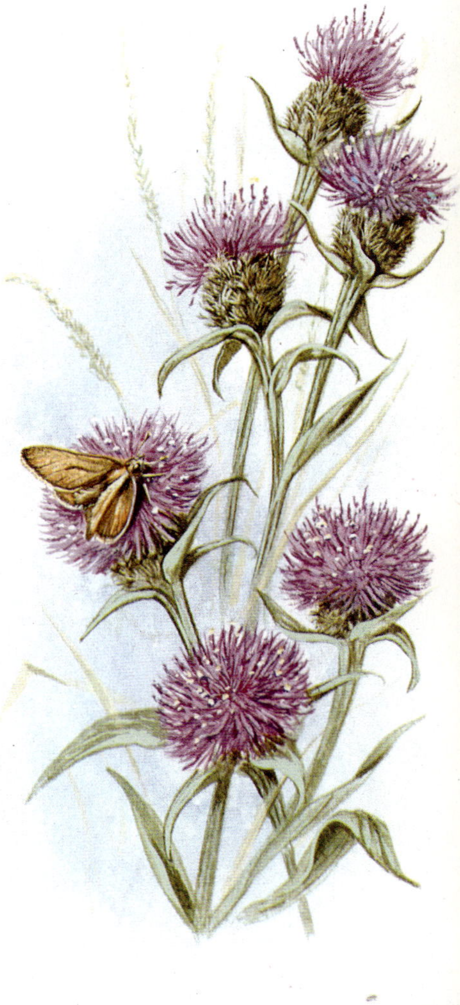

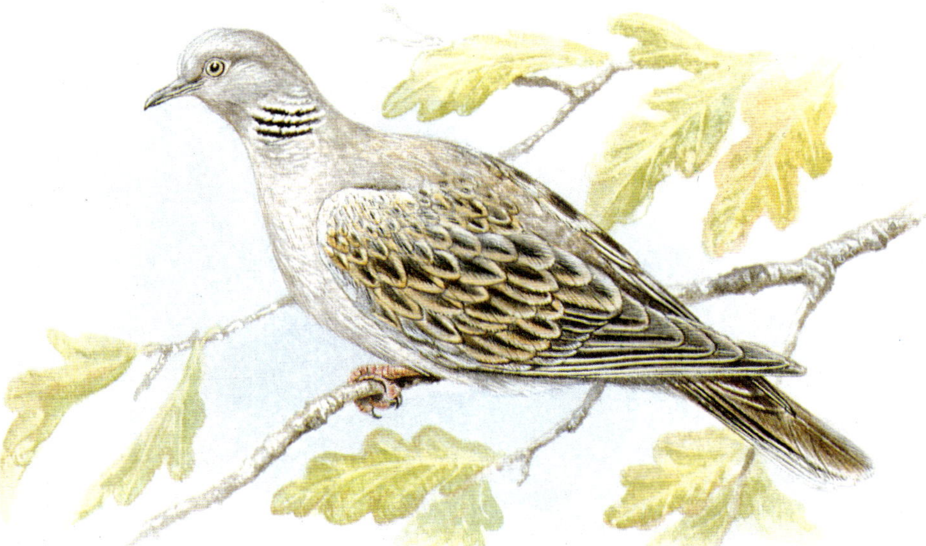

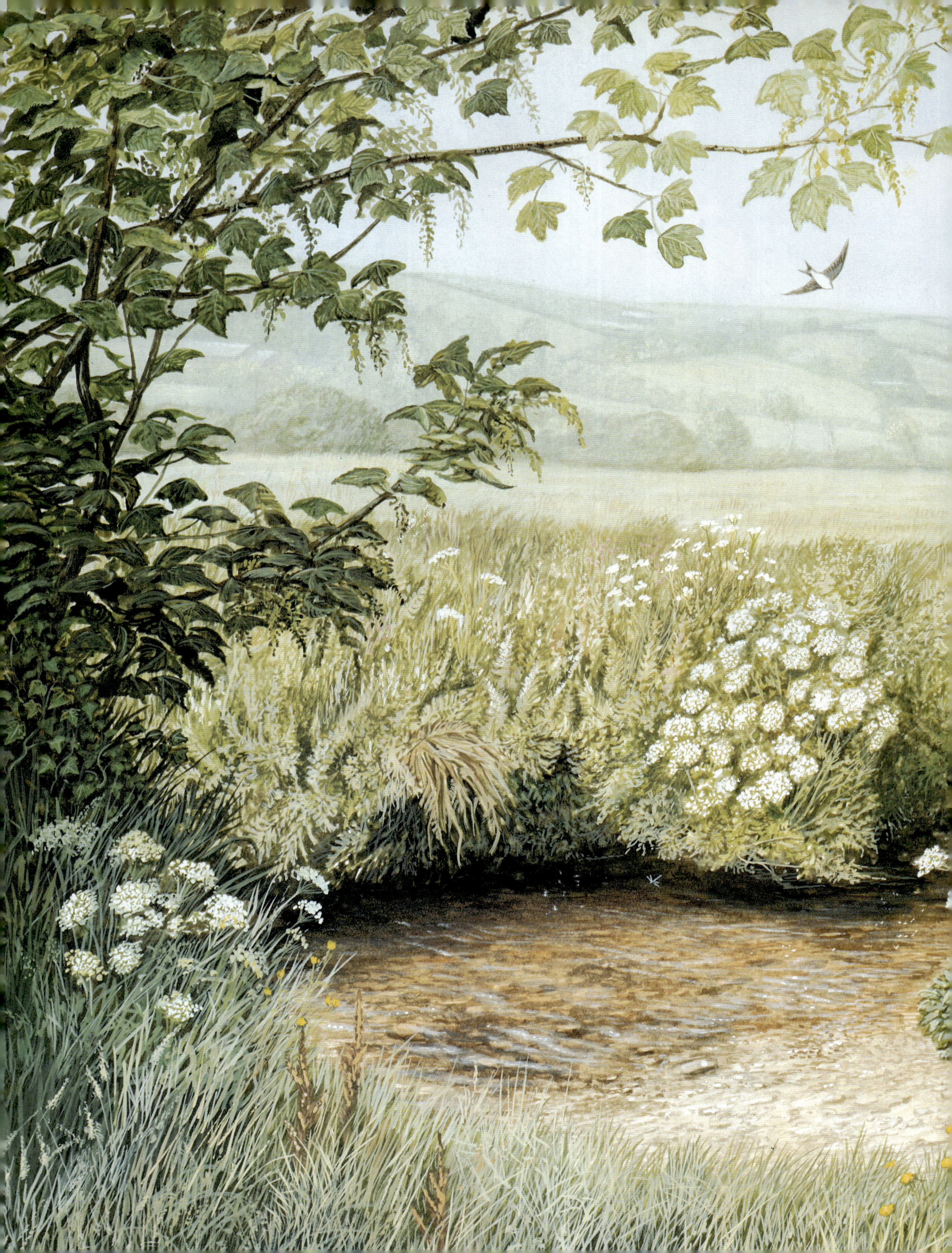

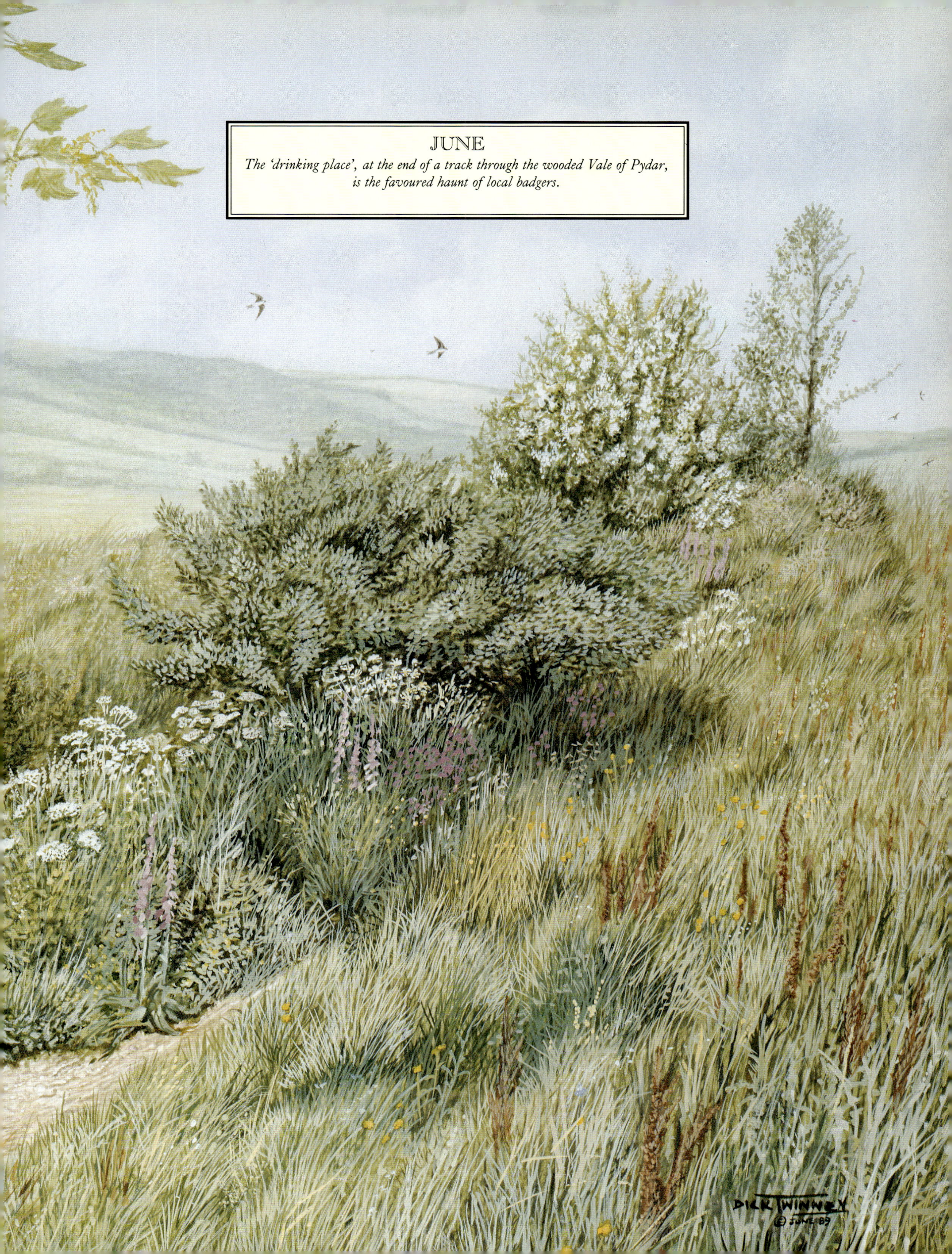

JUNE

The 'drinking place', at the end of a track through the wooded Vale of Pydar, is the favoured haunt of local badgers.

FIRST WEEK

FOX-CUBS

The summer has arrived. The long hot days are full of the hum of flying insects, fledglings cheeping and the rustle of small mammals in the hedgerow bottoms. As evening approaches rabbit kittens can be seen on the verges, cropping the ripe summer grasses. Many fox-cubs are taking their first look at the bright new world above ground, full of curiosity and fun they are delight to watch.

The cubs in the painting are around six weeks old, their home is an enlarged rabbit burrow in an old grass-covered bank. The immediate area around the earth is well worn with the coming and going of the vixen; many of the protruding roots have been chewed, I suspect, by the cubs trying out their new needle-sharp teeth. The whole area is brightened up by vivid blue patches of germander speedwell, although I have used some artistic licence in the placing of the flowers in the painting.

Having hand raised several fox-cubs, some from just a week old, foxes are very special to me and my family. At the time of writing we still have three foxes living with us which, for one reason or another, cannot be returned to the wild.

At this point I am tempted to hold forth on the evils of hunting foxes in the name of sport and tradition. I will control my desire. As an artist I am possibly over sensitive and over sentimental, but I fail to see the justification for pursuing any wild animal to a stressful and cruel death for the pleasure and self-gratification of so called sportsmen and women.

In the painting I have tried to capture the youthful curiosity of the cubs as they study the world about them. One peers across the fields, awaiting the return of the vixen, while another is showing an interest in a passing gatekeeper butterfly.

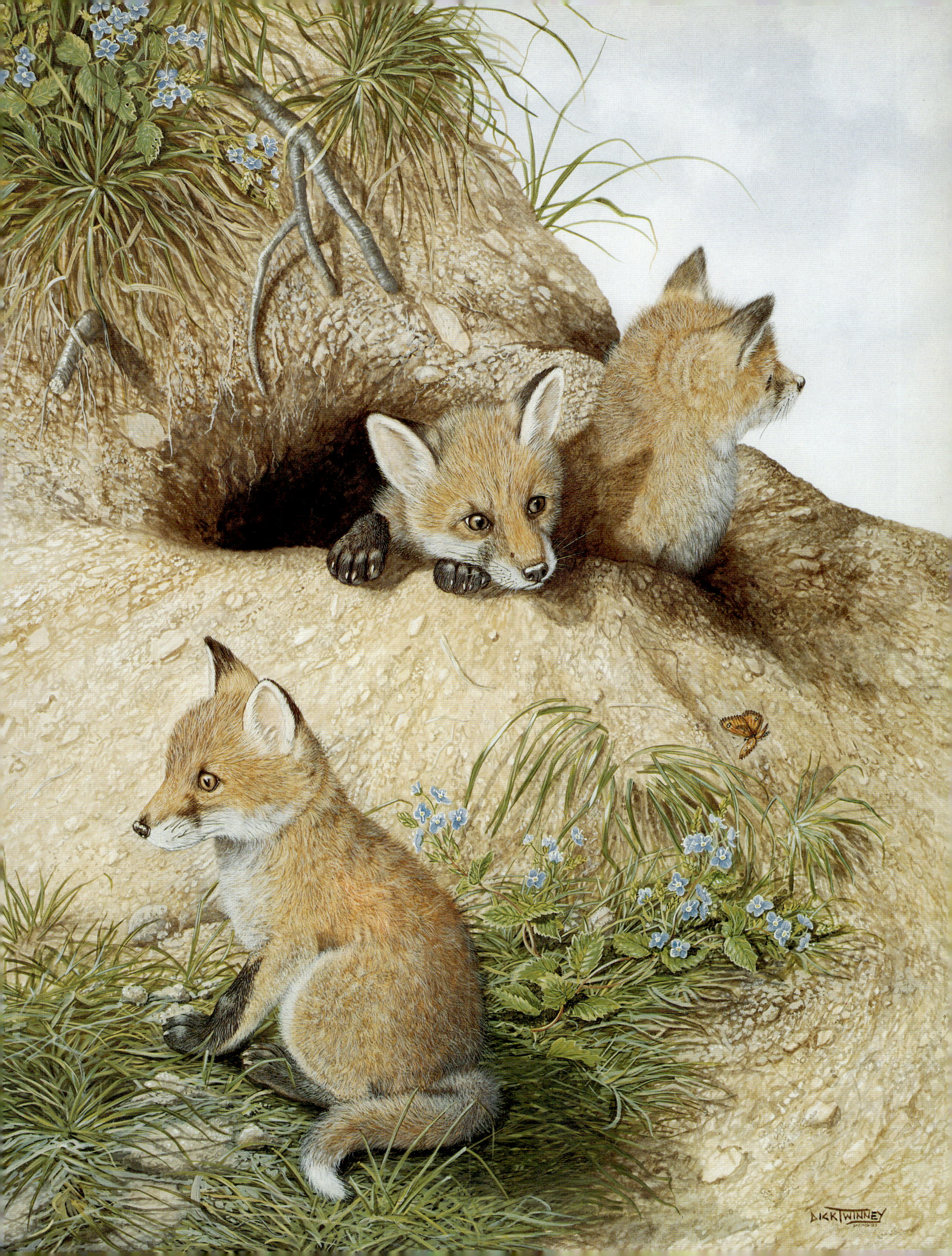
DICK TWINNEY

SECOND WEEK

DUNNOCK AND DOG ROSE

It was raining when I set off to gather material for a painting of a dog rose. My subject was a fairly large bush which I had been watching for several weeks waiting for it to bloom. It had now done so, standing out in a show of blazing pink between the more mundane hazel and blackthorn bushes. The stretch of hedge where this particular bush is situated has several other roses, including the white form of the dog rose, and some field roses, all adding beauty of colour and fragrance to the June hedgerow.

The summer rain shower had stopped, leaving the atmosphere fresh and clean, the smell of wet foliage and grasses scenting the air with a pleasant earthy aroma. As I continued on towards the particular rose bush my attention was drawn towards a plaintive piping bird-call from the wet hedge. A fluttering rustle, a scattering of raindrops and a small brown bird flew out from the hedge. Further on there was another call, another bird. It was a family of dunnocks, obviously sheltering from the rain. They were scattered up and down the hedgerow and the young birds had apparently only recently left the nest which was probably in the same hedge. The parent bird was agitated by my presence, as it kept calling as if to reassure the youngsters it was still around. I managed to spot two of the young birds, although I am sure there was at least two more.

On reaching my rose I became acutely aware of the immediate scene of natural beauty. The weak sunlight was filtering between the retreating rain clouds and causing the raindrops to glisten like many small jewels on the fresh green leaves. The spiders' webs, that were strung in festoons throughout the pink of the rose, were a delight to the eye and a pleasure to paint. I also could not resist including one of the young dunnocks in the picture.

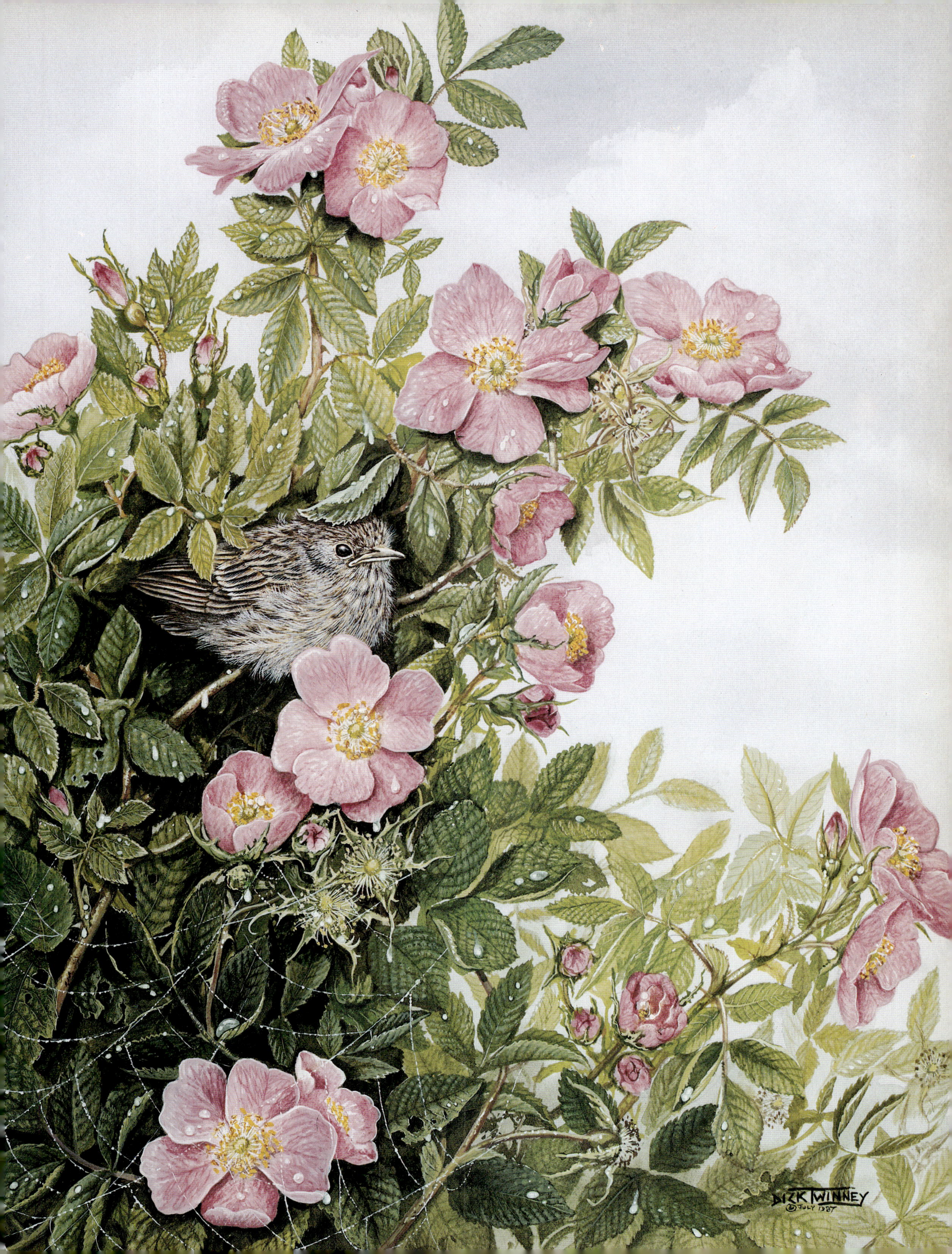
DICK TWINNEY
© JULY 1987

THIRD WEEK

FLEDGLING TAWNY OWL

Baby owls, without doubt, must be among the most appealing of all young birds, loved by both children and adults alike. Rarely a summer goes by that we do not have at least one baby tawny owl to raise, much to the delight of our children and friends.

Provided you have ascertained the correct diet, baby owls, as with other birds of prey, are easy to raise in captivity, readily taking food from the hand and soon adapting to their strange foster parents. We usually look after them until they are picking up food for themselves, then they are transferred to the local RSPCA centre where a good friend and bird expert has the more difficult and time-consuming task of gradually hacking them back to the wild. I am delighted to say this process is nearly always successful.

For this June painting I have chosen one particular character, affectionately known to us as 'Oggie'. He was extremely small when he first came to me, having been found in a local country lane, soaking wet and very weak, with no immediate sign of the nest site. Initially he had to be force-fed, but as his strength improved he was soon snatching food from our fingers. He remained in rather bad humour throughout his time with us, clacking his beak and fluffing out his soft feathers, with his eyes wide and staring defensively. He looked more comical than aggressive, but this belligerent attitude was something to be encouraged for he would stand a greater chance of survival once returned to the wild.

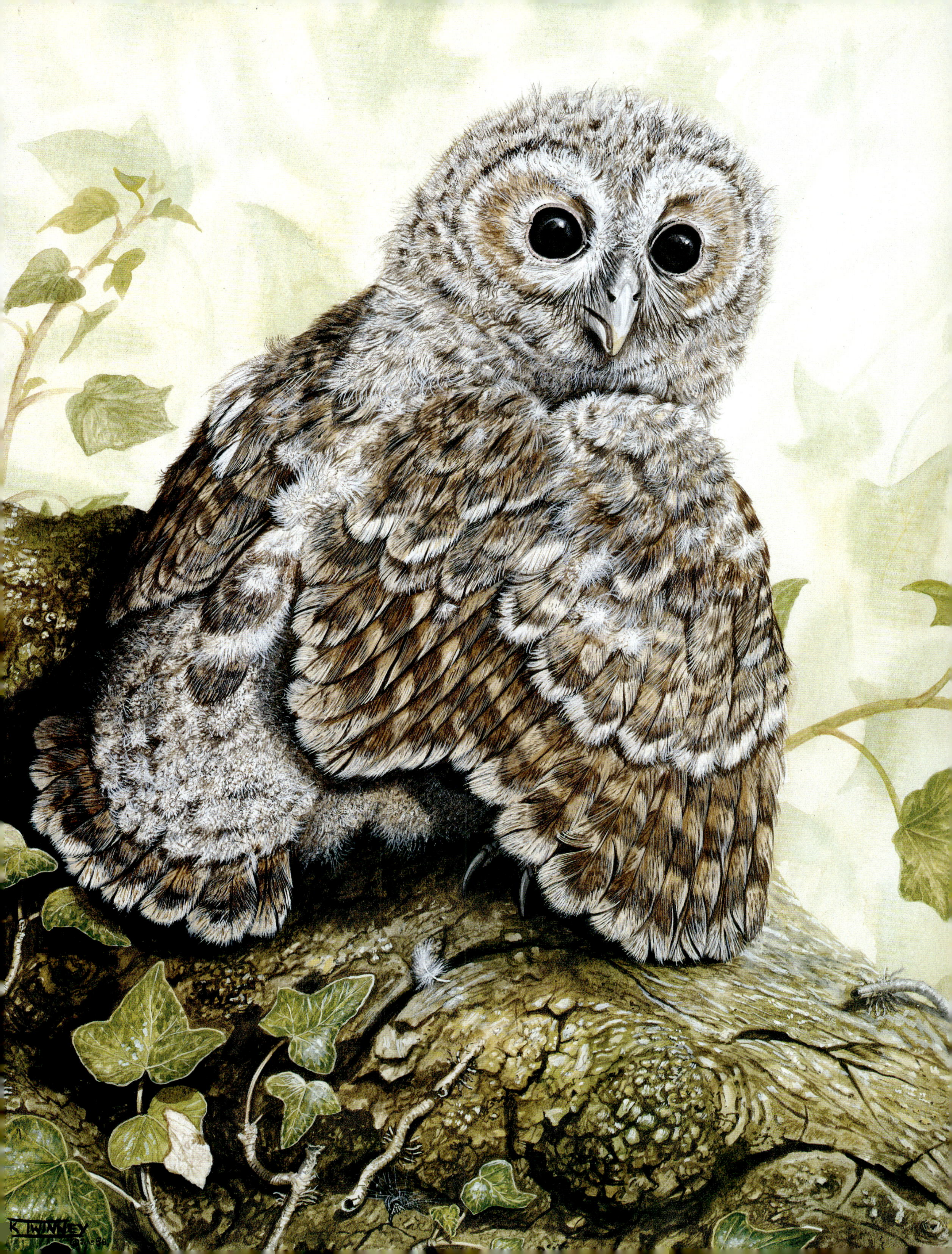
K TWINNEY

Fourth Week

SPECKLED WOOD, ORANGE TIP AND CAMPIONS

Although I have specifically featured red campions in this June painting, they are the one plant that can be seen flowering in Cornwall at almost any time of the year. During the summer months the roadsides and hedgerows are a mass of pink and red campions. Being so common, it is a plant often taken for granted. It is a great favourite of mine, although a difficult subject for the artist as the flowers have an almost fluorescent glow which is very hard to capture in watercolour. Not so the charmingly named mouse-ear chickweed whose pure white colouring is straight out of the paint box. They are also included here.

The choice of butterflies for this time of the year is vast, as most species are on the wing. Blues, browns and whites can all be seen, adding a moving cavalcade of colour to the hedgerows, as they move from one nectar-rich plant to another.

Two hedgerow regulars are the speckled wood and orange tip. The male orange tip featured here is easily recognized, his distinctive coloured wing tips showing up clearly as he flies past. The female butterfly is not so easy to identify, as she lacks the orange colouring and can be mistaken for one of the other whites.

The speckled wood, when first observed from a distance, appears to be a rather dull brownish colour but on closer examination the dark chocolate brown is seen to be delicately patterned with pale yellow and black spots, making it a very attractive butterfly indeed. Both male and female are similar although the male is smaller and darker.

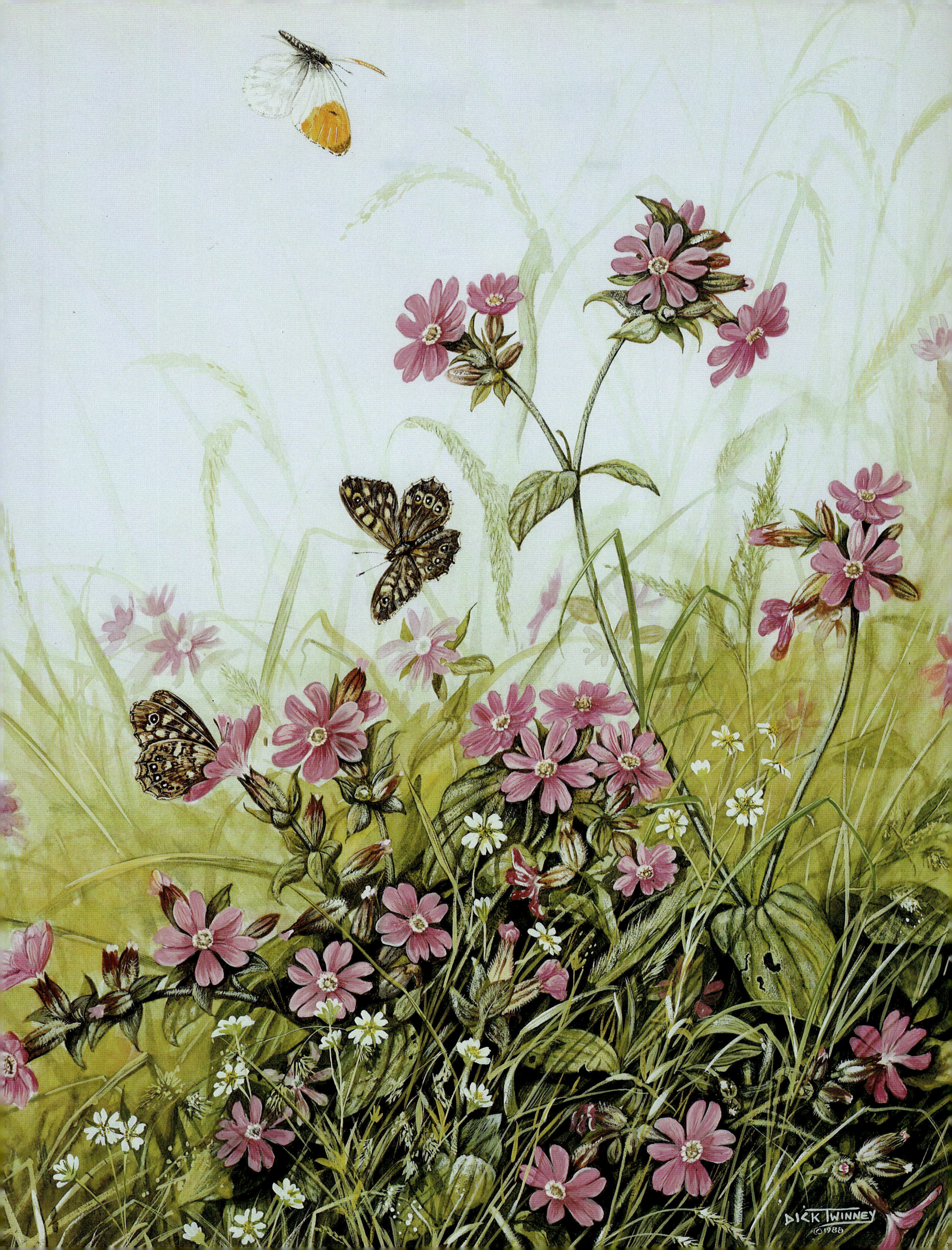
DICK TWINNEY
©1988

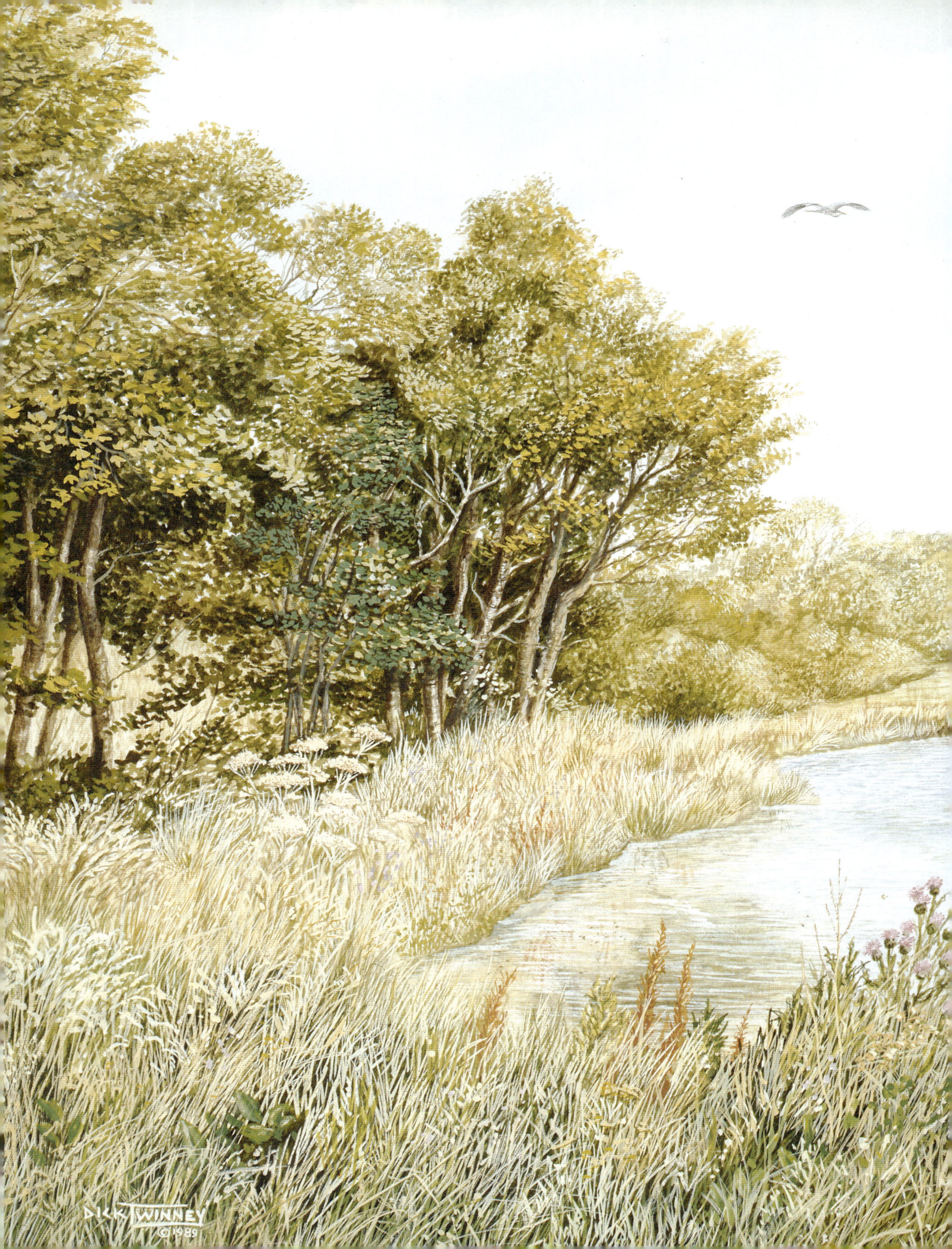
DICK TWINNEY
©1989

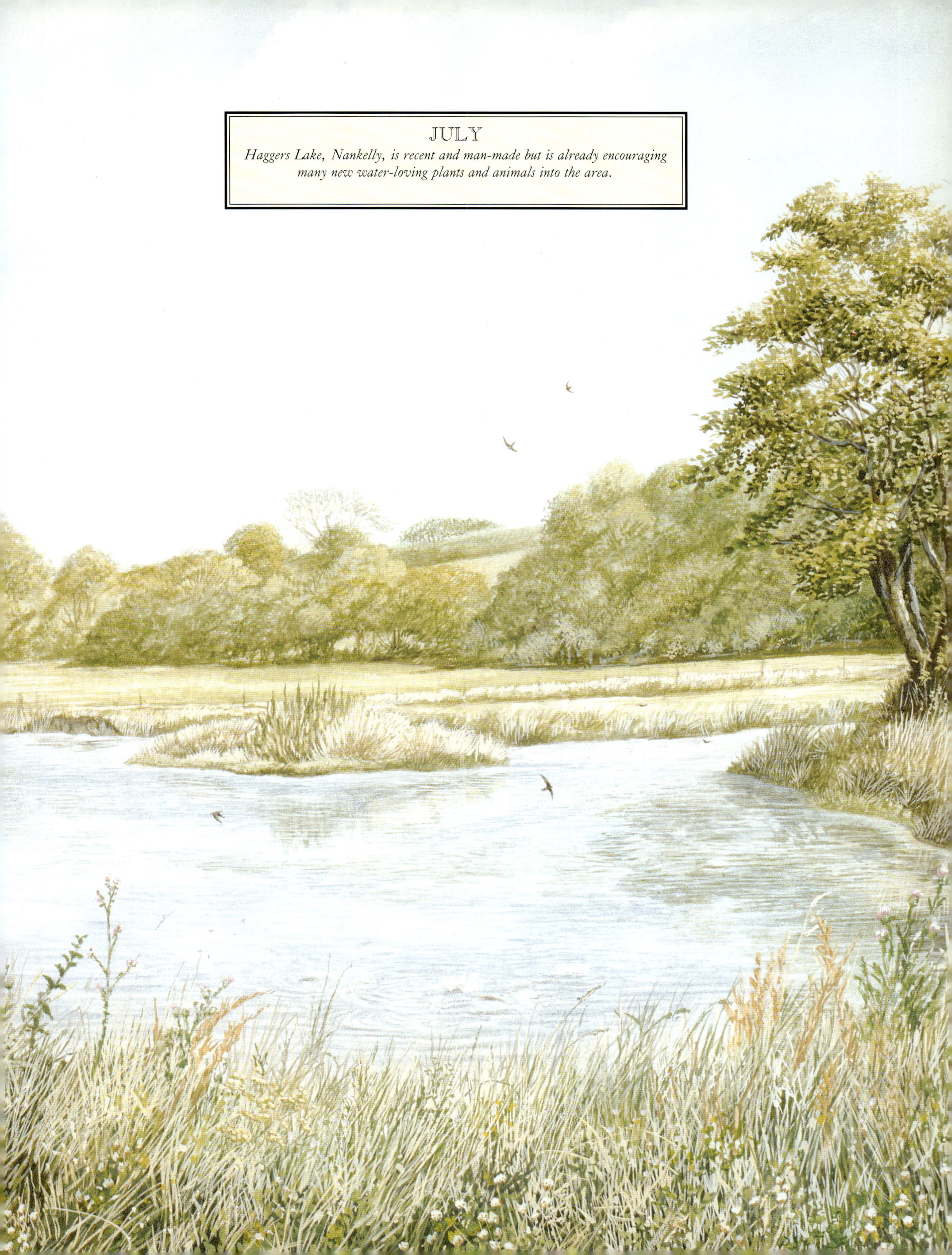

JULY

Haggers Lake, Nankelly, is recent and man-made but is already encouraging many new water-loving plants and animals into the area.

FIRST WEEK

VIXEN

As I walked slowly down the old well-worn badger trail, thinking to myself about the generations of 'brock' that have used this track, my dog Ben bristled and started forward: something was on top of the hedge just in front of us. At first I thought it must be a pheasant, but I was wrong for standing there in full glory was a beautiful fox – the slighter build and narrow head characteristics of a vixen. She looked over her shoulder, fixing her yellow, cat-like eyes upon us; I was able to study her rich red coat and take note of the scent gland mark on her tail. I quickly committed this majestic sight to memory and seconds later she was gone, disappearing silently into the scrubby area beyond. Restraining Ben from following, I felt that familiar tremor of excitement which comes from seeing a wild animal, at close quarters, in its natural habitat.

The vixen had chosen the perfect stage for her appearance – a hedge that had been built between a row of ancient, weather-worn oak trees, their powerful, gnarled and twisted roots making interesting abstract designs as they grew downwards among the assorted stones that created the hedge.

It was obviously a favourite resting place for the fox as the grasses were well flattened and a slight hollow was worn into the soil on the hedge-top. It was an excellent vantage point. Foxes like to sleep well above the ground, often climbing quite high into trees and on to the tops of buildings.

I used our own pet vixen, Smokey, for the finer details of this painting. In turning my brief encounter into reality I returned many times to the scene of the meeting to make sketches, collect stone samples and twigs, or fresh green oak leaves for the studio work.

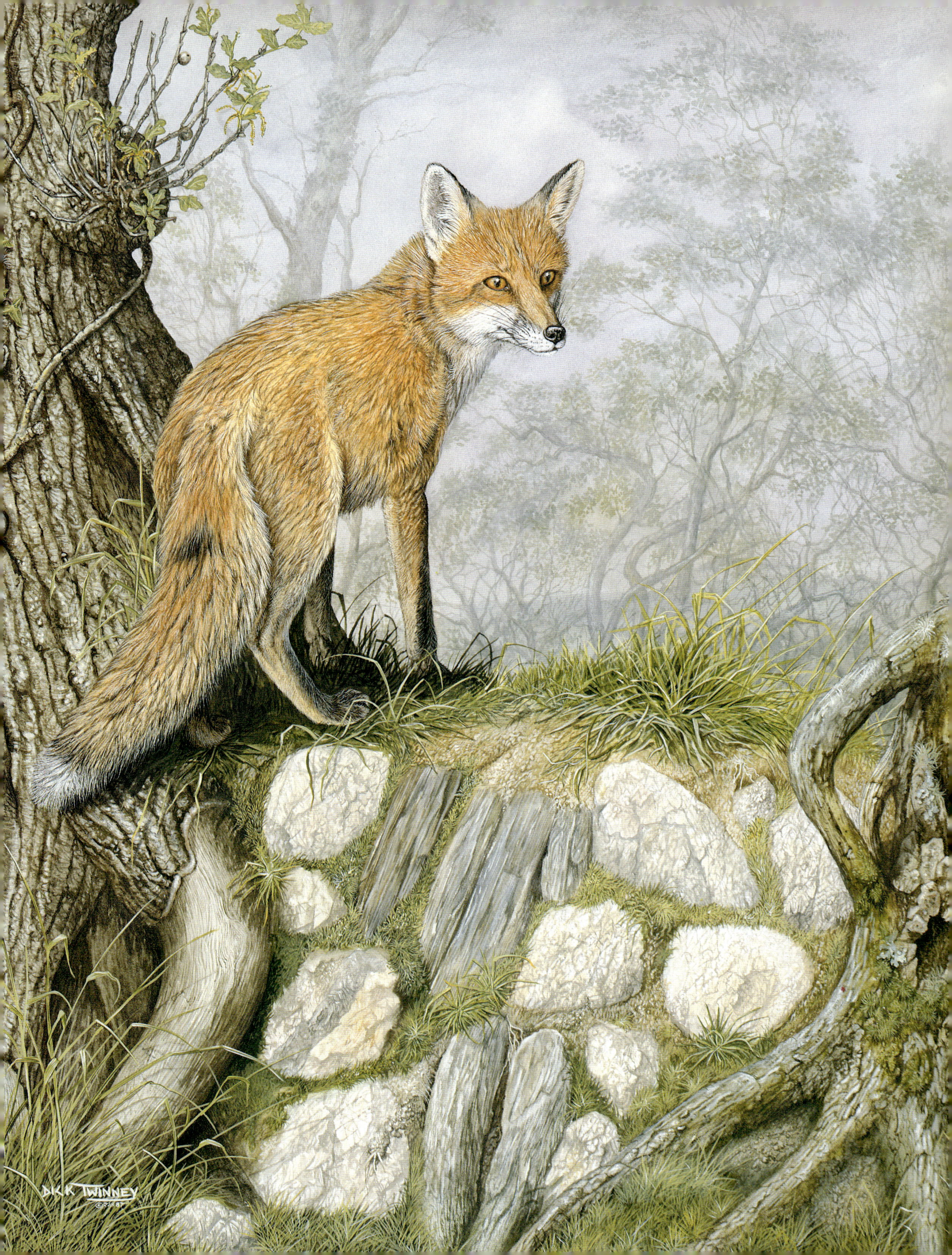
DICK TWINNEY

SECOND WEEK

GOLDEN-RINGED DRAGONFLY

I am often asked how I choose the subjects for my paintings. Fortunately, this is not a problem, there being such a variety of flora and fauna in so many diverse habitats. I usually have a rough idea of what I want to paint during a particular month, but I frequently change my mind, as with this painting.

I initially set out with sketch-book and camera with the intention of gathering material for a painting of butterflies in the hedgerow. I wanted to paint several different species of one plant, such as hemp-agrimony, a plant much loved by butterflies. However, it being a dullish, humid day, no butterflies were on the move apart from the occasional speckled wood.

After watching a large clump of hemp-agrimony for some time in the hope it would attract some flying visitors, I decided to continue along the hedgerow and was rewarded by the sight of a magnificent golden-ringed dragonfly. I followed it down the hedge-side as it patrolled on loud, vibrating wings, its large compound eyes scouring the area for flying prey. It alighted on some hemlock water-dropwort and allowed me to approach to within a few inches. I have often found that although dragonflies have excellent eyesight and can obviously identify intruders, they will tolerate the situation before eventually taking flight.

On close observation dragonflies are impressive creatures, especially the larger species such as this female golden-ringed. I had found my subject! The plant she had used as a resting place would make excellent background foliage. Add one yellow unbanded form of the banded snail with which the area abounded and I had created my picture.

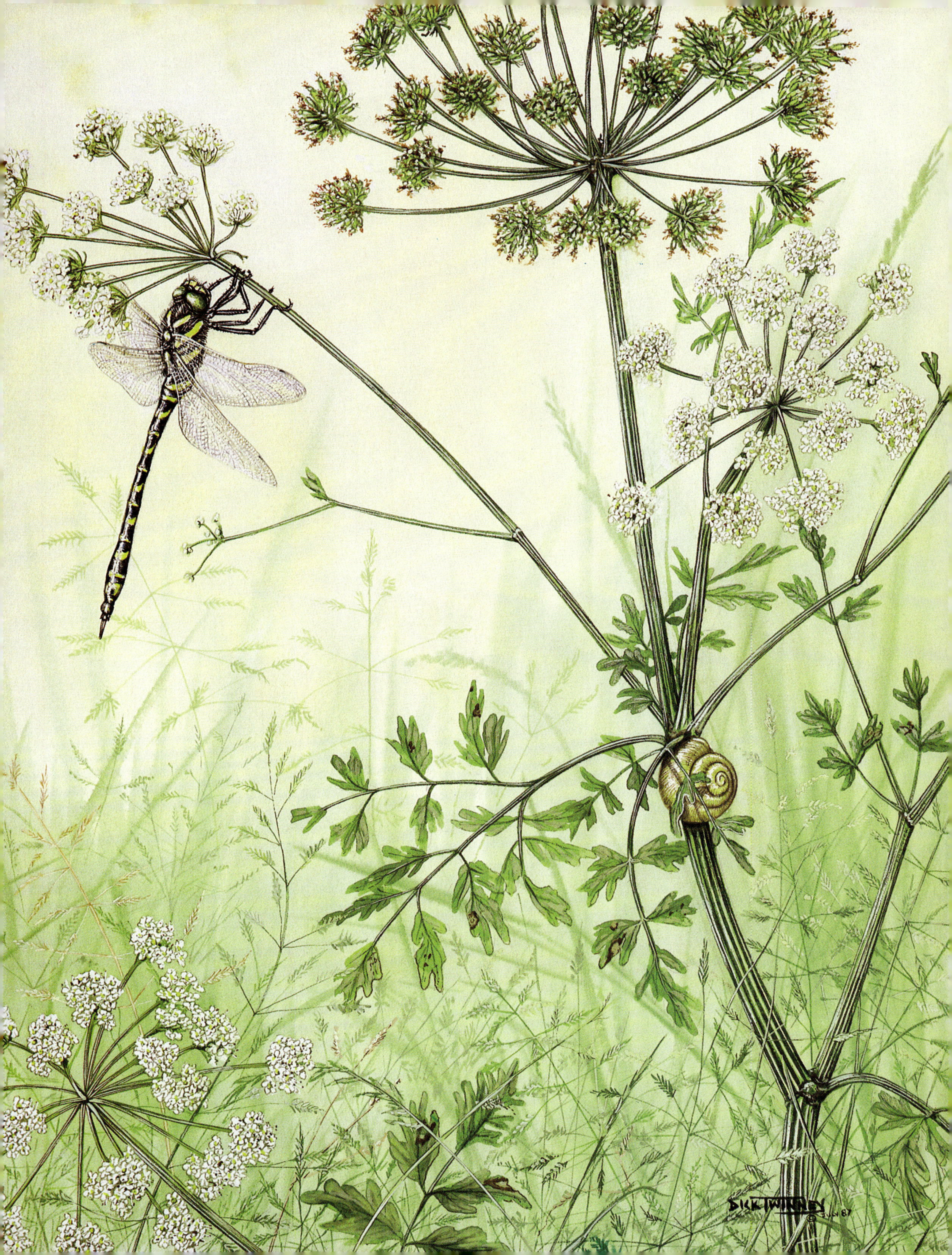
DICK TWINNEY

THIRD WEEK

KINGFISHER AND FLAG

For this composition my first intention was to paint only the flag, or yellow iris. It is at its best in mid-July, giving a beautiful show around the verges of our garden pond. However, having recently watched a kingfisher darting and diving along one of the local rivers, I decided to combine both water residents in one painting.

Before I could start I had to solve one rather interesting problem. As it was my intention to keep the painting simple, I did not wish to include any other foliage such as branches or roots, which are the kingfisher's more usual perches. I had to ascertain whether the flag would make a suitable perch and take the kingfisher's weight. With the aid of a flag from the pond and a lump of my daughter's Plasticine weighing thirty-seven grammes (the average weight of the kingfisher, I discovered), I found the sturdy plant was well able to improvise as a 'kingfisher perch'.

The flags were a joy to paint, having most complex and interesting flower heads when in full bloom and forming strange curling shapes as they wither and die. I could not resist including the old case of a dragonfly larvae which I had discovered earlier on one of the flag stems, a reminder that not all things in nature are aesthetically beautiful.

The kingfisher featured is a female, distinguished from the male by the orange underside to her bill, the bill of the adult male being all black. At this time of the year many parent birds are busy raising a family, which is very exhausting work. There can be six or seven fledglings in a brood and each one can consume up to eighteen fish a day.

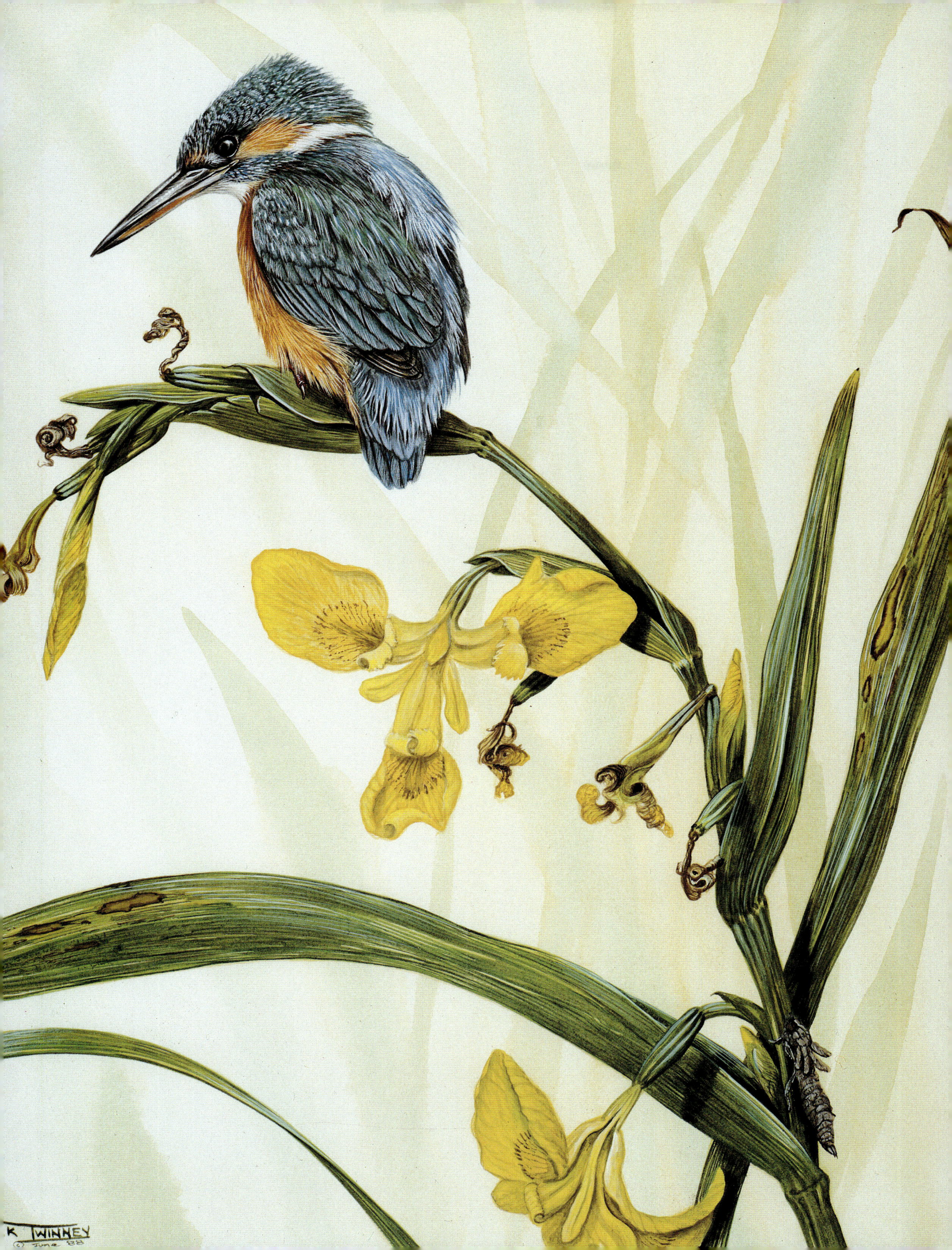
K TWINNEY
© June 88

FOURTH WEEK

HARVEST MICE

One of the most interesting and delightful residents of our fields and hedgerows is the diminutive harvest mouse. I found a used harvest mouse nest last October and it has been sitting on a shelf in my studio waiting for the correct time of year to be included in a painting. I have situated the nest in a clump of soft rush from the same field corner where I found the old nest last year.

The nest is a true work of art about the size of a tennis ball. It is a complex structure of neatly shredded and woven grasses and when completed has no noticeable entrance hole. In my painting I have shown the nest under construction, the nesting materials still being green and a visible hole where the mouse has entered to furnish the interior, which is lined with finely chewed grass or thistledown, making a snug and soft bed for the young mice. The nest is built by the female mainly at night, but the painting is set in the early morning to enable me to show off the rich yellow colouring of the buttercups and the russet orange pelage of the mice.

Having kept harvest mice briefly in captivity for the purposes of close observation, I was particularly struck by their climbing ability. They are able to run up the most flimsy of grasses and stalks – harvest mice are unique among British mammals in that they possess a truly prehensile tail, which they use most effectively as a fifth limb. It was thought that the harvest mouse was on the decline due to more intensive arable farming methods – its traditional habitat being cereal fields. However, it seems to have adapted well to change, moving into reed beds and hedgerows in which to live out its short but active life.

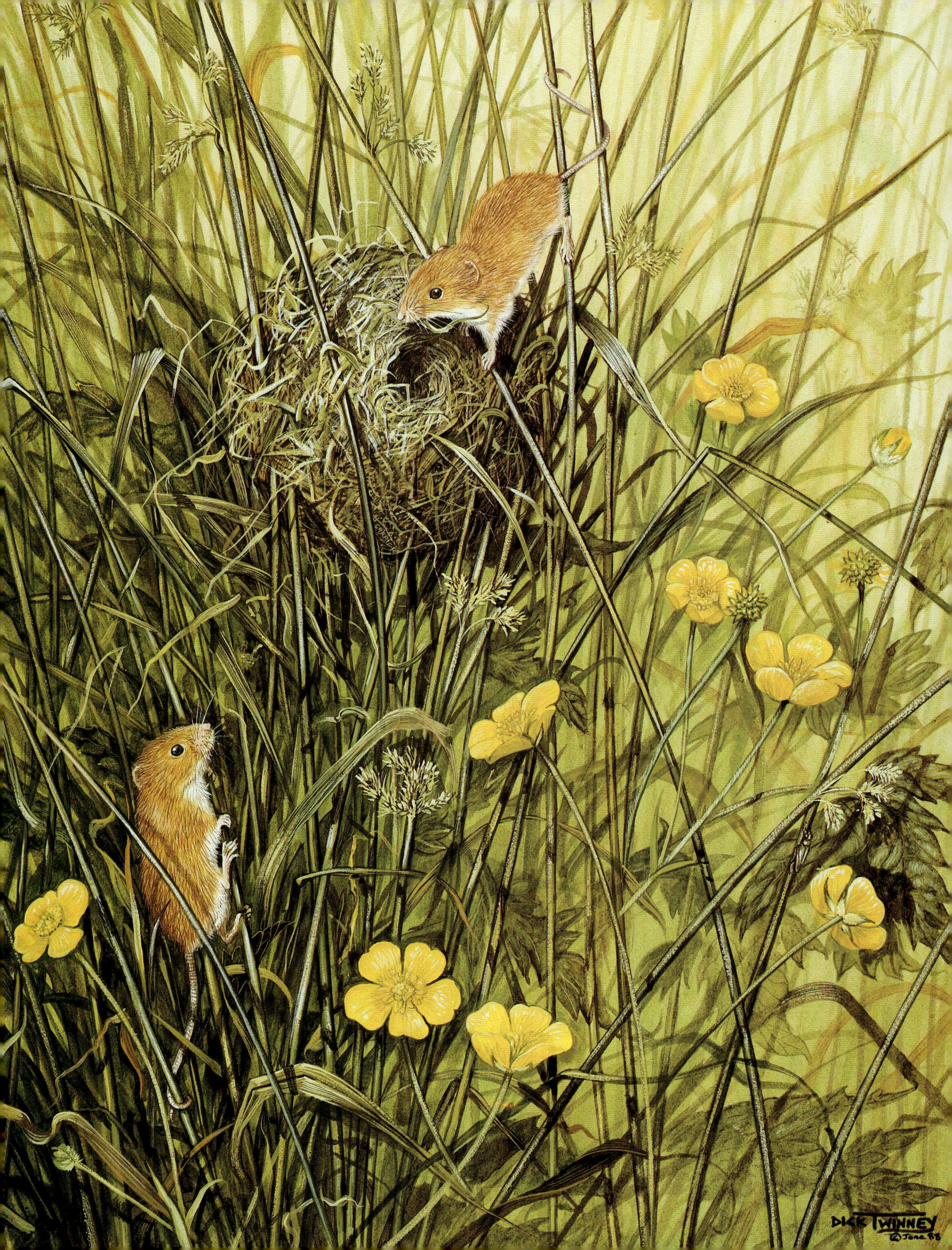
DICK TWINNEY
© June 88

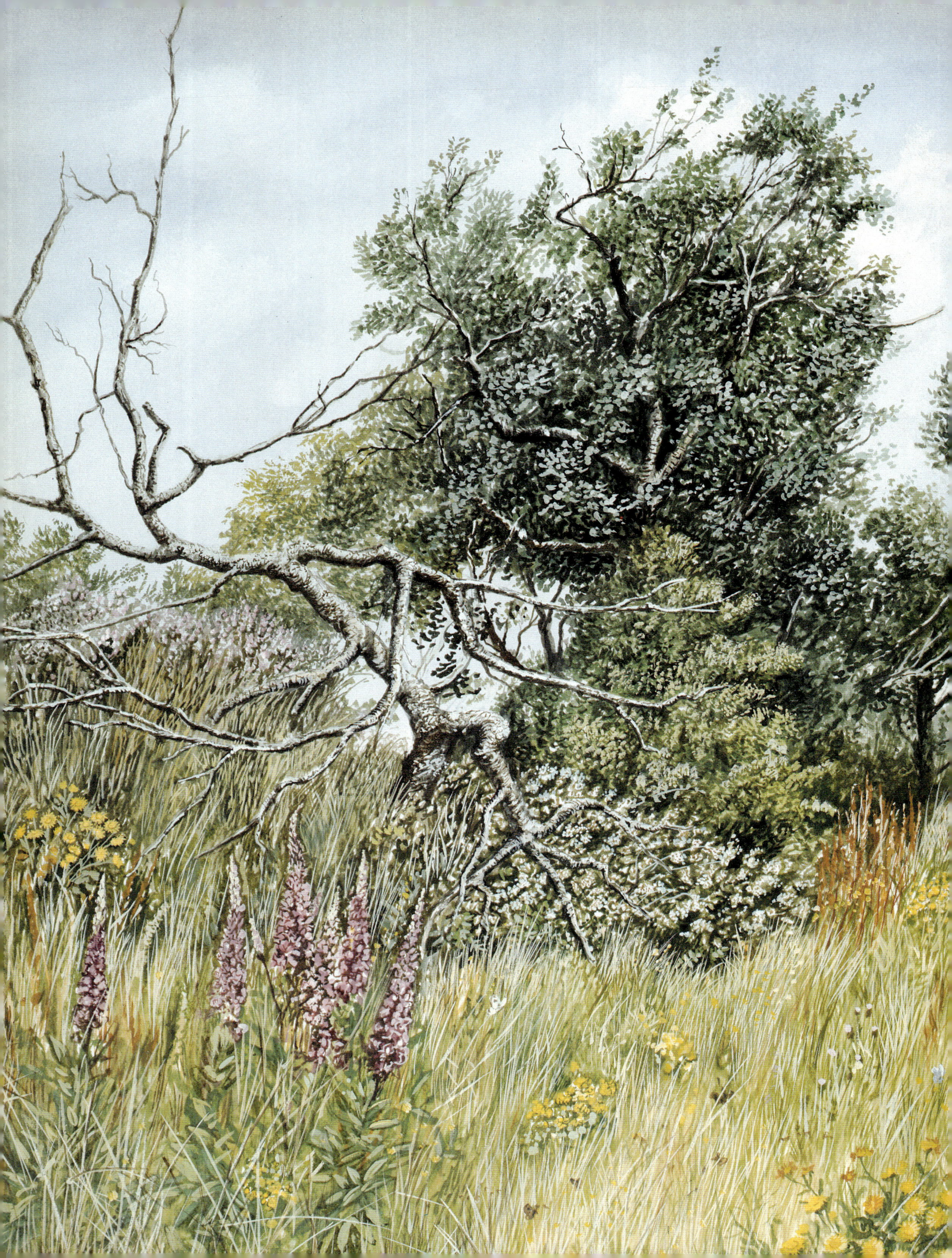

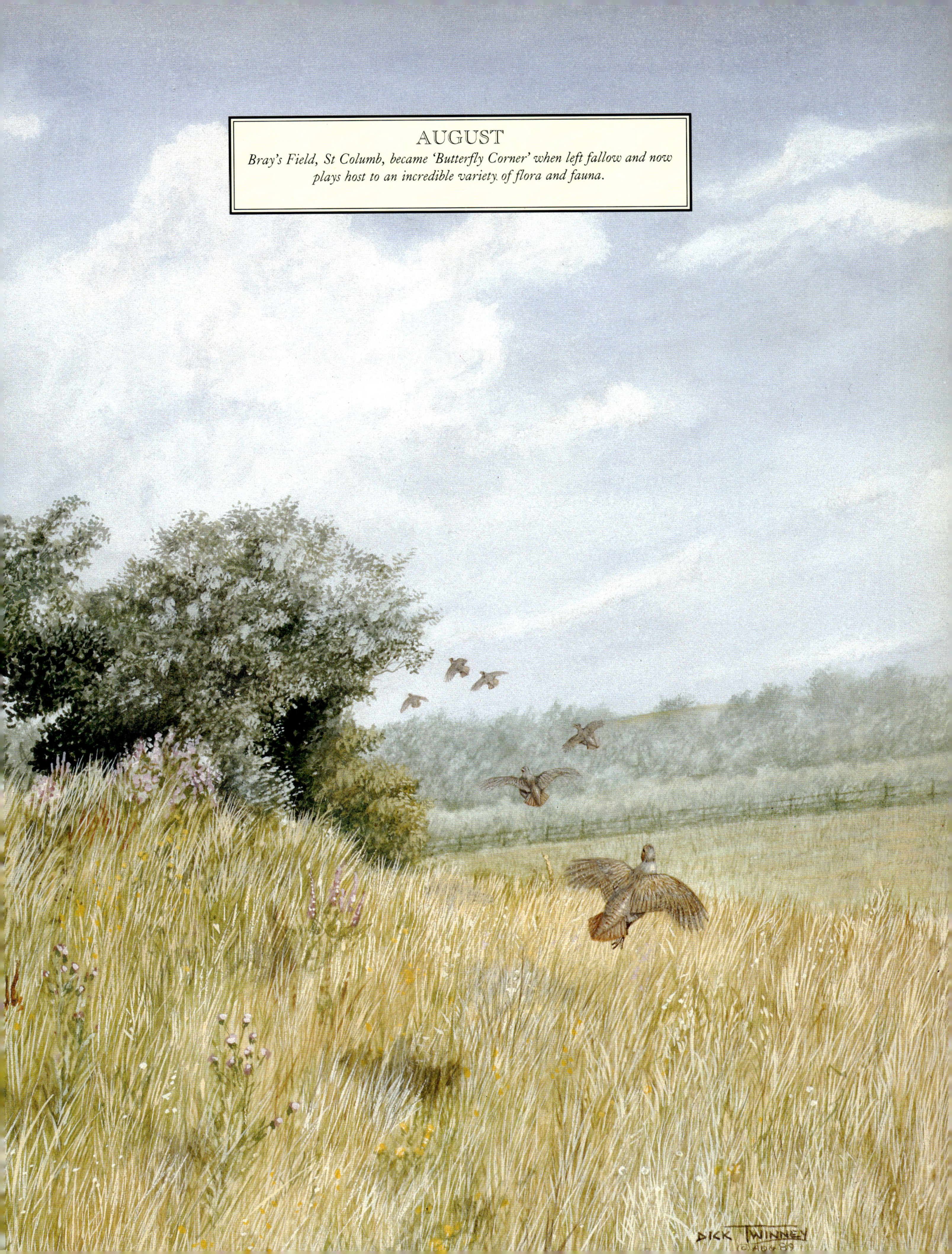

AUGUST

Bray's Field, St Columb, became 'Butterfly Corner' when left fallow and now plays host to an incredible variety of flora and fauna.

First Week

YOUNG BLACKBIRD

Over the years we have had a great many fledgling birds brought to the house. A good percentage should have been left where they were as almost certainly the parent birds would have been in the vicinity and are far better equipped to raise their offspring than human foster parents. The appeal of baby birds is immense and I can fully understand a well-meaning person, often a child, finding a seemingly abandoned orphan and feeling they must 'rescue it'.

Obviously if it is in immediate danger, on a road or within reach of cats, it could be moved to a safer place. The parents will still find it, as most fledglings can make their whereabouts known, particularly the young blackbird illustrated here in an elder bush, whose strident call can carry great distances.

Injured fledglings are a different matter and the one I have used as a model for the painting was brought to us suffering from the after-effects of a magpie attack. Magpies are terrors at this time of the year, taking large numbers of fledglings. Unfortunately these vicious pied raiders appear to be on the increase.

Young blackbirds are usually easy to raise, readily taking offered food from the fingers and loudly letting you know when they want 'topping up'. They are one of the most expressive of birds, capable of looking surprised, angry, amused and belligerent, as I have shown here. We have provided a home for a flightless male blackbird for many years and his beautiful song is a pleasure to hear, particularly during spring and early summer when he is in full voice.

Elder grows everywhere and is very common among the hedgerows, which is good news for a great many creatures (including home-made wine enthusiasts) who make use of the vitamin-rich fruit in the autumn. Here we see the flowers only just forming. Elder is a delight to paint as the branches form many interesting shapes; they are very brittle and often snap off, only to regrow at another angle from the broken end.

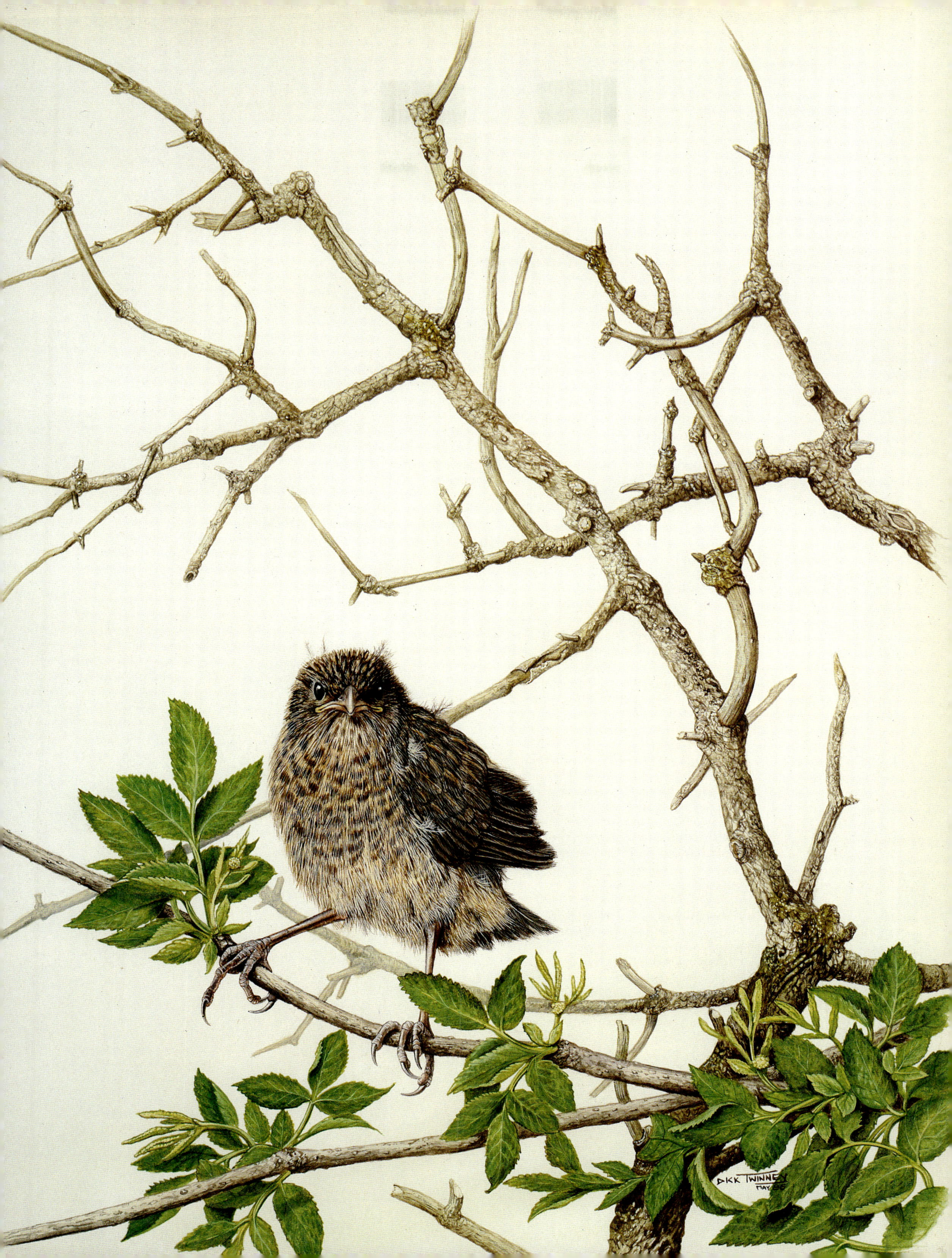
DKK TWINNEY
MAY 86

SECOND WEEK

BUTTERFLIES ON BUDDLEIA

No wildlife garden is complete without at least one buddleia bush. We have five in our garden and I intend planting more new colour strains in the near future; it will be interesting to see whether these have the same magnetic attraction for butterflies and moths as the more common lilac buddleia.

Most flying insects, particularly butterflies, are greatly attracted to the buddleia; it is fitting, therefore, that it is also known as the 'butterfly bush'. Originally a native of China, it is now well established in Britain, both in our gardens and in the wild. Our family never tires of watching the buddleia in the summer months, always hoping to see a new visiting species of butterfly or moth.

Among the most regular visitors to our butterfly bushes are red admirals, small tortoiseshells (I once counted seven of these on one flower spike), commas, peacocks, painted ladies, speckled woods, coppers, browns and various members of the white family. Day-flying moths such as humming bird and bee hawk moths are frequently seen alongside hoverflies and bees.

During the hours of darkness many nocturnal species also make use of this heavily scented and nectar-rich bush.

For this painting I have featured small tortoiseshell (top), peacock (centre), large white and painted lady. I make no apologies for expressing my preference for this particular shrub as it is a constant source of inspiration and pleasure, its regular visitors providing an ever-changing kaleidoscope of moving colour, from June to the second half of October.

As well as catering for the needs of nectar-feeding flying insects, the buddleia's leaves also provide a food source for many larvae, beetles and weevils. These include some very brightly coloured caterpillars. Three of the most frequent visitors are the caterpillars of the vapourer, the dot and the mullein moths.

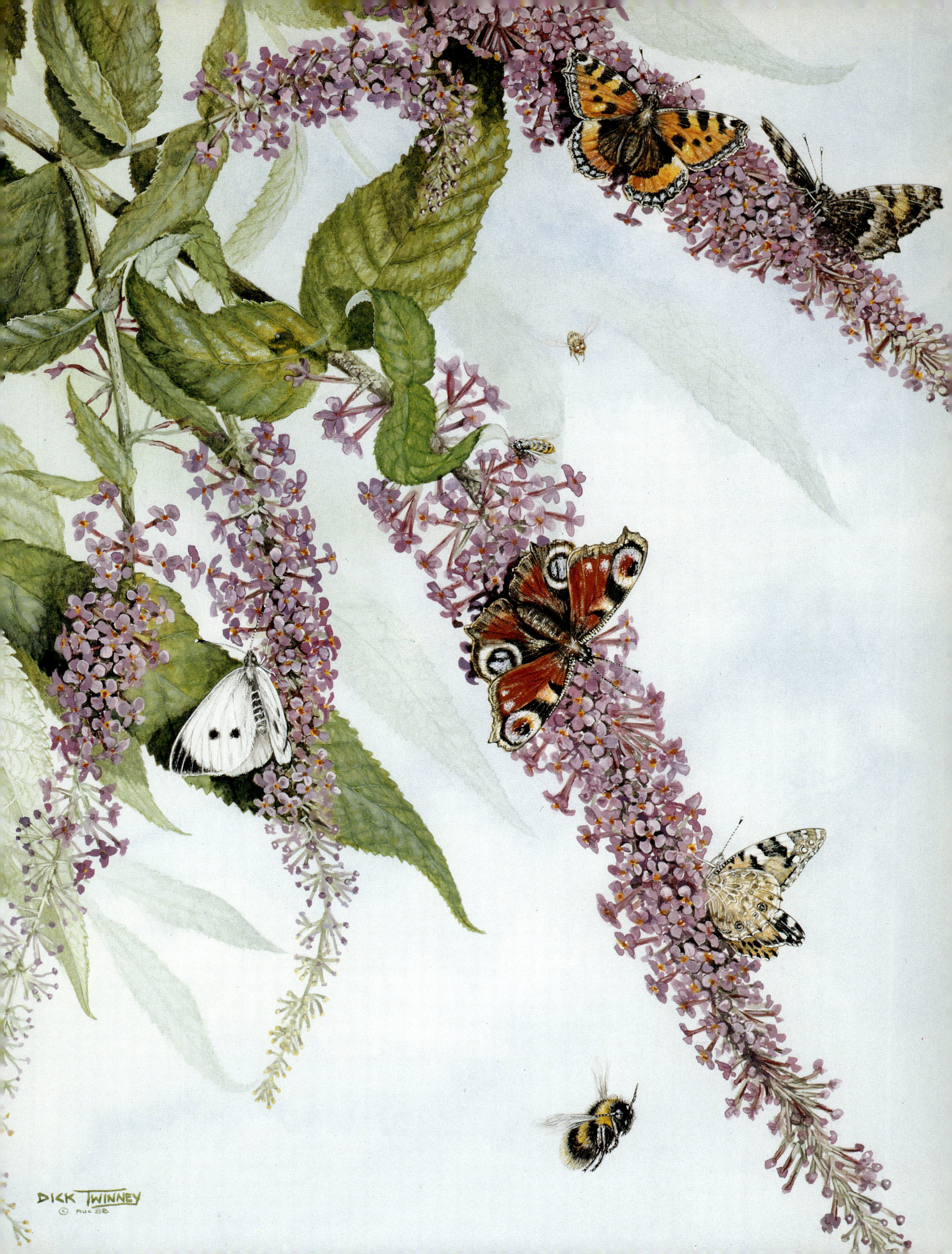
DICK TWINNEY
© AUG 88

THIRD WEEK

FIELD VOLE FAMILY

Walking through neighbouring fields, just after the summer barley had been harvested, I discovered several field vole nests. Some had been destroyed by the combine harvester but others had survived thanks to their location in deep ruts in the ground. A temporary respite, I fear, as any surviving baby voles quickly become prey to the many crows which descend on the field, attracted by left-over grain.

Field voles are one of our most abundant small mammals and can be found in almost any location, provided there is long grass or vegetation for cover. One particular family lived in an overgrown corner of our garden where they had built their nest under some old roofing sheets. I have always been fascinated by small mammals, and have kept or handled most species. I can remember as a very young boy getting up at five in the morning to go on vole-hunting forays on the railway embankment near my childhood home in Teignmouth, Devon.

For this August scene the voles are busy taking advantage of discarded ears of barley. Although primarily grass feeders, field voles will also eat seeds, cereals, bulbs and fungi. The young voles in the painting are not long out of the nest and are full of youthful curiosity as they explore their habitat among the stubble. At this time they are at their most vulnerable, being the prey species of so many of our predators, including owls, kestrels, foxes, stoats, weasels and the domestic cat. For this reason voles are prolific breeders, having a succession of litters from early spring to late autumn.

In deference to my wife I have included one of her favourite flowers in the painting: the aptly named scarlet pimpernel, which grows in abundance in this particular field, covering the ground with its long, straggling stems.

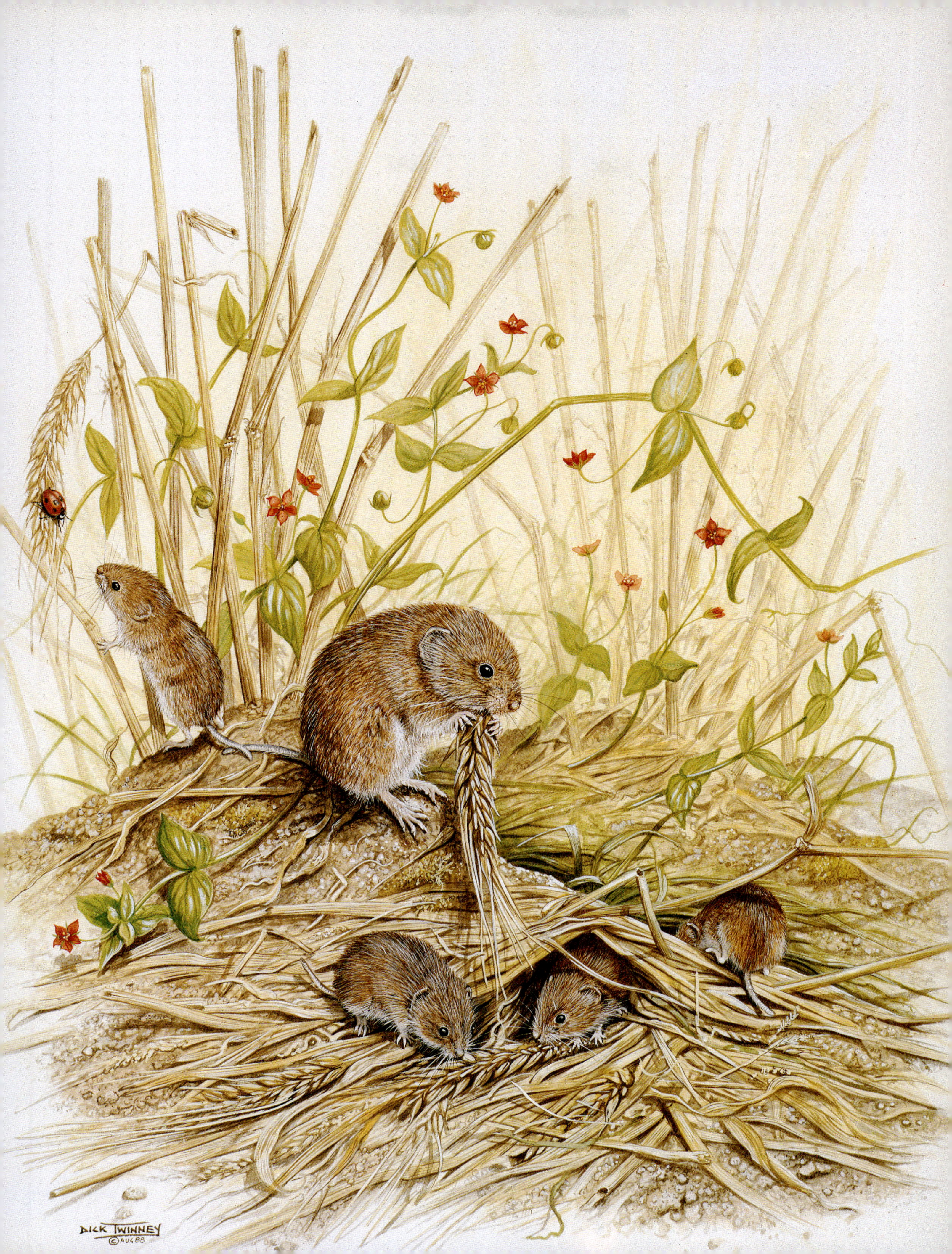
DICK TWINNEY
©AUG88

FOURTH WEEK

STONECHAT AND HEATHERS

Up on the moors and heaths the various heathers are coming into full bloom, the orange-buff areas of dried summer grasses are gradually brightened by a vast coloured carpet of the mixed lilacs, pinks and purple flowers of the bell heather and ling.

The nearest moor to my home is Goss Moor and although in no way as large or spectacular as the better known West Country moors such as Bodmin, Dartmoor and Exmoor, it is nevertheless a very interesting area to visit, being rich in flora and fauna. Rarely a week goes by when the whole family does not blow the cobwebs away during a walk on the moor with the dogs. It is partly a way of mixing business with pleasure for I am one of Goss Moor's voluntary wardens for the Nature Conservancy Council.

One of my favourite moorland residents is the stonechat, a brightly coloured extrovert which is easily identified as he sits in full view on his regular perch, surveying his territory. The hen bird's plumage is basically similar but much more muted and without the striking black head. Stonechats are resident all the year round and benefit greatly from the generally mild winters in Cornwall. They can become quite numerous during a good breeding season, experienced females sometimes having up to four broods. Stonechats often form family parties, keeping in touch with each other noisily as they flit from shrub to shrub, their most common contact call resembling the clicking of two pebbles, hence their name.

Also included in the composition, well camouflaged among the bell heather, is the caterpillar of one of our most attractive moorland insects, the emperor moth, which I found when gathering material for this painting.

A couple of years ago we kept an emperor moth caterpillar, monitoring its life cycle until the eventual emergence of the moth from the cocoon in the spring. After being greatly admired, it was returned to its natural habitat.

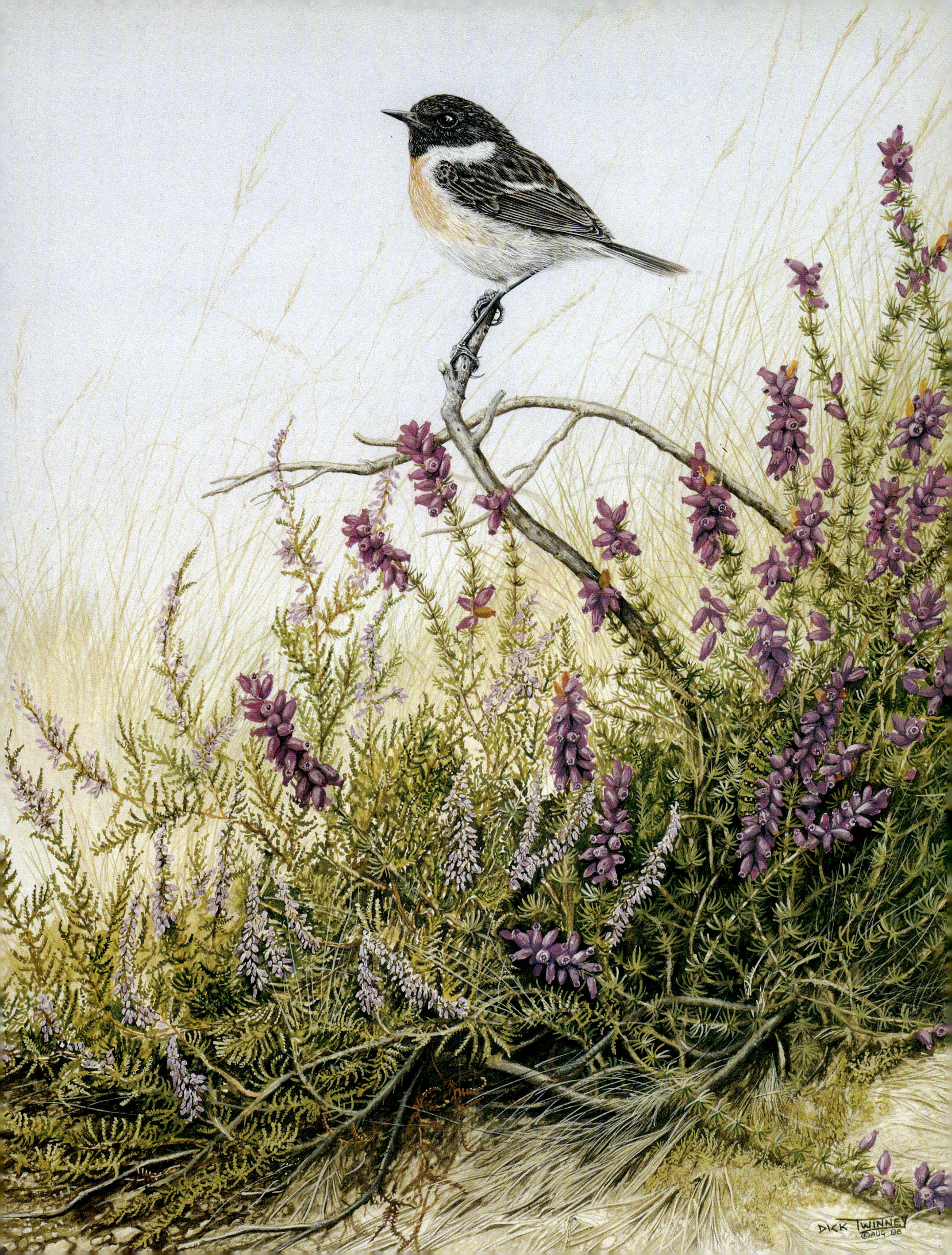
DICK TWINNEY
©AUG 88

FIFTH WEEK

KESTREL IN CORNFIELD

In this painting for the last week of August the harsh, bright heat of midsummer has gone, ripening the field of oats in its passing. We are left with a softer and more mellow warmth, a golden glow from the ready-to-harvest oats which wave slightly in the gentle evening breeze, creating an aura of peace and tranquillity. However, very soon the combine will do its work and the landscape and atmosphere will be changed once again.

Meanwhile the male kestrel rests on a favourite perch in the corner of the cornfield, the busy days of raising a brood over for another year. He fluffs out his feathers and tucks one sharply taloned foot into his chest, a certain sign of relaxation in a bird of prey. Some small noise distracts him momentarily, a mouse in the corn, the distant cry of a cock pheasant, just normal country evening sounds and no cause for alarm.

I have used our own 'Kes' as the model for this painting. He has been in our care now for over ten years after damaging his wing in a car accident. He came to us via Mousehole Bird Hospital, which at the time did not have the facilities to care for him. He has settled down well to a life of captivity, sharing a large aviary with two tawny owls, each species totally ignoring the other. Although Kes has a permanent disability and would not survive in the wild, a licence is still required before he can be kept in captivity.

The kestrel is Europe's most common bird of prey and a true falcon, best appreciated when on the wing, showing off its flying skills. It is widely distributed and can be seen in all types of habitat. One of its favourite haunts in Cornwall is the cliff-tops, where it is frequently seen hovering in the updraughts as it searches for small rodents and insects.

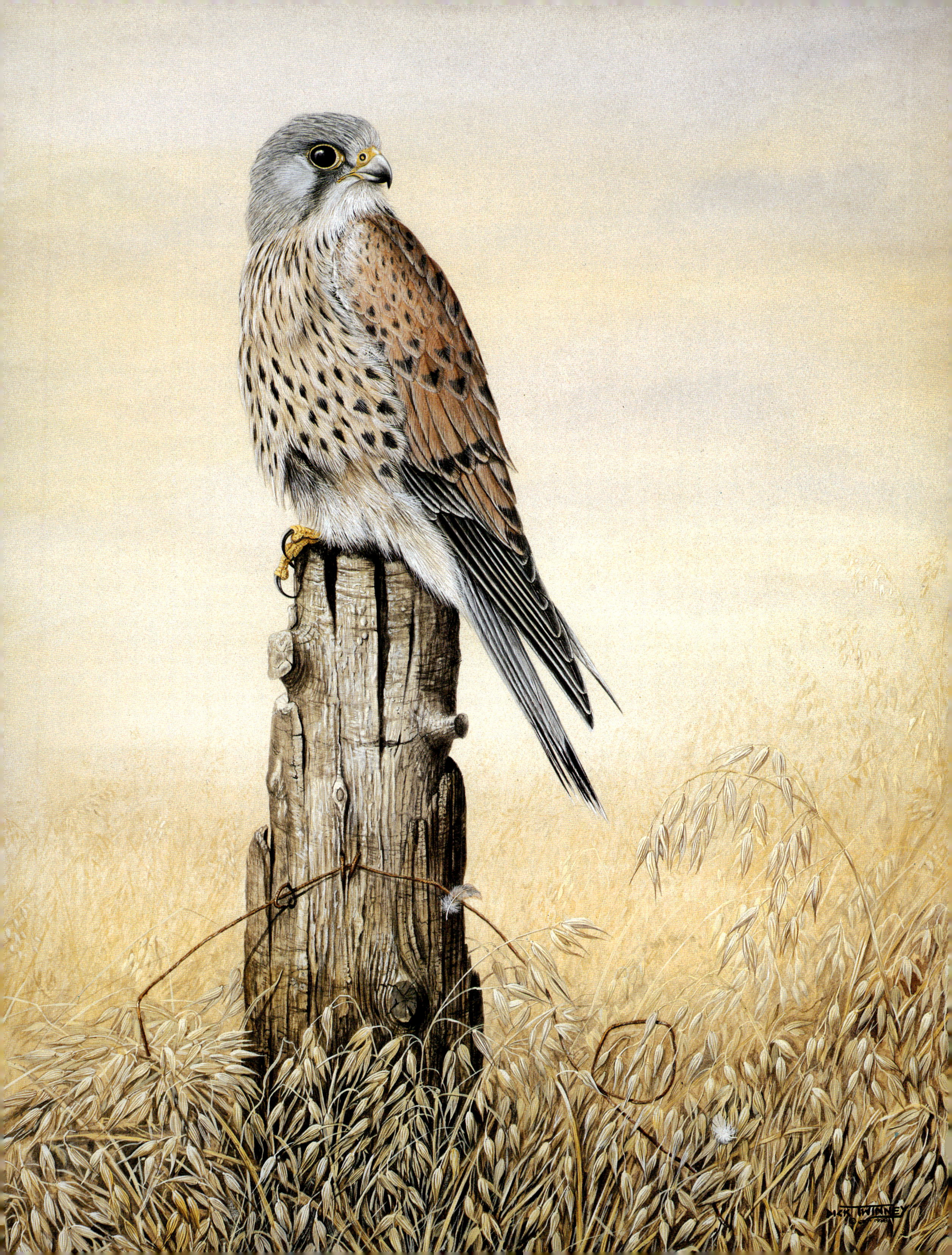
DICK TWINNEY

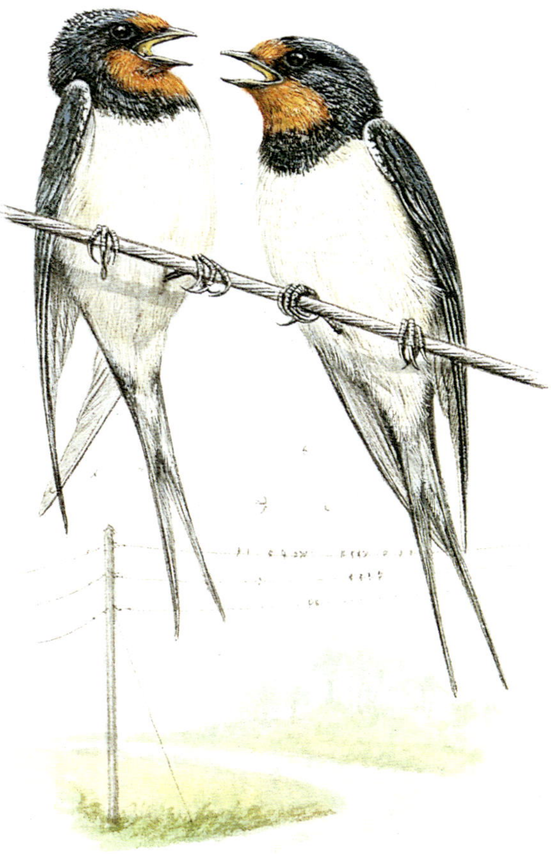

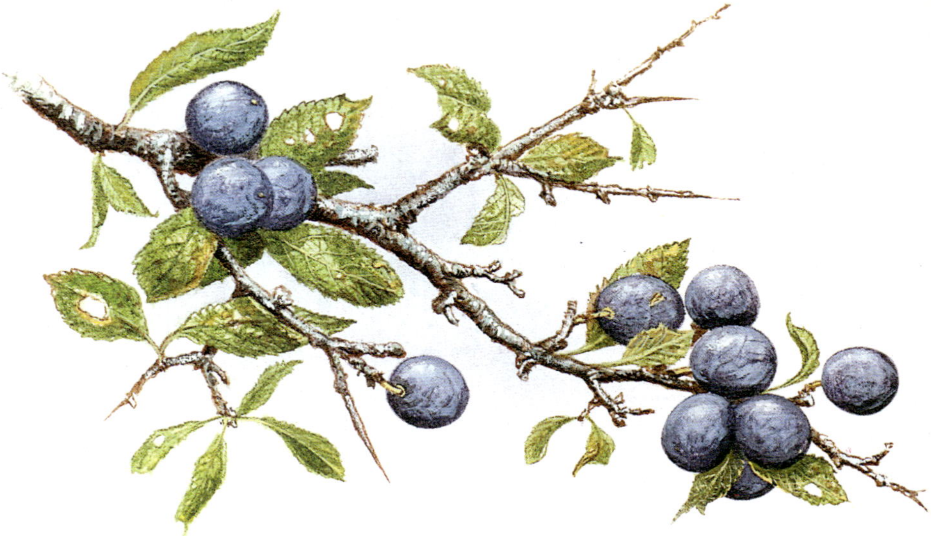

AUTUMN

If I had to choose one season in which to paint it would almos certainly be autumn. Many look upon this season with sadness a time of memories, the old age of nature's life cycle. For m autumn is the most delicately coloured and interesting o seasons, a time of fulfilment, when spring and summer's work i done.

The hedgerows and trees are laden with the fruits which are th culmination of complicated liaisons between insects and flowers. It i the time many fungi appear, some colourful and deadly, others, suc as field mushrooms, a much appreciated addition to our diet, as we as to the daily food intake of many animals. Rosehips, haws, acorns sloes and blackberries are all there for the taking, along with the swee chestnuts and hazel nuts. Nature's food store is at its most abundant.

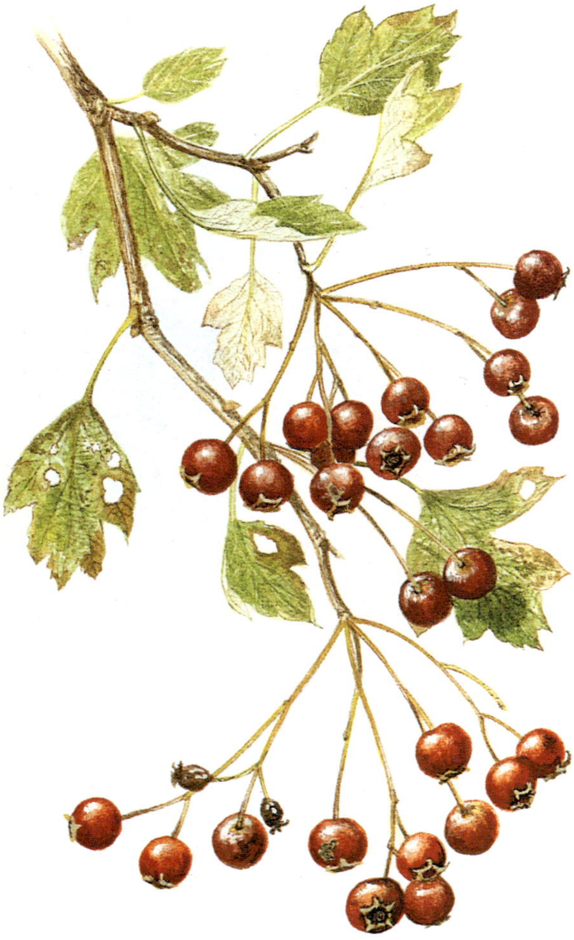

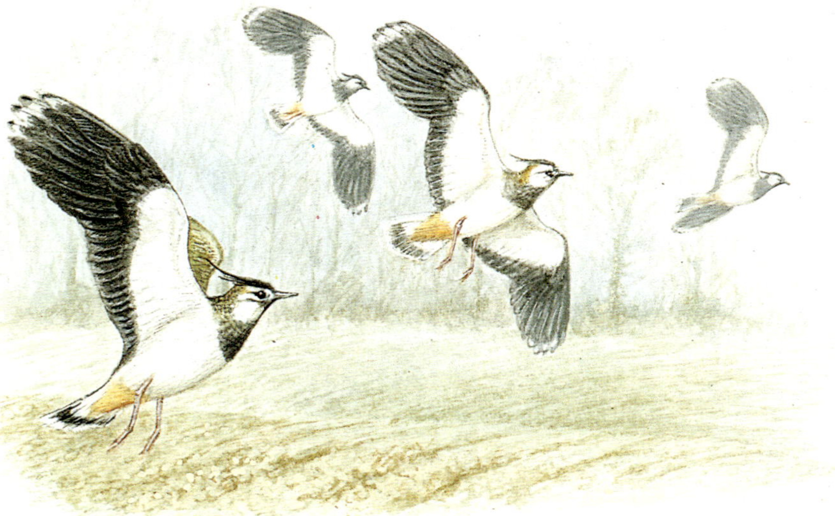

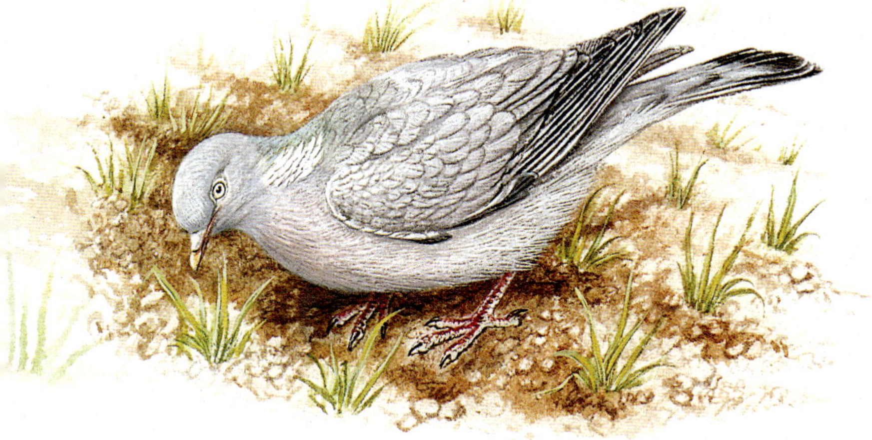

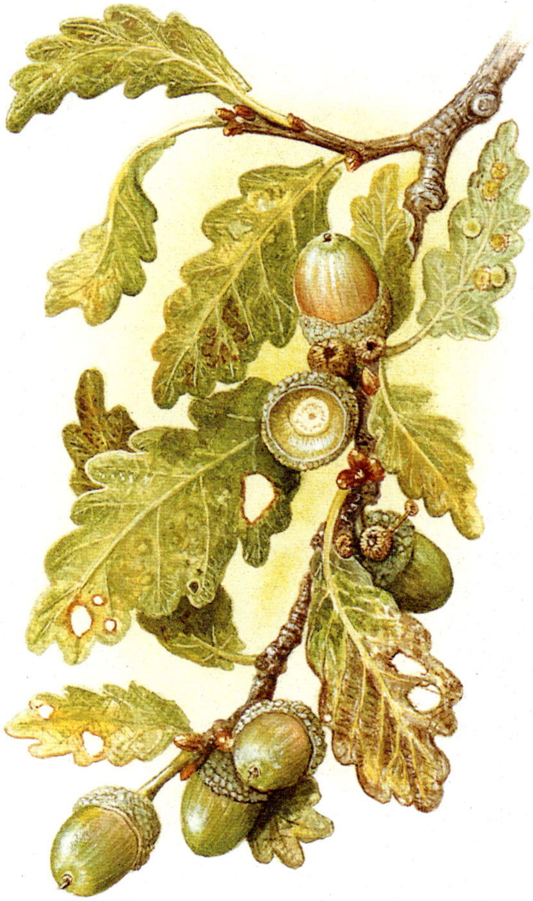

Birds and mammals take full advantage of all the food on offer, ilding up reserves of muscle and fat, either to sustain them on their ıg flights to warmer climes, or to see them through the harsh onths of winter.

Swallows gather on telegraph wires in chittering rows, while ıer birds such as pigeons, starlings and lapwings form large flocks. any small mammals prepare to hibernate and others, such as the y pygmy shrew, feed voraciously on insects, slugs and worms while s particular food source is still available.

Late-flowering plants such as the Michaelmas daisy and water ınt still attract many butterflies, including the red admiral and mma, who will also feast upon fallen fruit in our orchards.

In the mixed deciduous woodlands the full beauty of autumn is show, particularly during October when the many different tree ecies put on a varied display of reds, browns, russets and golds, a for both artist and country lover alike.

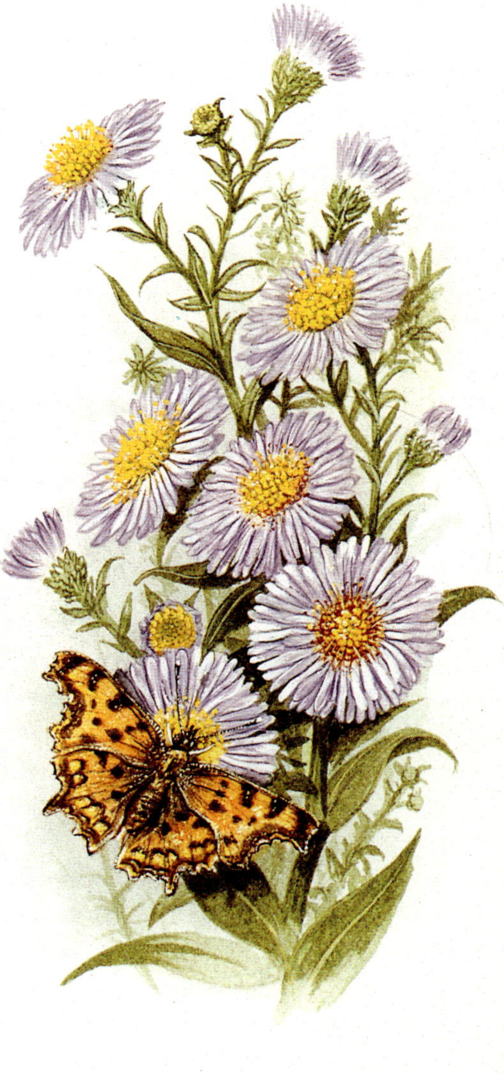

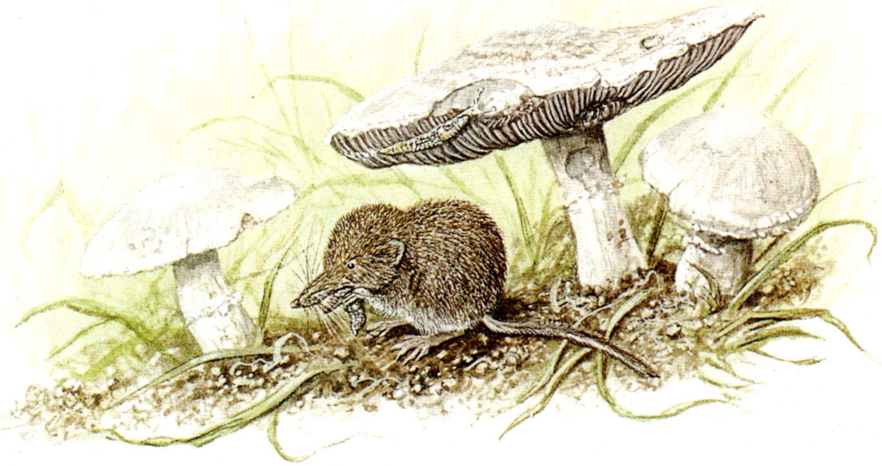

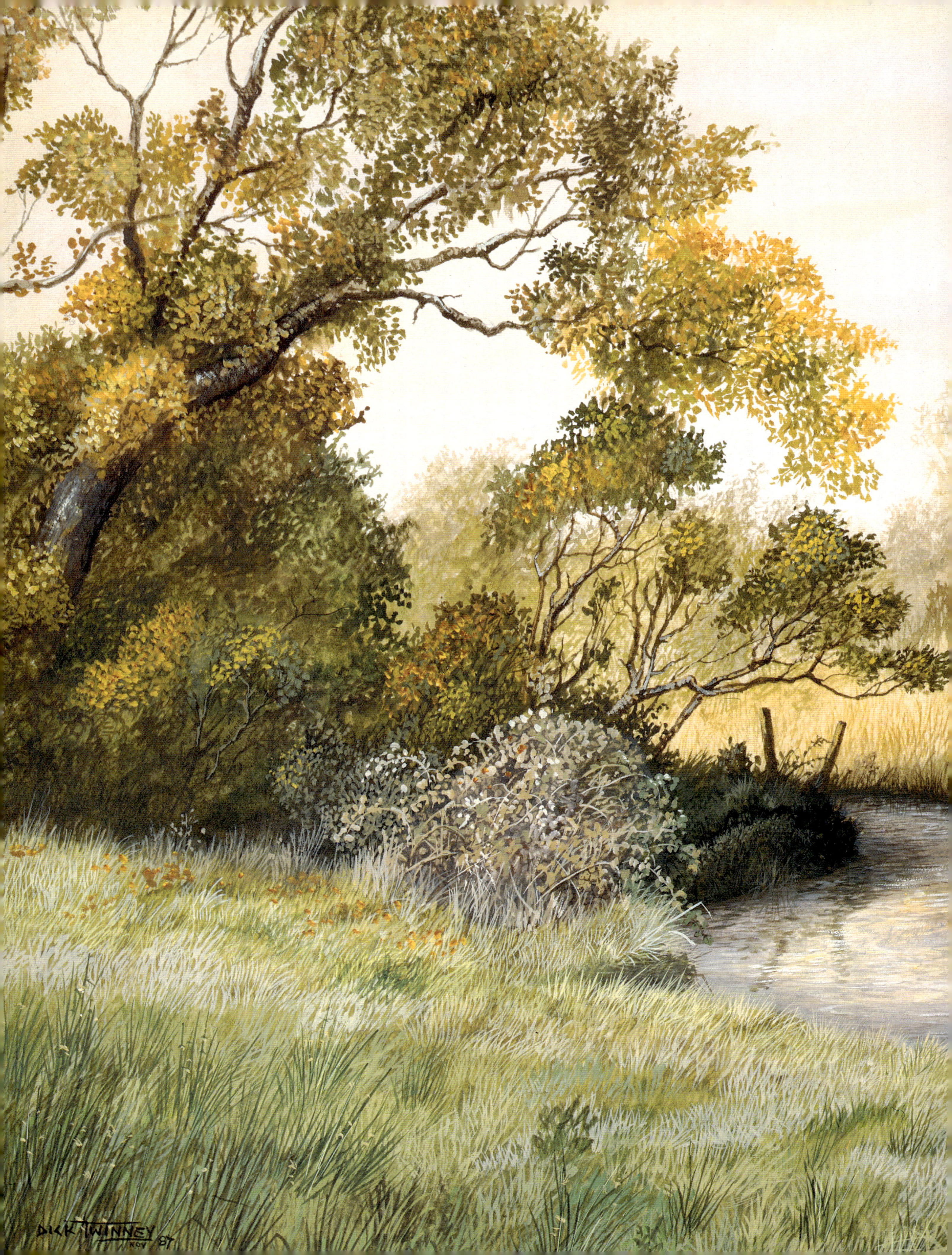
DICK TWINNEY
NOV 87

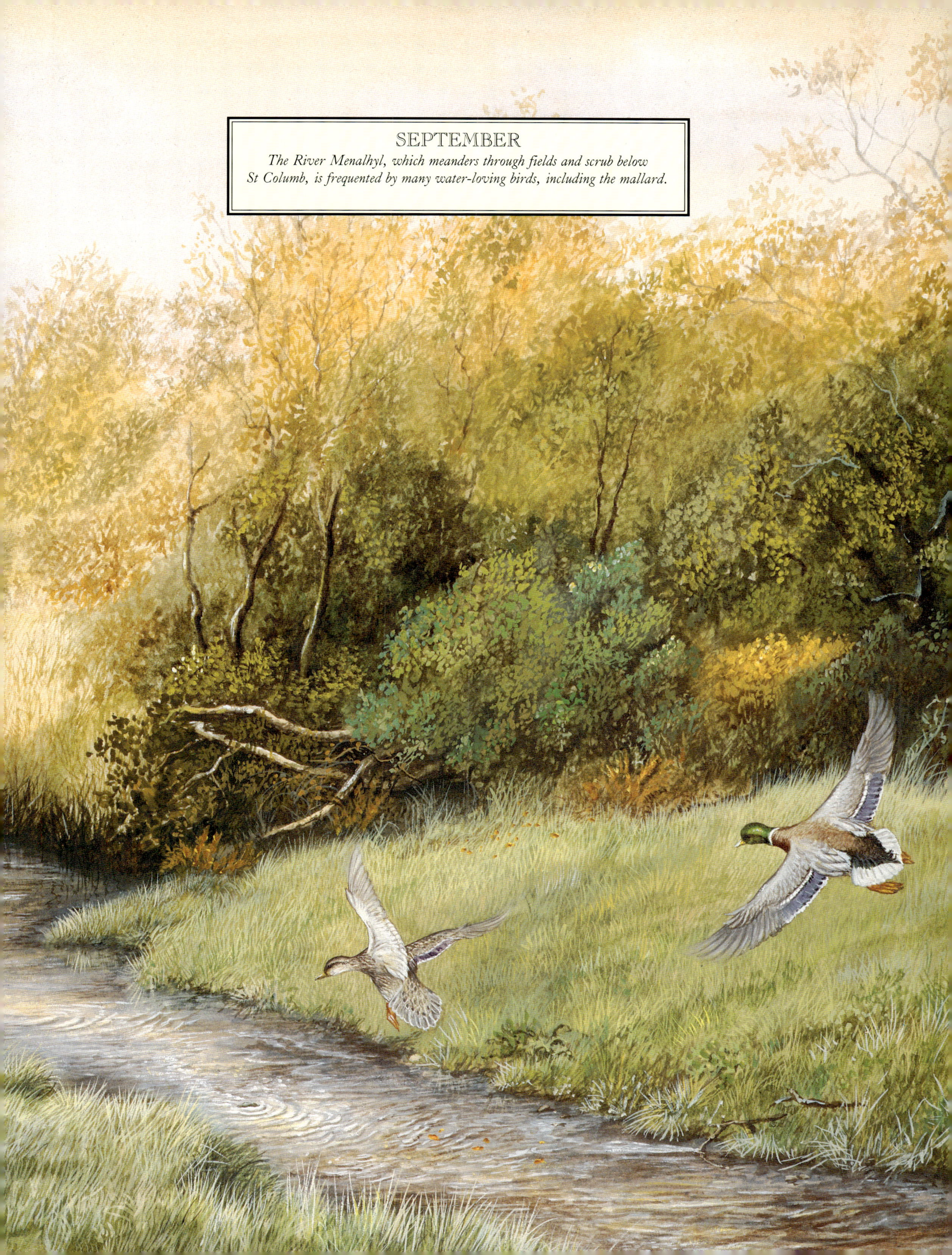

SEPTEMBER

The River Menalhyl, which meanders through fields and scrub below St Columb, is frequented by many water-loving birds, including the mallard.

First Week

BUTTERFLY CORNER

If ever an area illustrated the importance to wildlife of farmers leaving odd small areas free from cultivation, it is this natural, wild garden in one of our nearby meadows, which I have named 'Butterfly Corner'. The complete area is shown in the landscape for August.

The corner of the field is bordered by a drainage ditch which always, even in the driest weather, contains water. This makes ideal damp conditions for fleabane (yellow flowers) and the sneezewort (white flowers). Completing the flora in the painting is purple loosestrife.

Although I have featured only three flowering plants the choice is vast – I could have included bird's-foot trefoil, hemp-agrimony, yellow bartsia, various chickweeds and clovers which all grow in abundance alongside a multitude of different grasses. The area is also backed by blackberry bushes which also add variety to the corner.

Naturally, with so many different flowering plants offering such a vast array of fragrances and nectars, the insect life is abundant and varied. Over the summer months we have recorded most of Britain's more familiar butterflies here. In the painting I have included the small skipper (top), common blue, both male and female (male in flight), two six-spot burnet moths and a meadow brown, all regular visitors to Butterfly Corner. The long, hot summer of 1989 brought ideal conditions for observing butterflies and moths, especially the attractive and distinctive six-spot burnet moth (a day flier).

I get great satisfaction from working on this type of painting, being right down among the flowers and grasses on a sunny day in the meadow with sketch-book and camera at the ready, never knowing what small creatures will enter my immediate field of vision. I cannot think of a better way of earning a living.

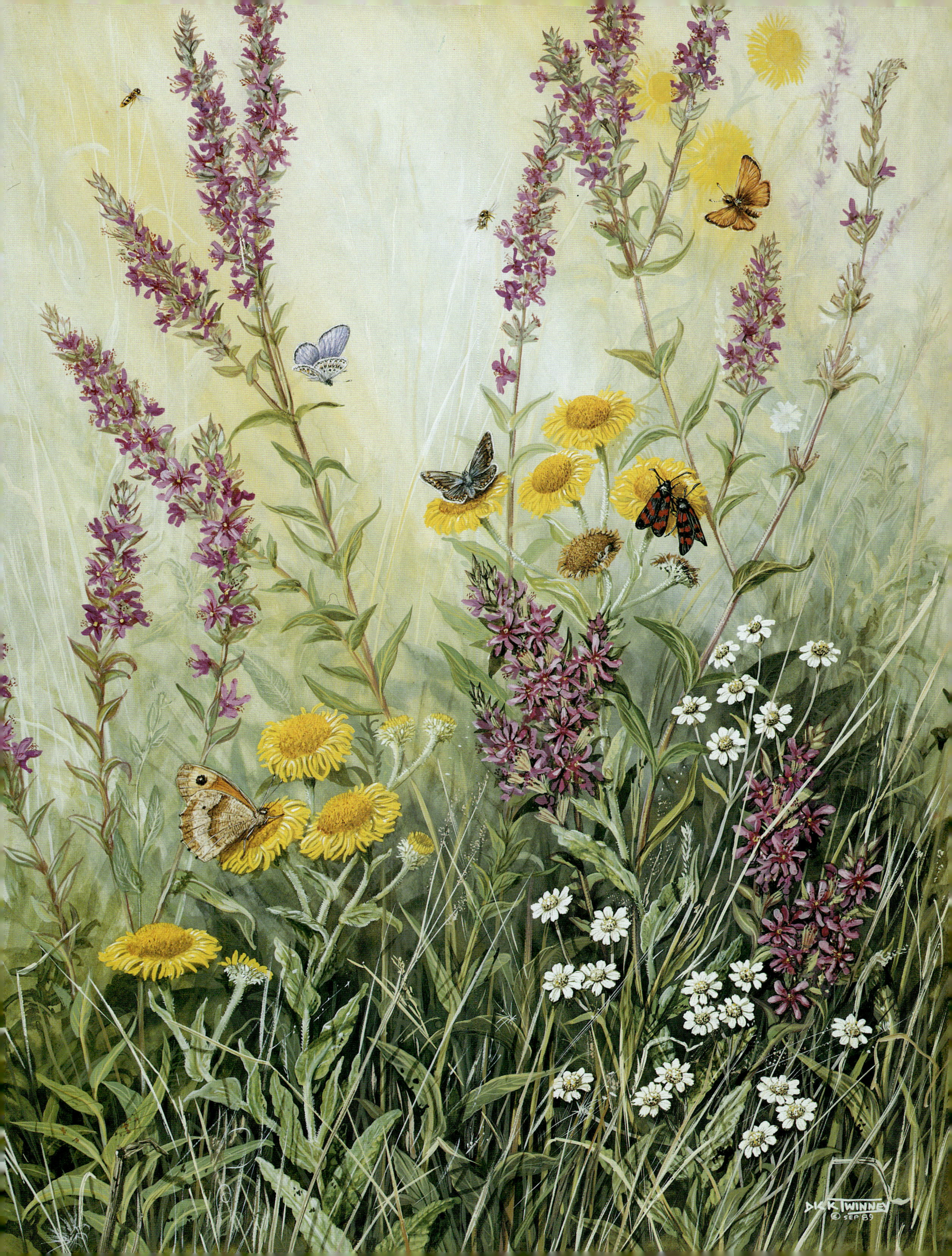
DICK TWINNEY
© SEP 89

Second Week

BARN OWL

On silent outspread wings the barn owl drifted ghost-like across the fields and hedgerows, dipping and wavering with just the occasional flap to keep airborne, patrolling its territory as it had done for many years. Times have changed, however, and it now has the new bypass to negotiate; its path cut across the owl's traditional hunting grounds and, worst of all, caused the old barns, which had been used by generations of owls as nest sites, to be destroyed.

The fast-moving traffic had claimed two of the owl's last brood and a poisoned rat another. We must help the barn owl to adjust to modern agricultural methods by providing suitable alternative nest sites where its traditional homes are being destroyed. Steps must also be taken to encourage captive breeding to help replace the inevitable road casualties. It saddens me to think that one day our British countryside may no longer be graced by this truly beautiful bird and the eerie screech of the barn owl will cease to be heard echoing across the meadows.

In flight the barn owl is at its most impressive, but in this painting the bird has just alighted on a favourite perch, disturbing an eyed hawk moth which was resting among the ivy. Its head swings round in surprise as the whirring of small wings attracts its attention.

Although it looks almost entirely white in flight, on closer inspection the back and tops of the wings are a beautiful dark golden-orange, flecked with black and white. The feathers are soft and flexible with finely fringed edges which aid its silent flight. The talons are very impressive, the needle-sharp claws bring a swift end to any small rodent unfortunate enough to be caught.

At this time of the year the parent barn owls are often seen hunting during daylight hours; their fast-growing brood are nearly fledged and need constant feeding.

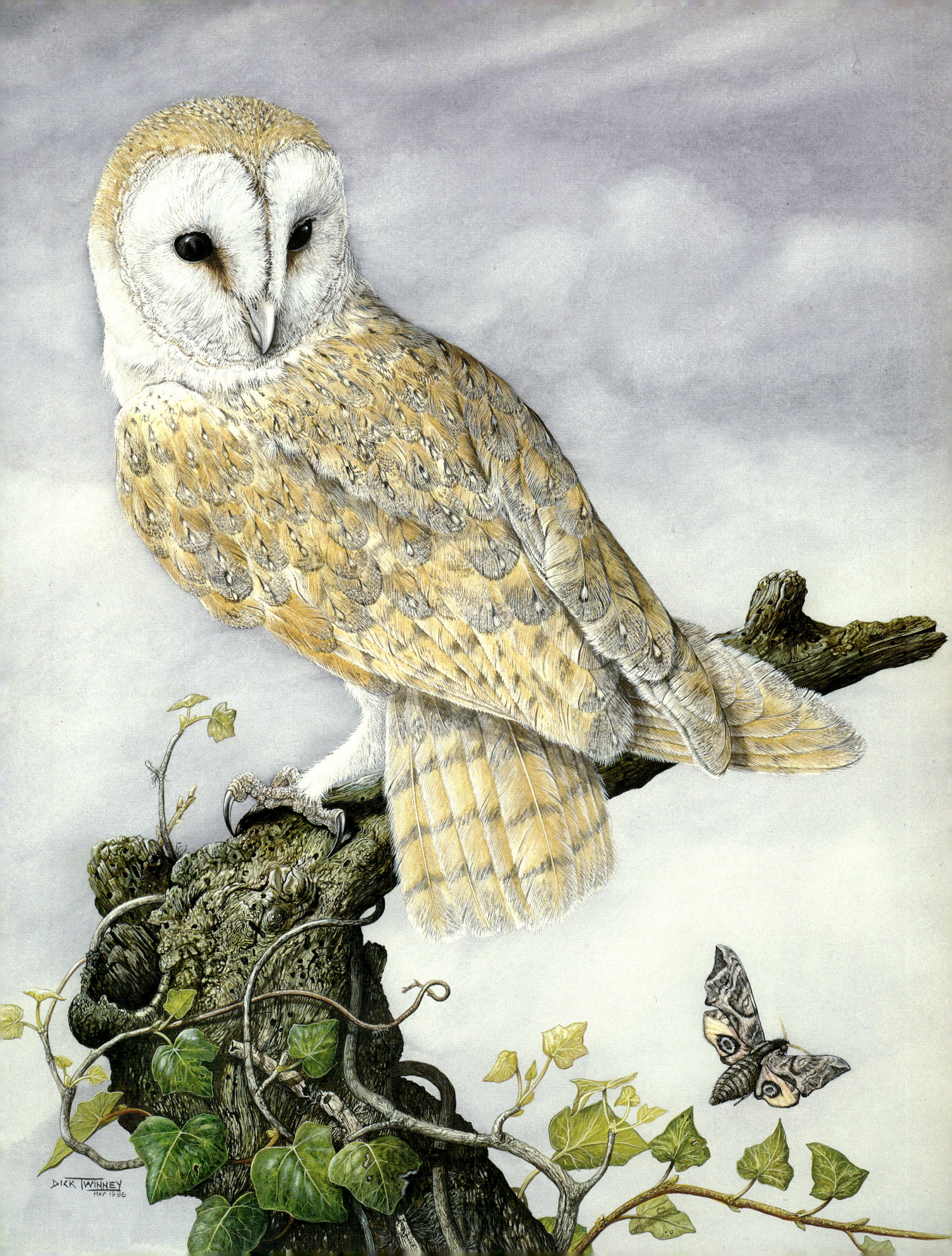
DICK TWINNEY
MAY 1986

THIRD WEEK

BADGERS – BEDDING CHANGE

The badger is one of Britain's best known and much loved indigenous animals. They certainly have a special place in the hearts of our family, for we have been involved with them for a great many years.

There are many badger setts in the near vicinity of our home but none quite as obvious as the one featured here, which is built in a bank right next to a popular public footpath. Being in such a noticeable place is probably greatly to the badgers' advantage, as any nefarious nocturnal human activity, such as 'badger digging', would immediately be detected by people living nearby. Unfortunately, despite all the hard work on the part of the RSPCA and badger-protection groups, the cruel and illegal practice of badger-baiting still goes on in isolated areas of the country, causing great suffering to badgers and, to a lesser extent, the hapless dogs. Public awareness and the reporting of anything suspicious is one way we can all help to eradicate this barbaric pastime.

In my paintings I always endeavour to depict the various creatures in an active role, going about their lives as naturally as possible, which is why for this September painting I have the badgers hard at work changing their bedding. This activity is typical of late summer and early autumn and one seemingly undertaken with great enthusiasm. In one place the path was nearly blocked by a huge pile of soil and old bedding which had cascaded down the bank. The fresh bedding, which in this particular sett consisted of grass and hay, is gathered at night from a nearby meadow and rolled into a large bundle which is held between the badger's chin and forelegs. The bundle is then transported back to the sett by way of an ungainly and amusing backwards shuffle.

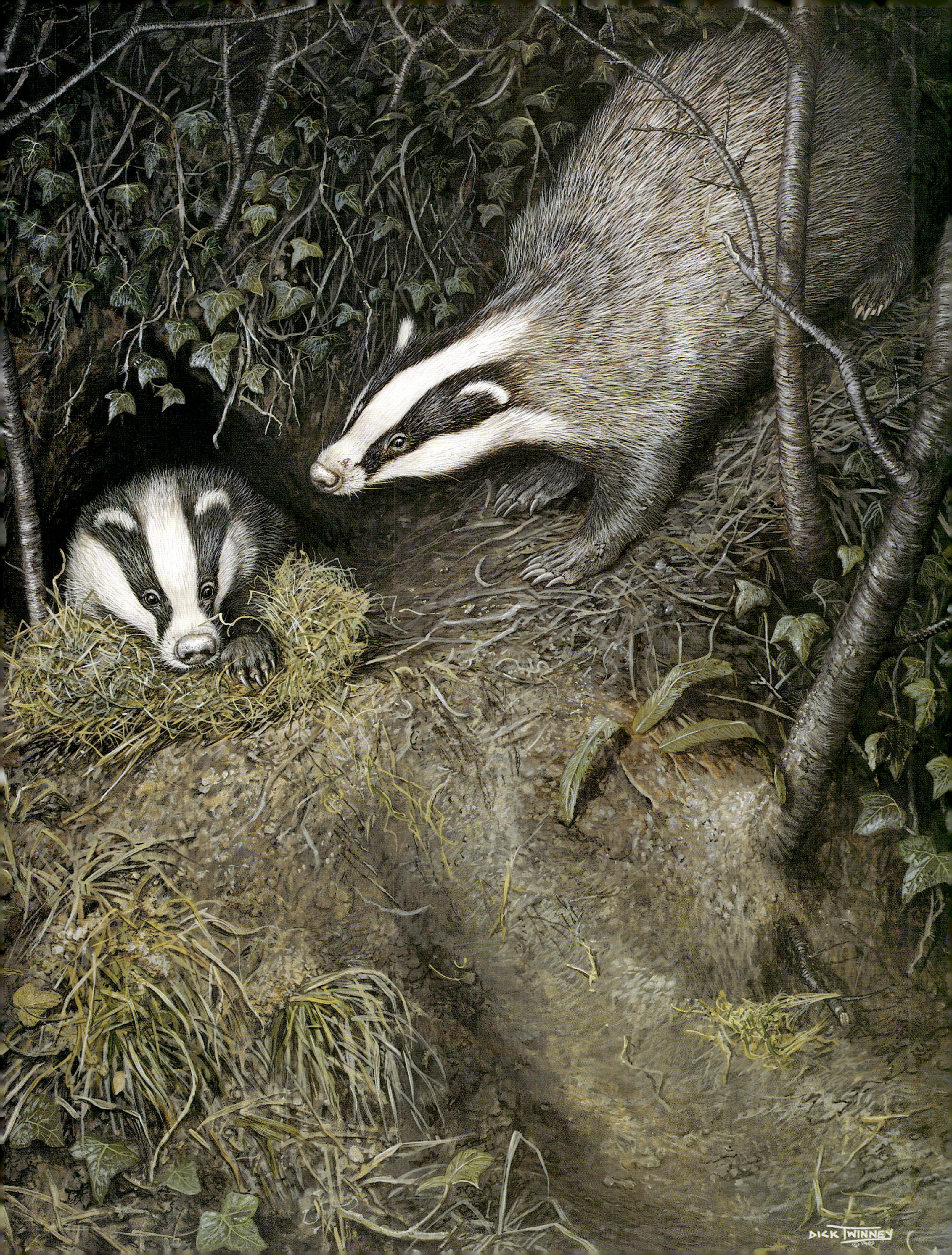
DICK TWINNEY

FOURTH WEEK

WATER SHREW AND WATER MINT

Back to Butterfly Corner for yet another painting. The small drainage ditch which supplies the life-blood for so many different wet-land plants is now almost choked with masses of water mint. This has been growing steadily throughout the summer and is now a mass of pale purple flowers. These are much loved by many flying insects, some of the most noticeable being the common blue, small copper and skipper butterflies. As with many garden varieties of mint, water mint gives off a very pleasant minty aroma when the leaves are crushed or when you walk through it.

The ditch itself is also a haven for many small animals – frogs, toads and newts all use it for spawning. Dragonfly, damselfly and caddis fly larvae can be found alongside many species of water beetle. One of the great joys of my 'job' is that I can still pursue the pastimes of my childhood, knee-deep in muddy water, with net and collecting jar, all in the name of research for my paintings!

In and around the bank of the ditch there are many small holes and runs, obviously made by mice, shrews and voles. The water shrew in the painting was drawn from a dead specimen which was found many miles from water lying in a lane. Perhaps it was dropped by a predator.

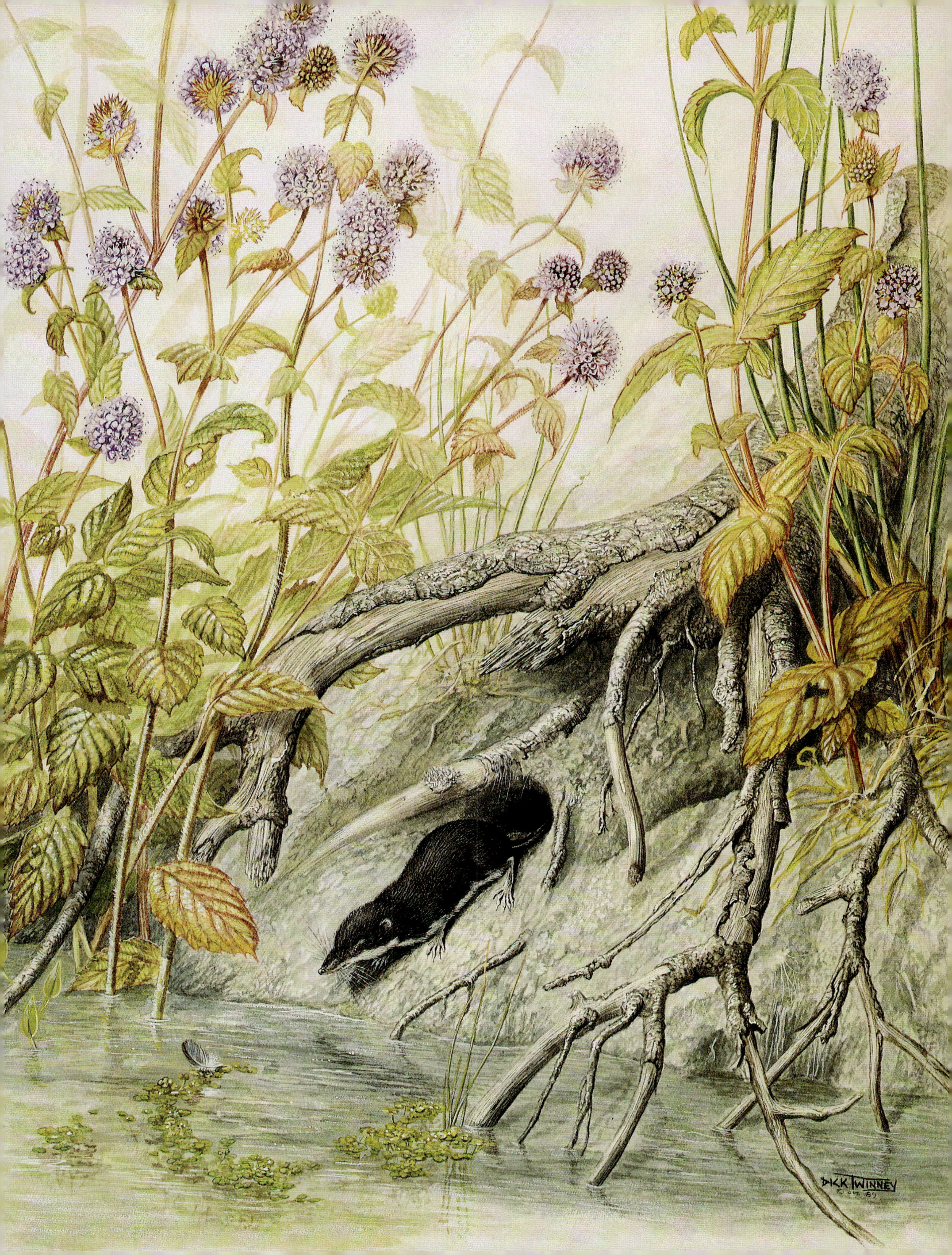
DICK TWINNEY

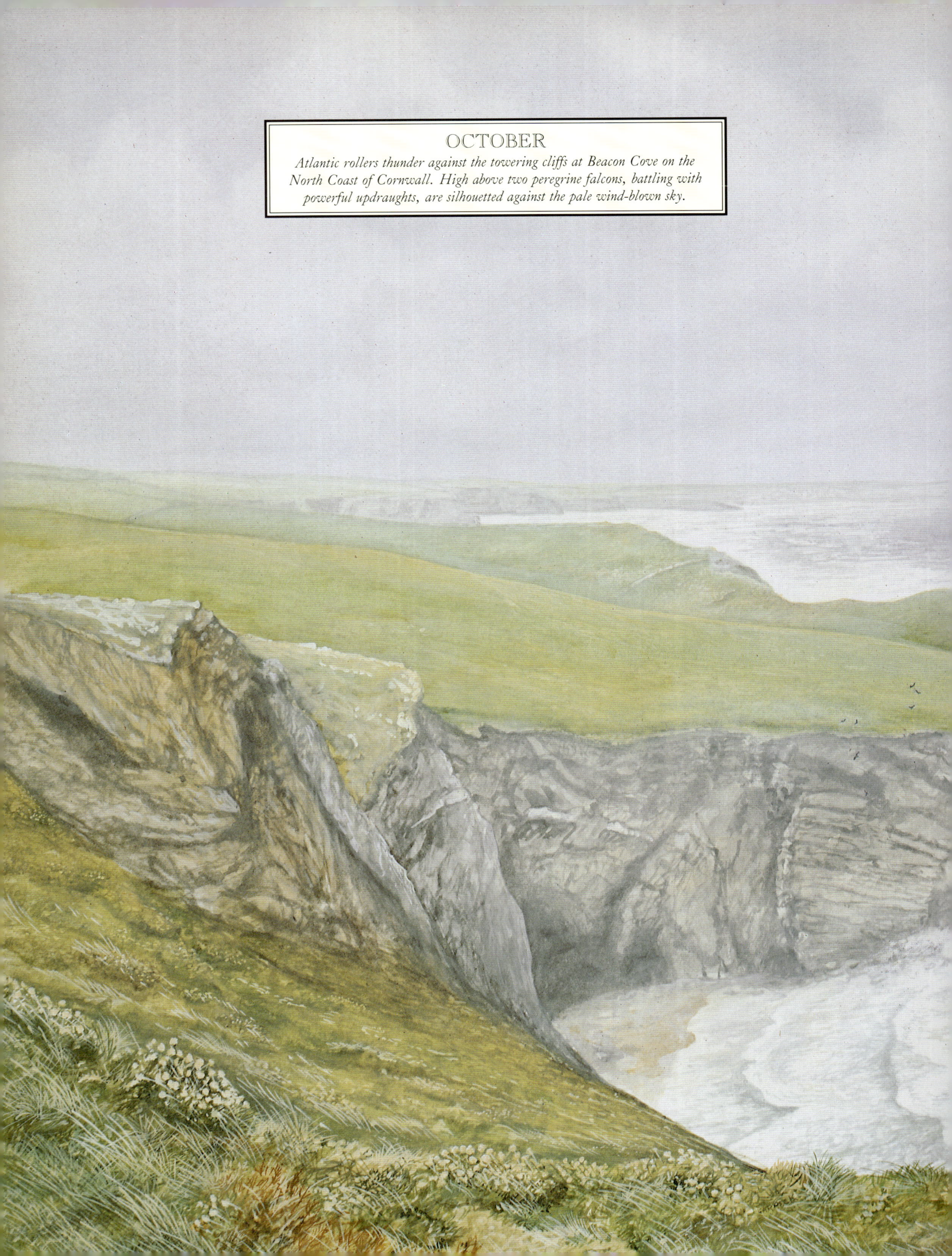

OCTOBER

Atlantic rollers thunder against the towering cliffs at Beacon Cove on the North Coast of Cornwall. High above two peregrine falcons, battling with powerful updraughts, are silhouetted against the pale wind-blown sky.

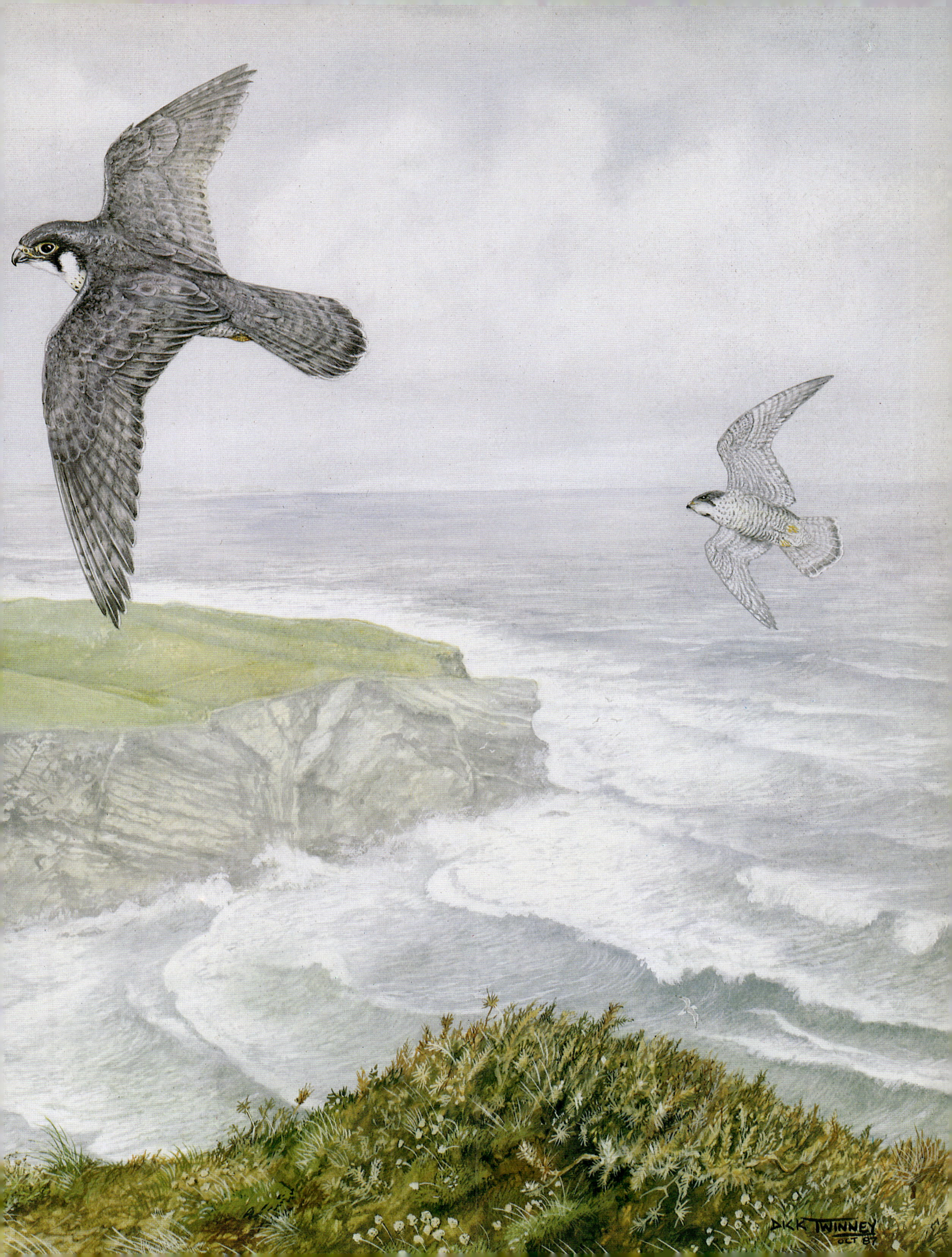
DICK TWINNEY
OCT 87

First Week

SUMMER'S END

Strictly speaking, October is well into autumn, but the picture I have painted for this first week in October could not have any other title. It has that feeling of spent life, of dying back. The rich greens of the meadow's edge have all turned various tones of brown. Nature's life force is now concentrated into the many seeds and berries which grace our fields and hedgerows. They will rely on a great many methods of distribution, some employing wind power, as in the case of the thistle family, while other seed pods have small hooks and spikes that become attached to any passing animal or clothing. Birds and mammals play an important part in the spreading of plant life by eating the many berries and fruits available at this time of year; the digested seeds are often left miles from the original source. Birds, in particular, are responsible for plants and shrubs becoming established in strange out of the way places.

I am especially fond of the muted colours which abound at this time of year. The strange shapes created by dying foliage has made this a very interesting painting on which to work. I have tried to capture a sadness, the end of something special. The inclusion of the discarded buzzard's feather and the delicate wing of the common blue butterfly all add to the evocative scene.

All the material used for this painting was gathered from one small field corner and set up in my studio. The orb web spiders came from the same area, which was a mass of cobwebs. The older webs were covered in grass seeds and various inedible parts of insects, beetle wing cases and the butterfly wing.

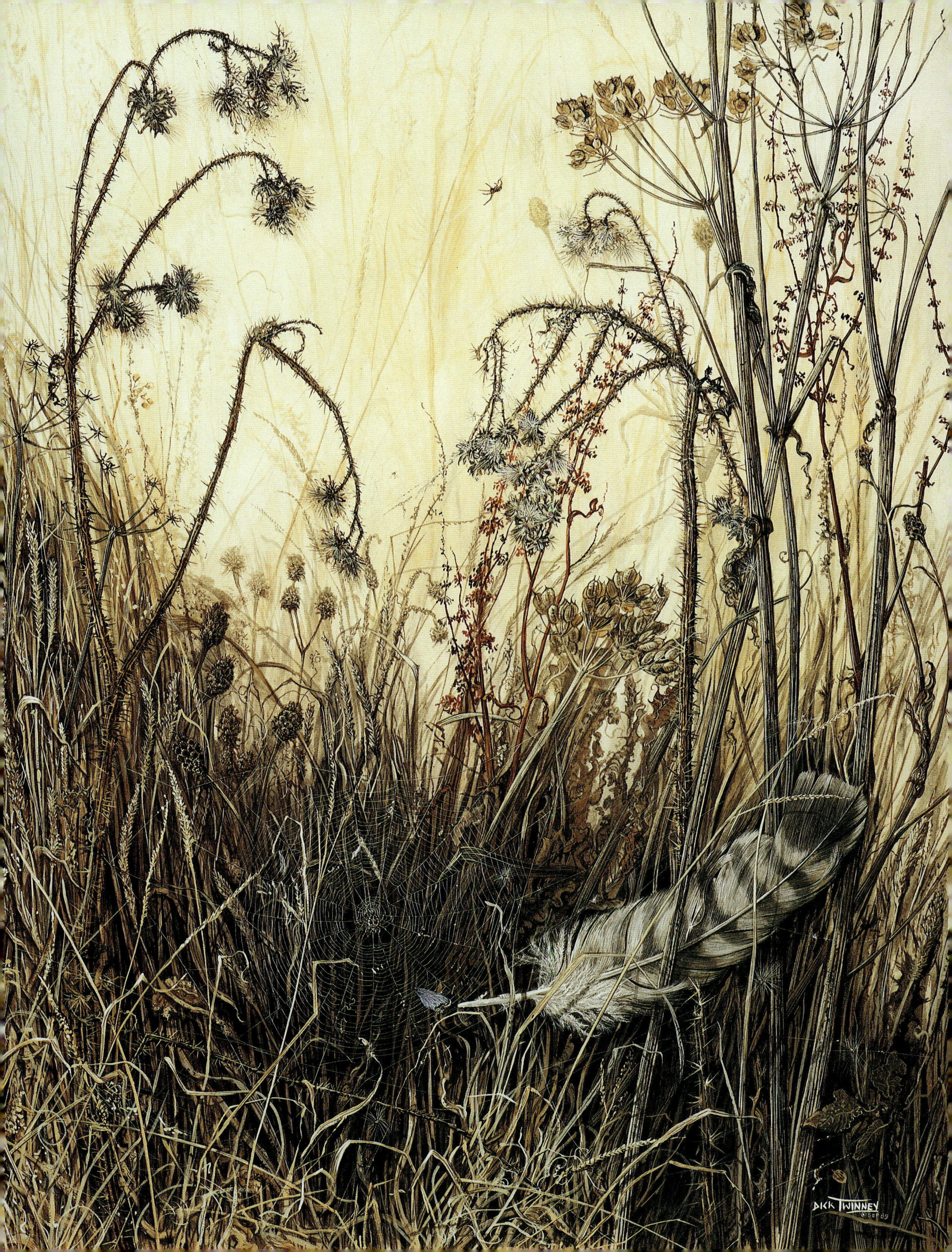
DICK TWINNEY
© SEP 89

SECOND WEEK

RED SQUIRREL AND SWEET CHESTNUT

Being one of our most delightful mammals, I could not possibly leave this little fellow out of the book, although it meant using another artist's field sketches, photographic and video references. Sadly the red squirrel is now very rare and I have not seen one in the wild since childhood. However, they are still numerous in some areas, particularly in Scotland.

They are the most amusing of creatures to observe, with comical mannerisms and jerky movements which I have tried to portray in the painting by showing the squirrel in a position of attention. Some movement or noise has attracted him, his body is tensed and vibrantly alive, ready for instant flight.

At this time of the year red squirrels are busy feeding and gaining strength for the coming winter months. Their coats thicken and darken and the ear tufts become very prominent. They do not hibernate but will remain in their dreys during bad weather.

The favourite habitat of the red squirrel is conifer woods, where the evergreen trees offer year round shelter and cover from predators and the firs provide food in the form of oil-rich seeds from the cones. Flower buds, leaves and nuts are also included in their diet as are some fungi when available.

I have put the squirrel in a sweet chestnut tree, as it is at its most attractive at this time of the year with the nuts starting to ripen off and the leaves just beginning to change colour. During the two weeks it took me to paint the foliage in this picture, the leaves changed quite considerably and many of the nuts ripened and dropped to the ground where their prickly protective shells burst open to provide food for the local grey squirrels and woodmice.

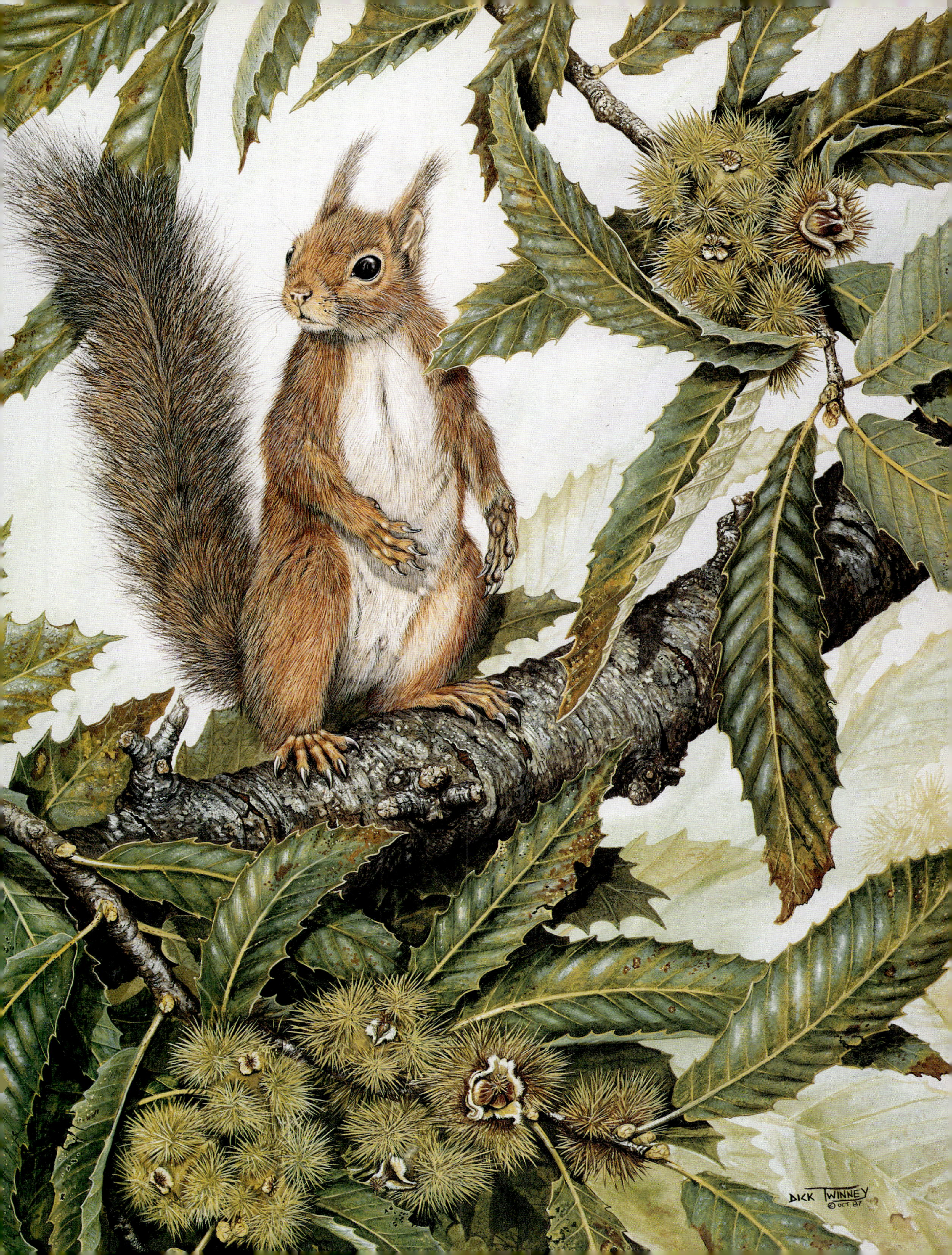
DICK TWINNEY
© OCT 87

THIRD WEEK

NUTHATCH AND ENGLISH ELM

The nuthatch is a delightful little bird. It is easily identifiable because of its striking plumage and powerful bill. Once a bird of broad-leaved woodland, it has now also moved into our parks and gardens. It will take full advantage of bird-table fare, particularly nuts, a great favourite, which are taken off and wedged into a suitable tree where they are hammered with the 'hatchet' bill until they crack open, hence the bird's name.

They are very interesting and amusing birds to observe, especially when they are busy searching for small invertebrates hidden under wood and in the bark of some old tree. They have great acrobatic skills and are the only British bird which regularly climbs down trees head first. I have chosen this bird for late October because you are most likely to see it during the autumn months when there is little foliage on the trees. You may be lucky enough to have one visit your bird-table.

For the painting I have put my nuthatch on an old elm tree – one of the few still standing since Dutch elm disease. Although it is completely dead it is visited regularly by nuthatches and woodpeckers and is obviously a home for many insects, spiders and beetles.

I have painted a complete section of the tree trunk to give a very dramatic and abstract effect, the thick, deep crevices showing up clearly in the bright autumn light, which comes from below. To avoid flatness I have used deep shadow around the curvature of the trunk. The nuthatch is working downwards and across, thus breaking up the continuous pattern of the bark.

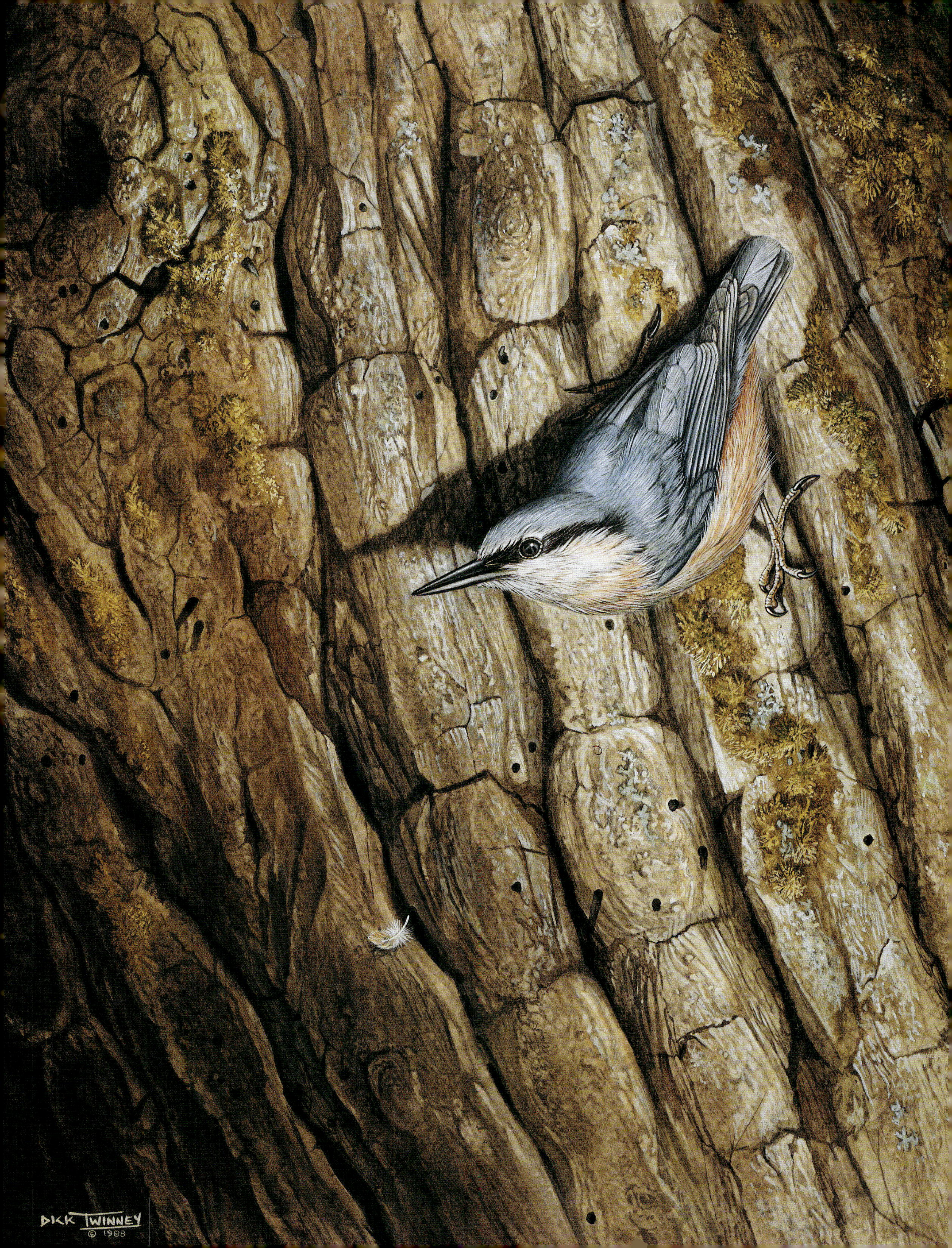
DICK TWINNEY
© 1988

Fourth Week

GREAT TIT AND NASTURTIUM

I did not have to travel far to gather material for this painting, just down to the bottom of the garden where one flower bed had been taken over completely by a great mass of nasturtiums. The long, hot summer of 1989 provided the ideal conditions for this particular plant, creating an amazing show of colour. Not being content to confine itself to the flower bed, it had spread outwards and upwards, covering the path and climbing over ten feet (three metres) up one side of an aviary, some of the rambling stalks being as thick as my finger. It flowered all summer long and even during the last week of October still had many blooms and opening buds. The large green leaves have provided a constant food source for many caterpillars, particularly those belonging to small and large white butterflies.

Many other insects seem to find this plant to their liking, the leaves providing shelter as well as food and the flowers a source of nectar. Because of this abundance of insect life the nasturtiums are regularly visited by many garden birds. I have seen, at different times, wrens, blackbirds, thrushes, hedge sparrows and blue and great tits, all busy among the plant's foliage. The thrushes, wrens and hedge sparrows work away near the ground after small slugs, worms and snails, whereas the tits flit acrobatically through the climbing stalks, searching for aphids and tiny winged insects. The nasturtium is certainly beneficial to a wildlife garden, not only providing a colourful profusion of yellows, oranges and reds but also attracting many varied forms of animal life.

I have chosen the great tit for this painting as it is the most frequent visitor to the plant. The tit's striking plumage is also a suitable companion for a colourful and striking flower.

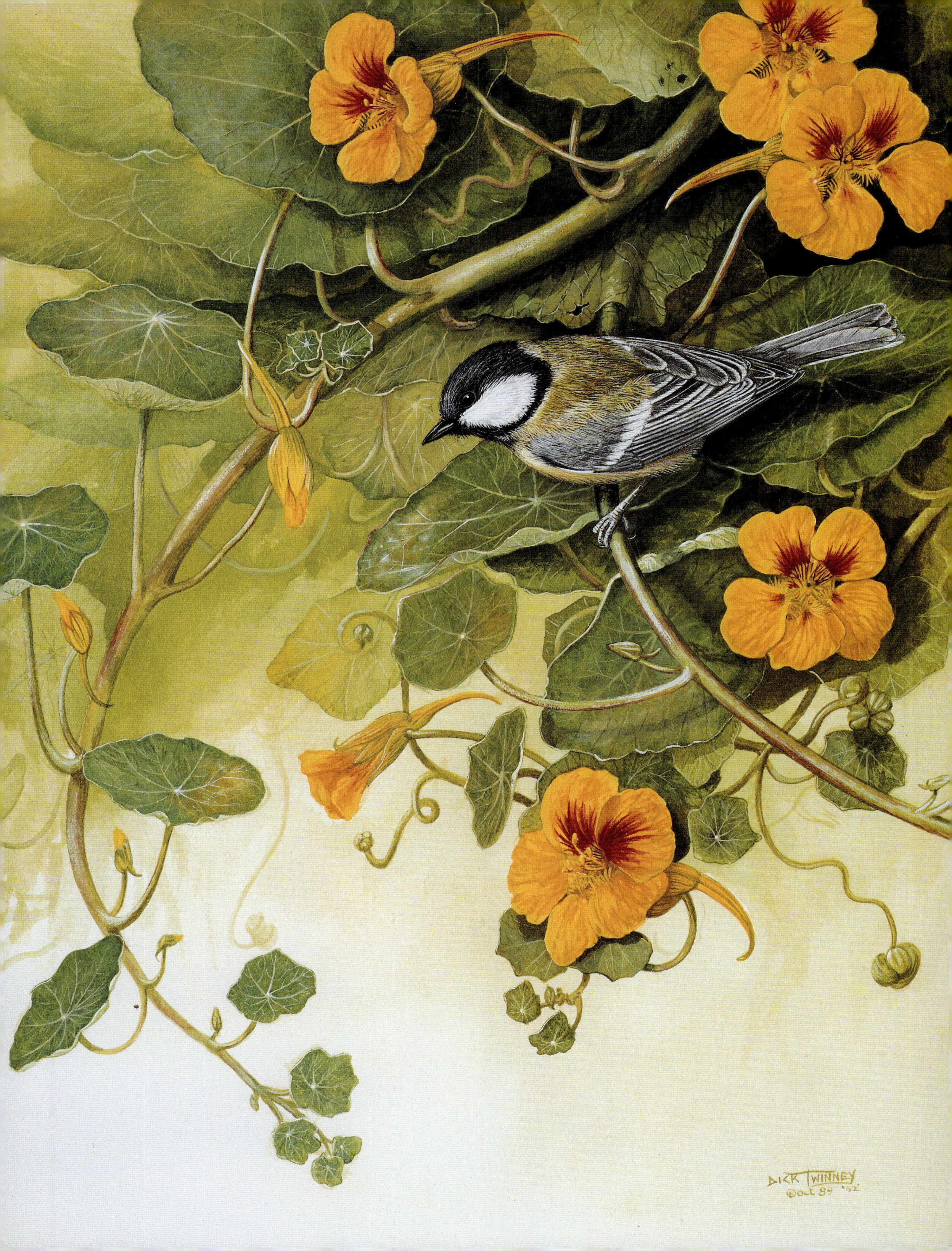
DICK TWINNEY
©Oct 89 '52'

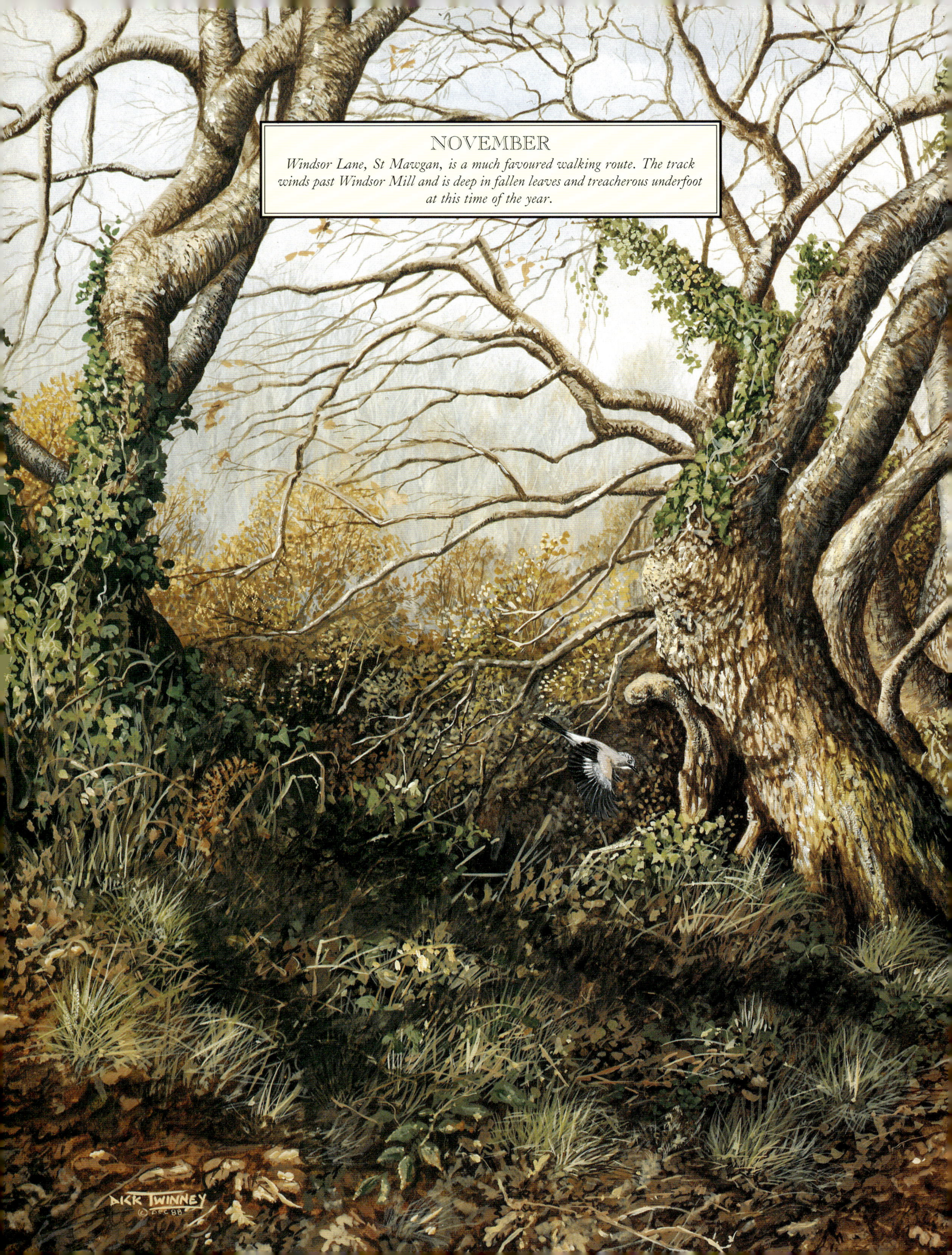

NOVEMBER

Windsor Lane, St Mawgan, is a much favoured walking route. The track winds past Windsor Mill and is deep in fallen leaves and treacherous underfoot at this time of the year.

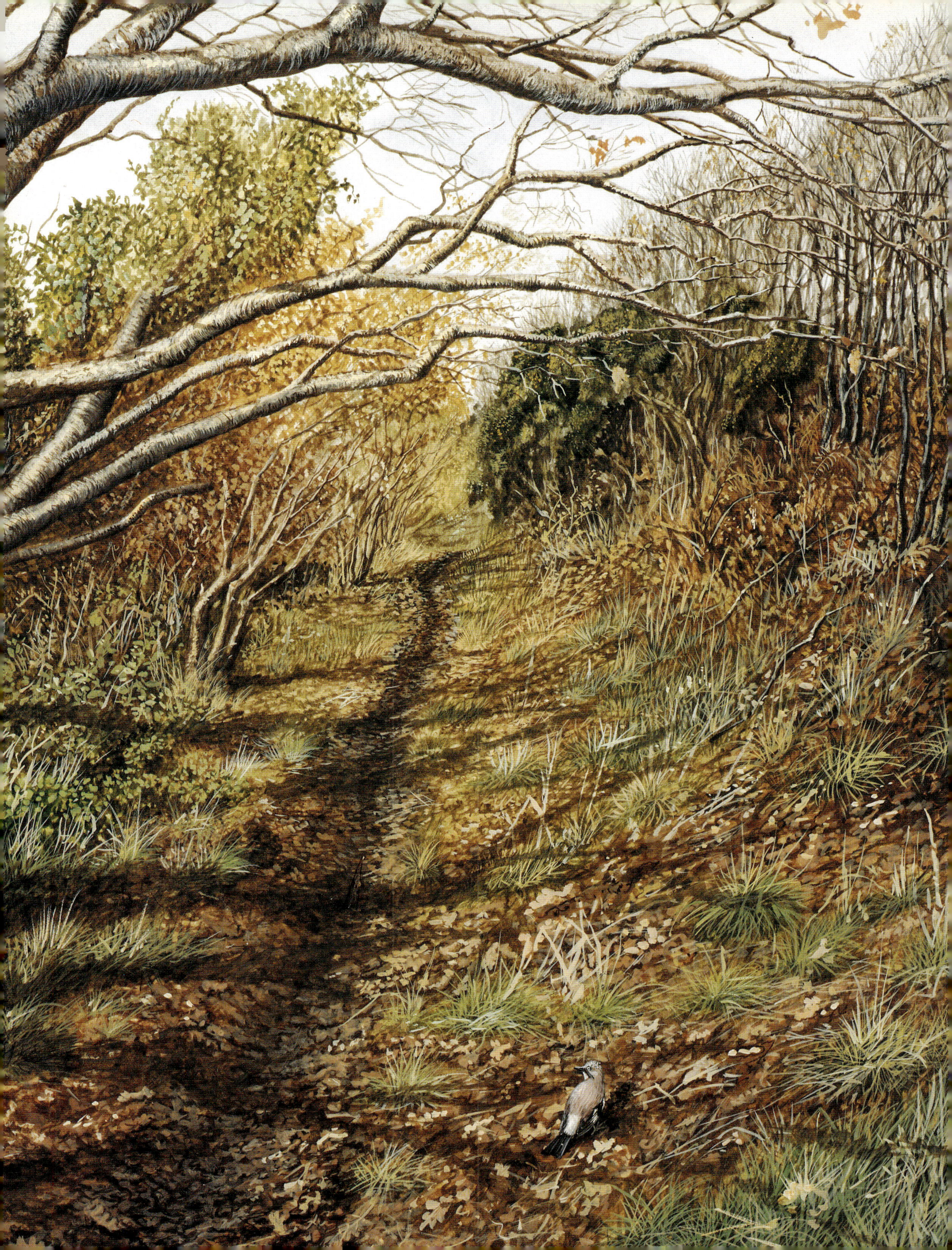

FIRST WEEK

BROWN HARE

The nearest moorland to my home and studio is Goss Moor, a small wild area full of ancient historical interest and abundant with many forms of animal life. Cornwall, being an area of so many differing landscapes, does not have much open countryside – the favoured habitat of the brown hare. However, Goss Moor is the exception rather than the rule.

Built for speed, the hare is larger and has longer limbs than the rabbit. The prominent black-tipped ears and large alert eyes are its main attributes for detecting danger, while its speed helps it to out run would-be predators.

The hare's brown-grey colouring enables it to remain undetected in the long moorland grass, especially when it crouches down in a small hollow or scrape (known as a form). Many times my heartbeat has quickened following the sudden appearance of a hare from virtually under my feet. The situation illustrated here was one such occasion in early November when the whole family, including the dogs, were walking on the moor, taking in the splendid views from this rugged upland area. Suddenly Ben, the largest of our dogs, dived into a clump of grass just in front of the party. Out sprang a splendid hare, which was up and away in seconds, easily out running the dogs. As it disappeared almost leisurely over a stone wall in the distance, I called our dogs back. The somewhat bemused expression on Ben's face seemed to say 'some rabbit that'.

For this painting I have tried to capture that moment as the hare springs to its feet, all senses alert, muscles quivering, so vibrantly alive, the master of its environment. There was never any danger of our dogs catching the hare. The fact that dogs are specially bred for hare coursing is totally abhorrent to me and my family.

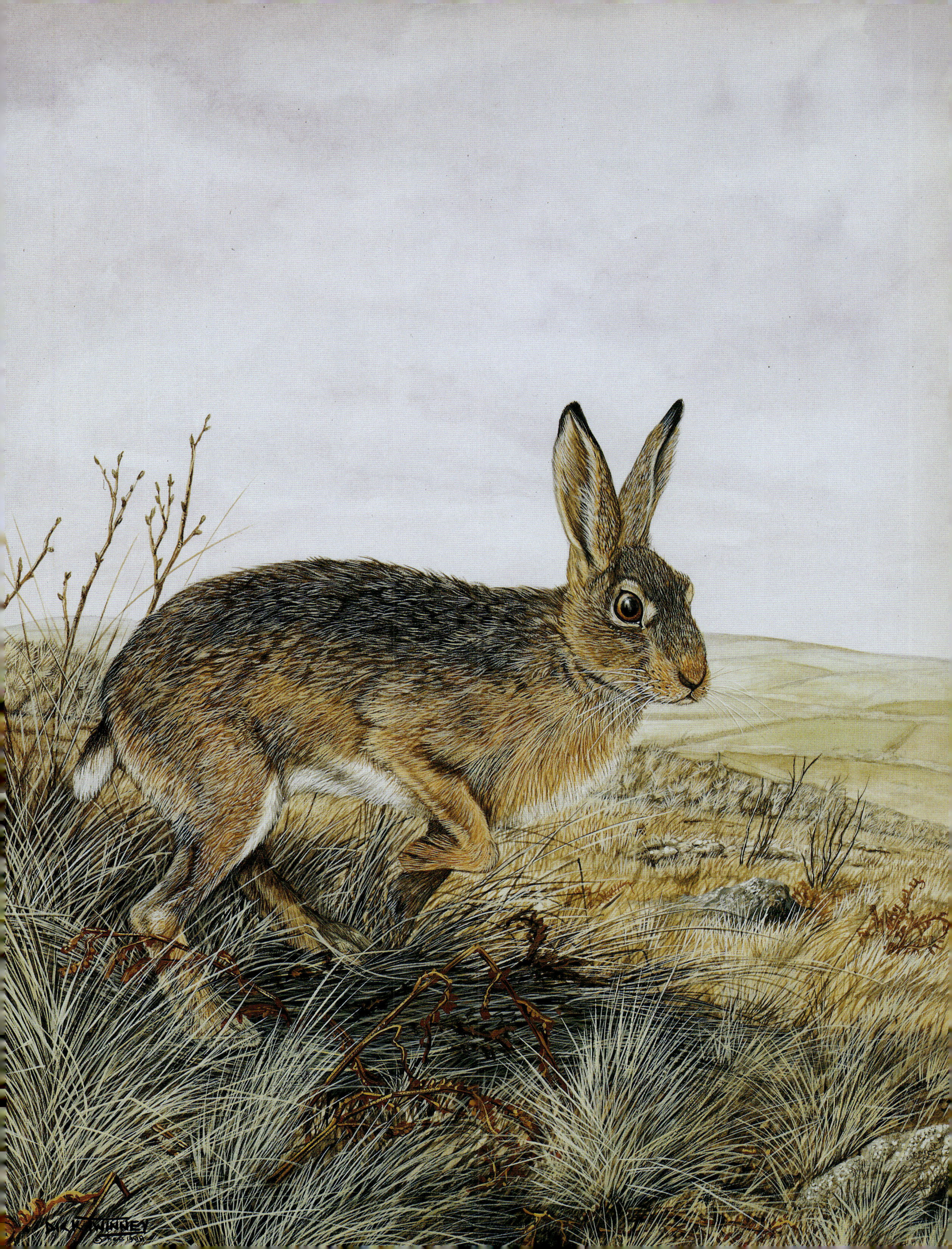

SECOND WEEK

BLUE TITS IN ENGLISH OAK

Autumn is one of the best seasons of the year for bird-watching. It is a time when many species are on the move, summer visitors going and winter visitors arriving, and some resident birds are forming large flocks. The tit family is no exception, gathering in chittering groups as they take over whole hedgerows and woods, busily seeking out small insects and showing off their acrobatic prowess in the process.

This painting was inspired by a most pleasant hour watching tits at work in one large oak tree. The tree was visited by great tits, coal tits and, most numerous of all, the blue tit. They were all very active, enthusiastically searching every nook and cranny, in typical tit fashion, for hibernating insects and larvae.

Having painted the great tit previously, I decided it was the turn of the delightfully coloured blue tit. Although a common garden bird, I never tire of watching them as they take peanuts and fat from the bird-table. They also find no difficulty in slipping through the one-inch mesh of our squirrel pen, cheekily stealing the food, often from right under the squirrels' noses.

The oak itself is a very special tree in Britain's countryside. Apart from living longer than any other native tree, it is also home for a rich variety of animal life. When exposed to fierce prevailing winds it is frequently battered into fantastical shapes. Even in our wooded valleys the wind often prevents the oak from standing tall, as can be seen in the landscape for this month.

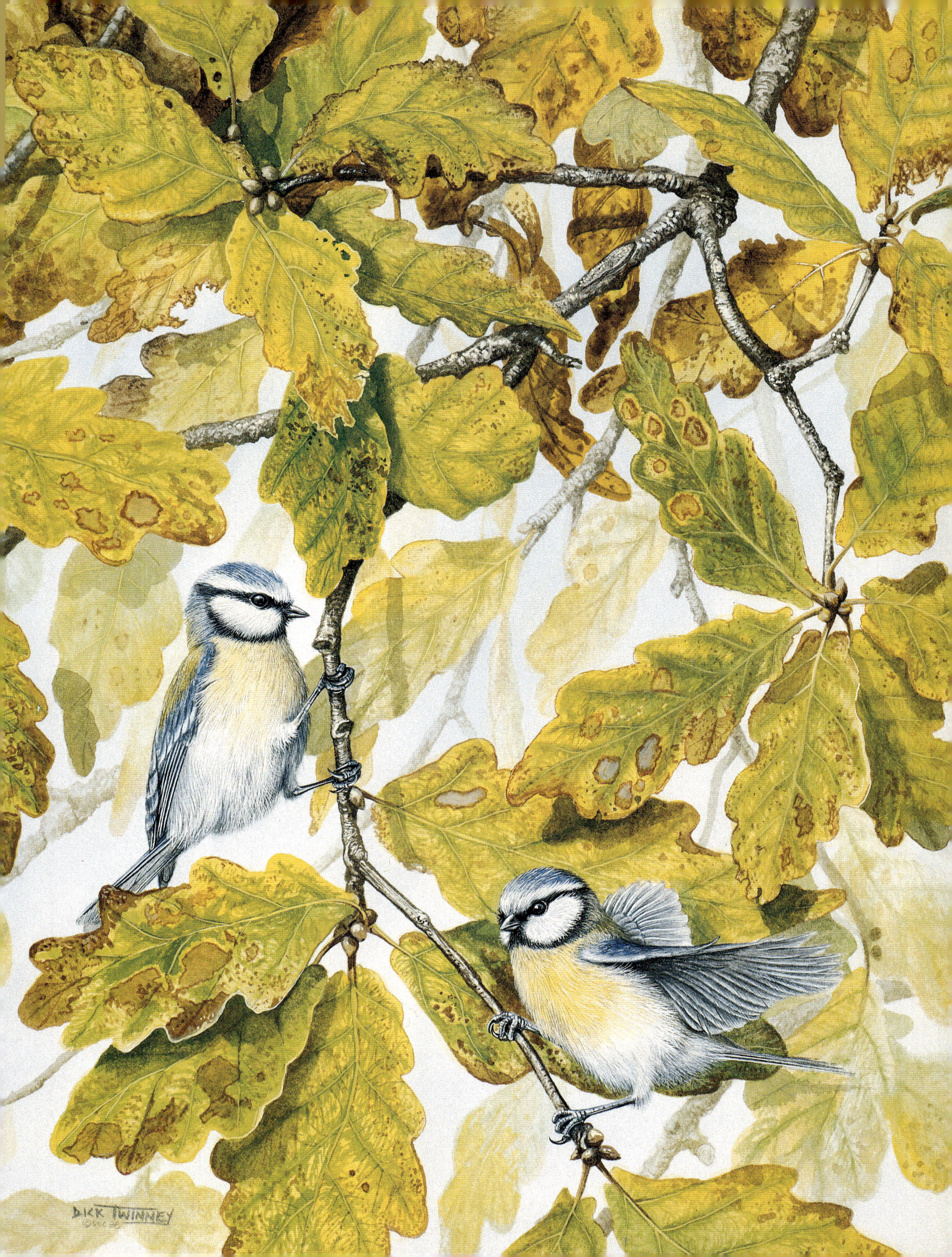
DICK TWINNEY

THIRD WEEK

GOLDCRESTS IN DOUGLAS FIR

Together with the similar but rarer firecrest, the goldcrest is Britain's smallest bird: it is just three and a half inches (nine centimetres) long. At this time of the year they form large flocks, often joining up with other birds such as tits and warblers. Their presence is given away by a high-pitched chirping song as they keep contact with other members in the flock while flitting from branch to branch in the search for small insects.

Coniferous forests are the favoured haunt of the goldcrest (see the March landscape) and we often catch glimpses of them as we walk along the tree-lined tracks. They are quite difficult to spot initially, being so tiny, but once discovered they seem to be unconcerned by the presence of humans and one can venture quite close before they fly away.

Some years ago, at about this time of the year, a small flock of goldcrests visited our garden. Once again it was their song that drew our attention. They systematically flew from bush to bush, totally engrossed in the need to explore every leaf, twig or crevice which might contain small spiders and aphids. They were delightful to watch, continually on the go, their movements best described as 'scurrying'. Once they had exhausted our supply of food they flew off to investigate another garden.

In the painting I have shown two male goldcrests engaged in a vocal dispute while the female (identified by her less fiery crown) looks on. They are perched in a Douglas fir. I chose this particular evergreen because of its interesting and attractive cones, which proved to be quite difficult to paint. The thin, delicate branches of the tree, with its tiny needles, give an overall feeling of airiness or lightness, which helps to emphasize the diminutive stature of the goldcrest.

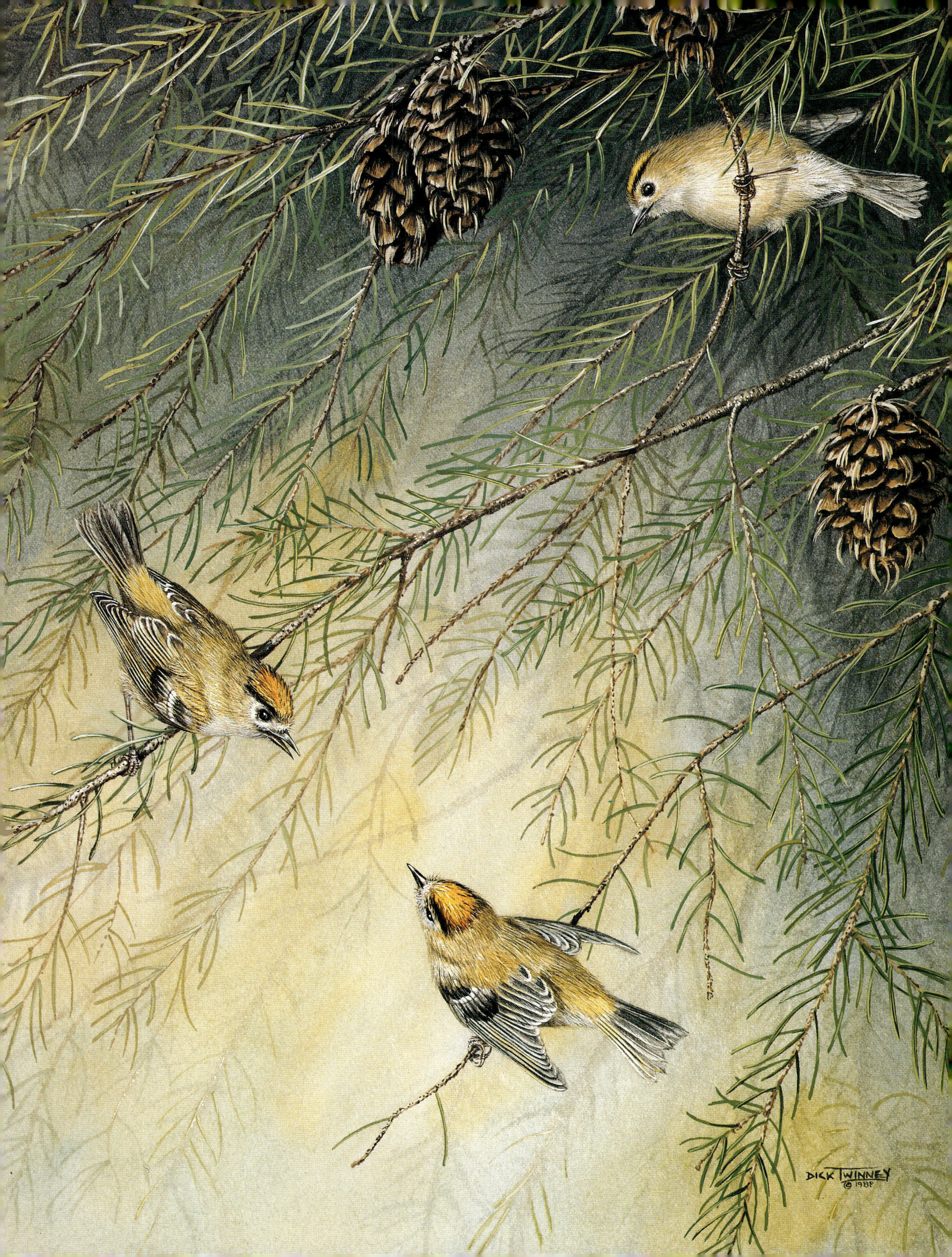
DICK TWINNEY
© 1988

Fourth Week

OTTER

The evening light gradually fades over the reed beds; the deep orange autumn sun reflects in the small stream; the twisted dried shapes of rushes form bizarre and abstract shapes in the deepening shadows. The scene is set to paint the otter.

During the daylight hours the otter has been lying up deep in the heart of the reed beds, safe from disturbance and sheltered from the elements. He now makes his way cautiously towards the water, testing the air frequently with small, nodding movements of his head. He reaches the stream and stops for a moment, his powerful webbed front feet resting on a soft mat of moss which adorns an old log. His fine head is briefly silhouetted against the evening sky before he slips silently into the water.

Due to the loss of natural habitat and the pollution of rivers, otters have become very scarce in many areas of the country. However, in Cornwall we are fortunate for there are still some in the wild. They are very secretive and you would be extremely fortunate to see one in its natural habitat. It has been many years since I was so lucky, although I know they inhabit our local river as I have found their tracks on several occasions.

There are two wildlife parks in Cornwall where this delightful mammal can be seen in captivity. One of the parks is a branch of the Otter Trust which has been extremely successful in breeding European otters and reintroducing captive bred otters to the wild. With the help of organizations like the Otter Trust, cleaner rivers and the availability of natural habitat, the number of otters should increase and the chances of seeing this delightful animal on our rivers will become less remote.

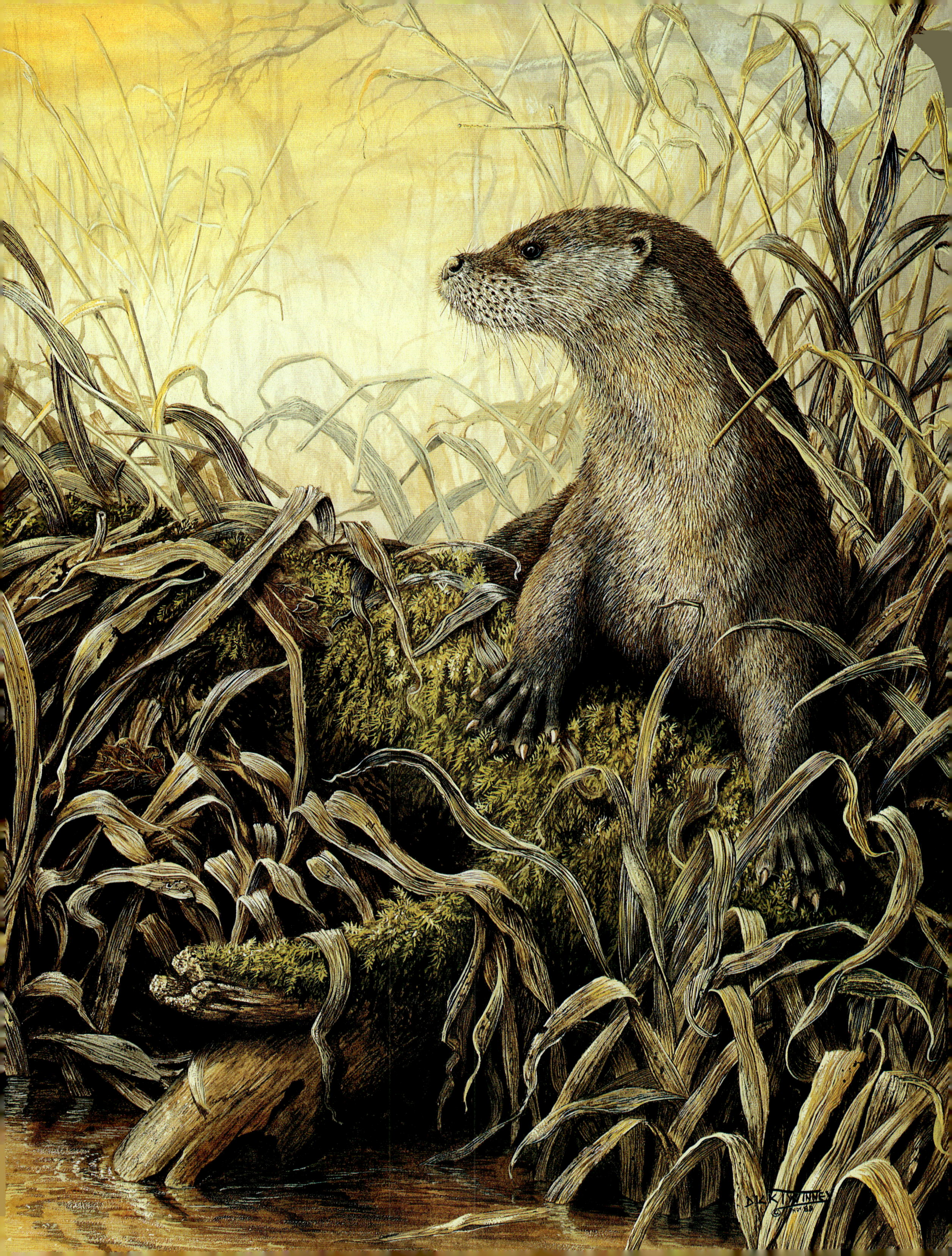

FIFTH WEEK

GREY SQUIRREL

Although not as attractive as the native red squirrel, the American grey has become a widespread addition to our wildlife, and is found in all types of habitat. It makes full use of the hedgerows both as a source of food and a place to nest; this great adaptability is one of the chief reasons for its phenomenal success.

At this time of year grey squirrels are busy burying surplus nuts and acorns; these subsequently become a useful source of food for the winter months ahead. The food store is relocated during the cold weather by scent.

The setting I have used for this painting is the base of a hazel hedge on the edge of Carnanton Woods near St Mawgan in Pydar, Cornwall, an area particularly abundant in squirrels.

The 'model' is our own squirrel Hansel, who along with his sister Gretal, was raised by a cat after the tree which contained their dray was cut down. The cat, which had lost her kittens and was still lactating, readily took on the two unusual charges. The young squirrels became firm favourites with the cat and her owners. As they grew in size and become active problems arose – there were many instance of ripped curtains and gnawed furniture. They were soon relocated to a large outdoor enclosure. I should stress here that they do not usually make good pets and can become very aggressive later in life. A licence is also required in order to keep them in captivity.

Hansel and Gretal, however, readily took to a life of captivity and kept us and the children entertained for many hours. They were extremely playful and liked nothing better than a bundle of fresh hay in which they would roll and dive, fluffing out their tails with obvious enjoyment.

Over the years they became great favourites with the local school-children. Gretal died aged six and Hansel eight months later, just before I finished this painting which I dedicate to them for the hours of pleasure they gave to the whole family.

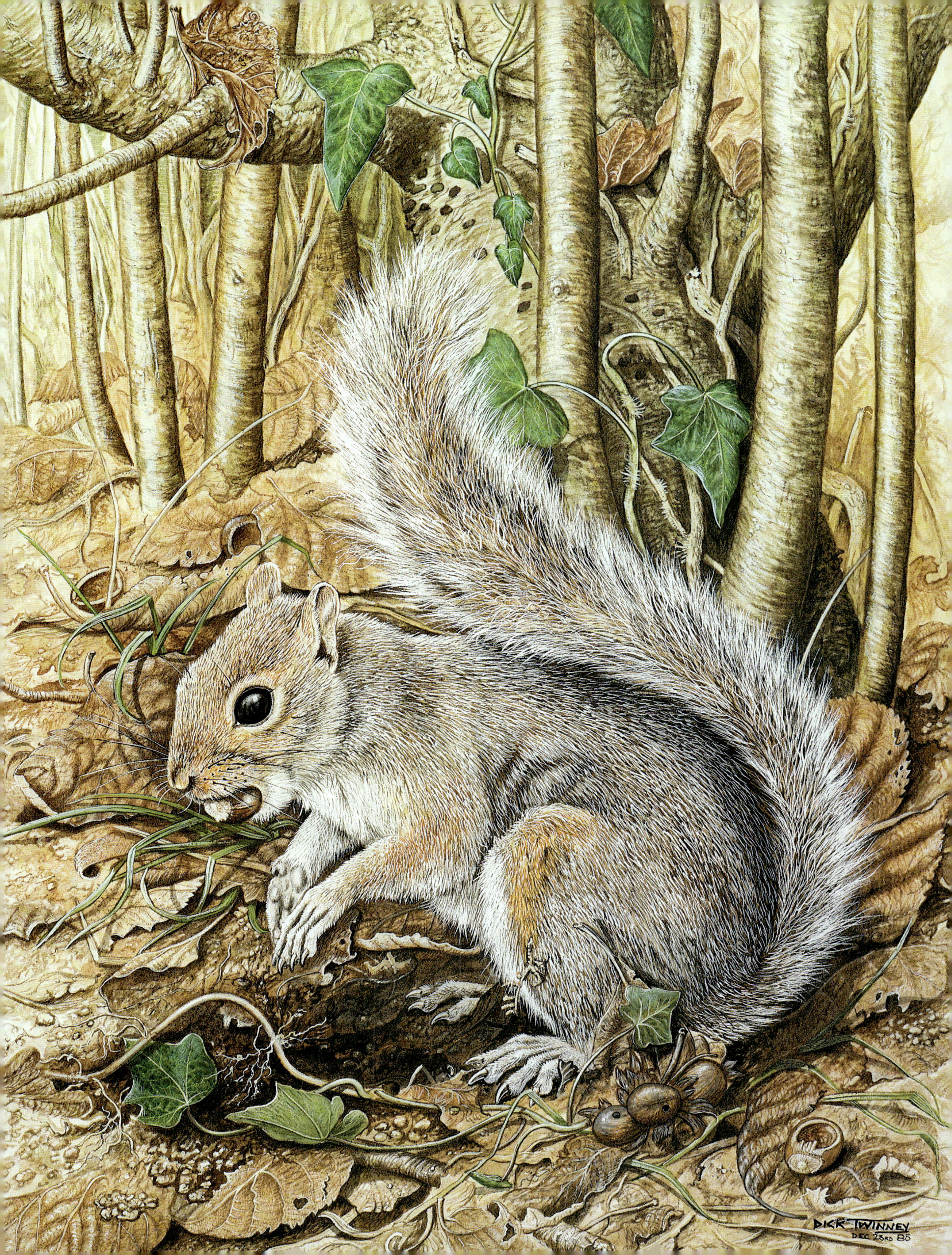
DICK TWINNEY
DEC 23RD 85

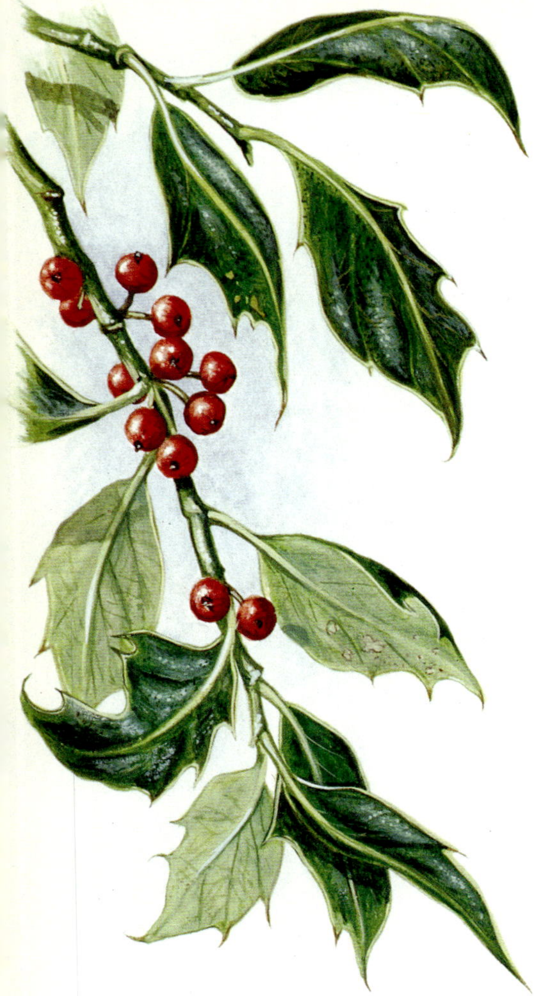

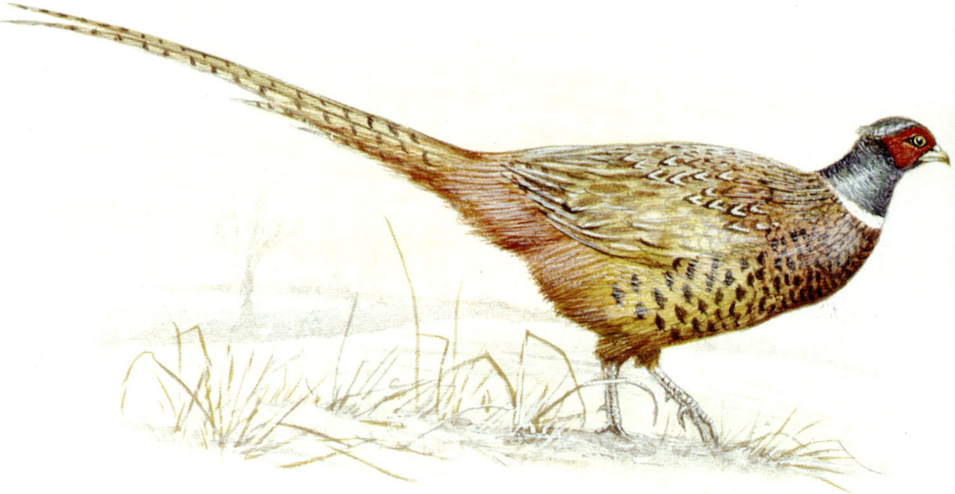

WINTER

Winter is a time of rest for much of the natural world. Plants lie dormant, patiently awaiting the warming earth to stimulate growth, and many mammals are conserving energy by hibernating in snug nests deep underground or in holes in walls or trees. Only the bird world is really active, with many species congregating in large noisy flocks. In the South-West keep a watch for winter migrants such as the short-eared owl and hen harrier, both of which can be seen on the moors; while open farmland is the habitat of snipe, lapwing and golden plover, all of which I regularly encounter on my winter walks.

Following winter snowfall much can be learnt about local wildlife from their tracks. The regular trails of resident badgers are criss-crossed by those of other travellers, from tiny shrews to foxes. Here we see where a fox has been sniffing around some rabbit diggings and we can follow the easily identified pheasant footprints with the tell-tale drag of its long tail.

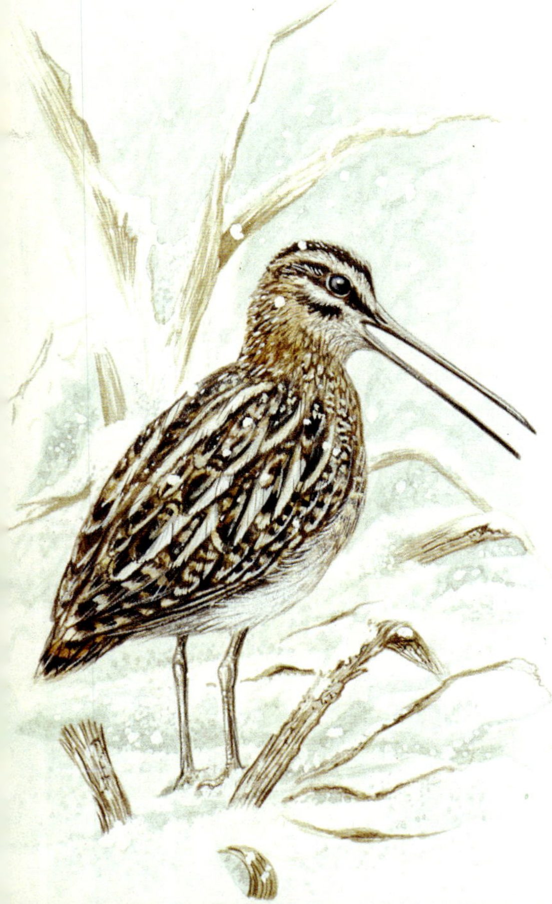

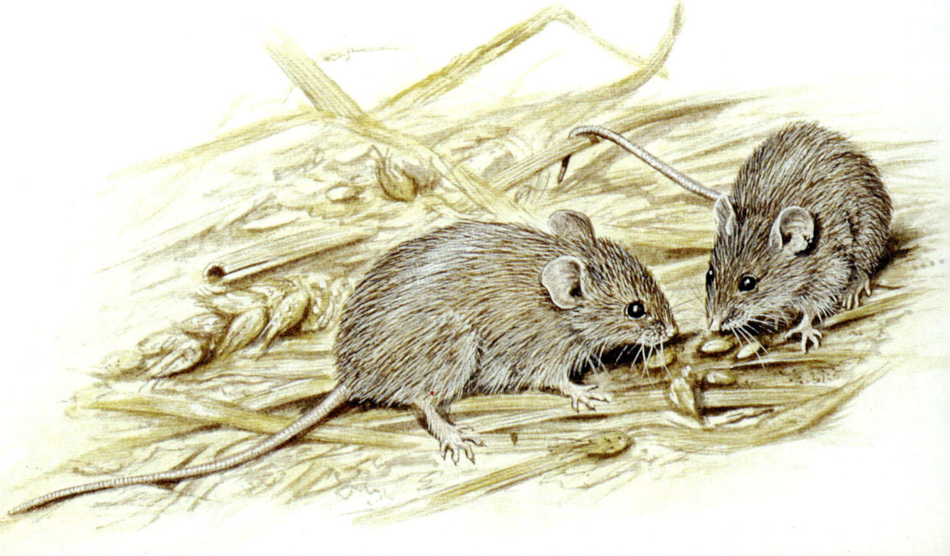

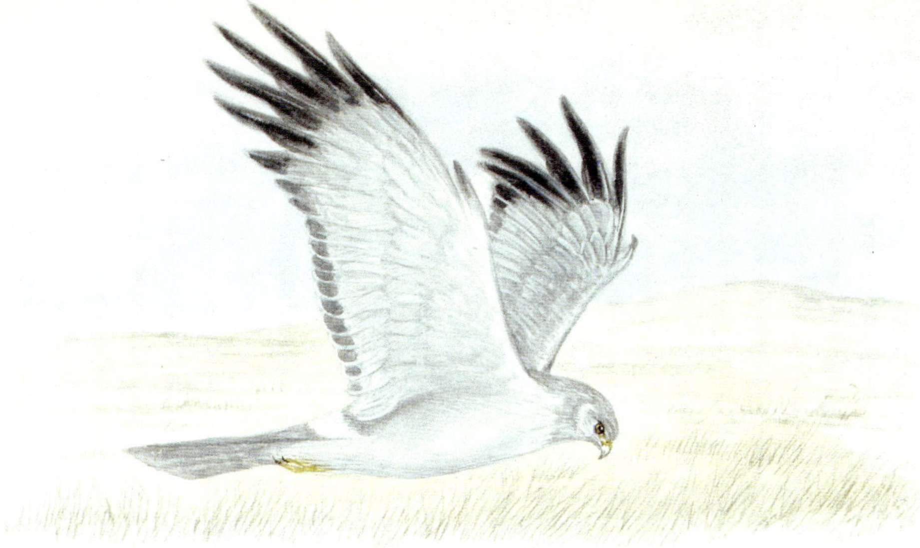

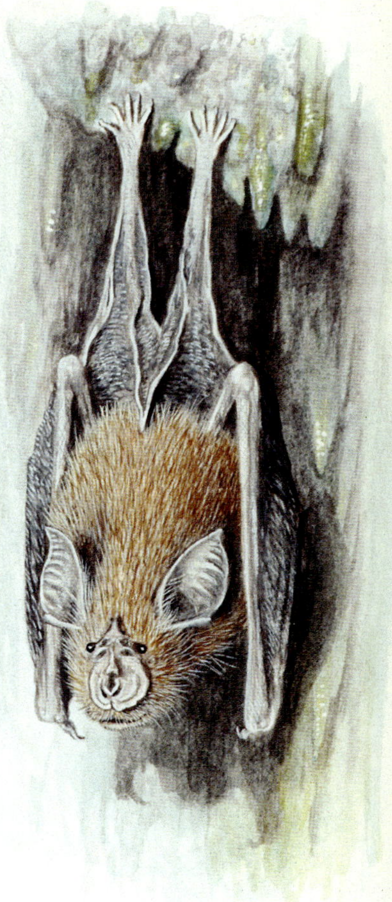

All reptiles and amphibians hibernate at some stage during the winter months. However, in the far west of the country there is often frog spawn in January, although this early spawn is sometimes rendered infertile by prolonged freezing conditions.

Some animals hibernate deeply, while others will venture forth should the winter sun encourage more appealing temperatures. Such intrepid creatures include the hedgehog and many species of bat, such as the greater horseshoe and pipistrelle who will often leave their winter roosts in caves, dead trees and attics for a brief evening flight. The house mouse takes full advantage of its association with man and, by living in our houses, sheds and barns, can remain active all winter.

Although the weather may be bleak there is still much beauty to be found in the countryside. Many bright fruits such as the berries of the evergreen holly add colour to a winter's hedge, while the dried seed heads of thistles and teazles form interesting shapes in the dull, grey monotone of a winter landscape.

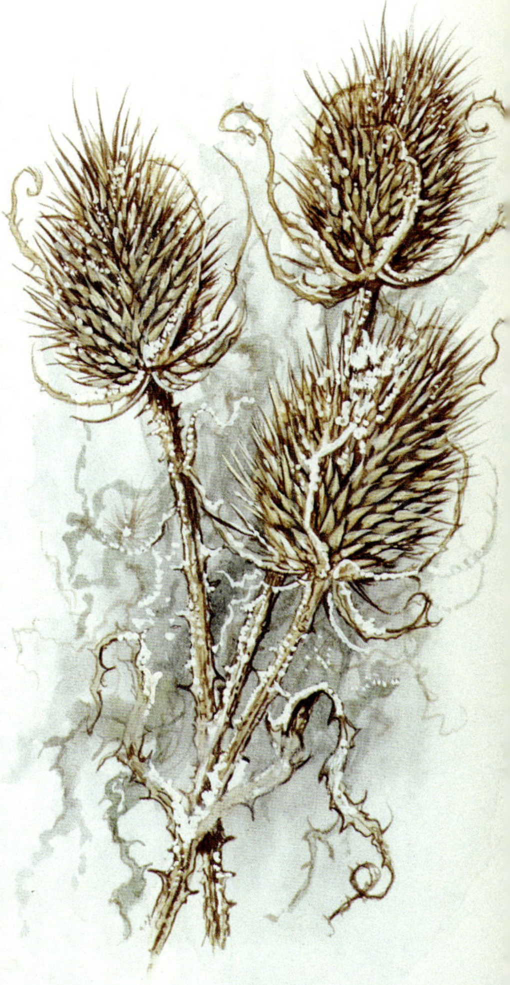

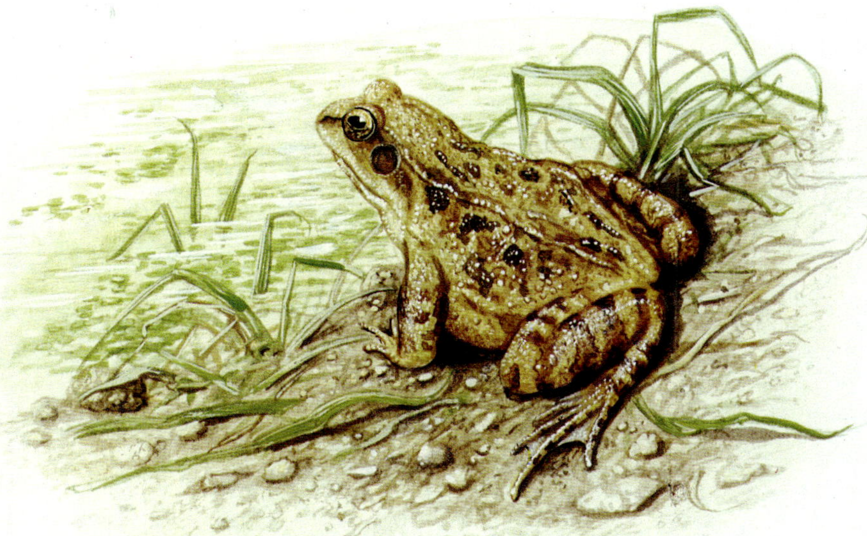

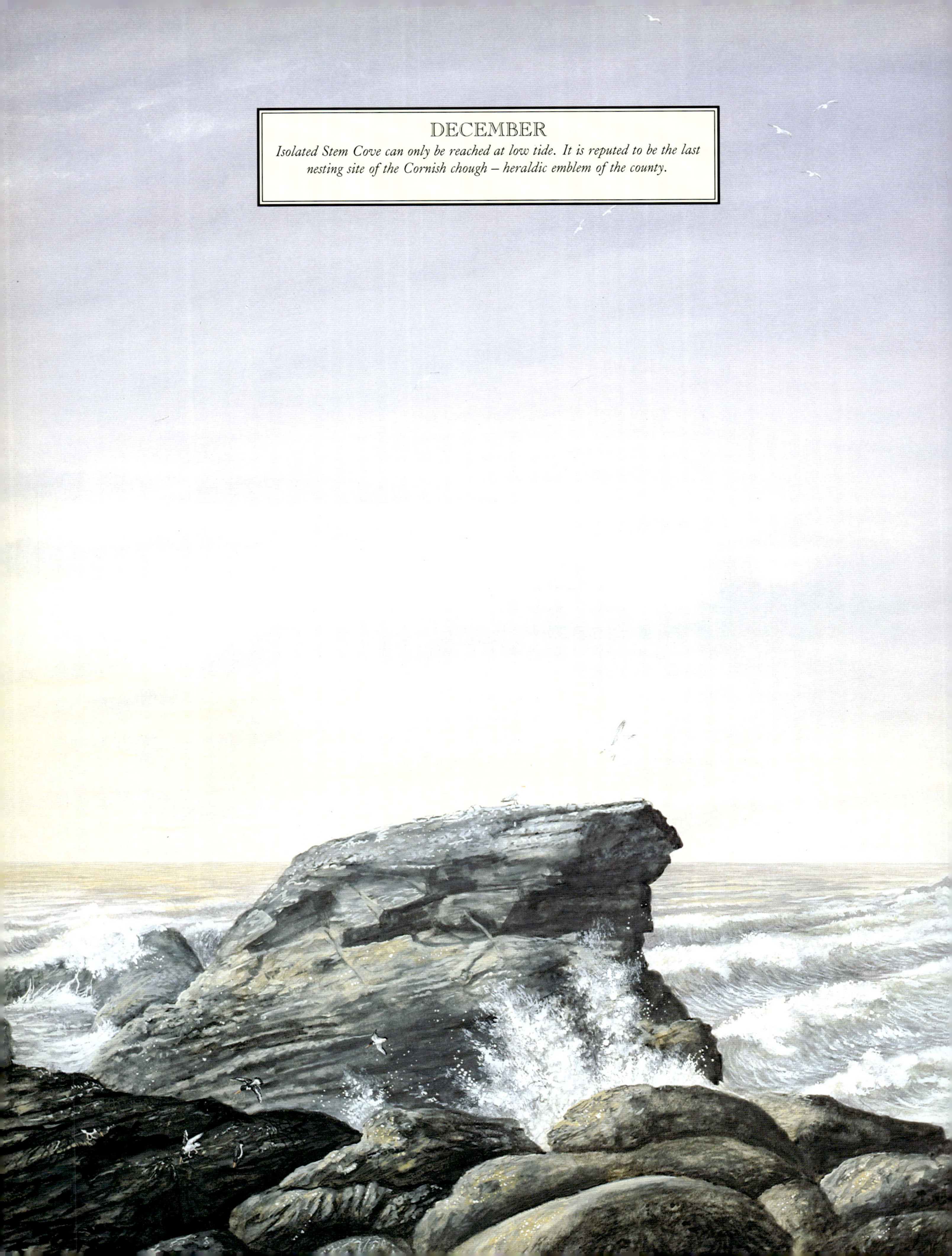

DECEMBER

Isolated Stem Cove can only be reached at low tide. It is reputed to be the last nesting site of the Cornish chough – heraldic emblem of the county.

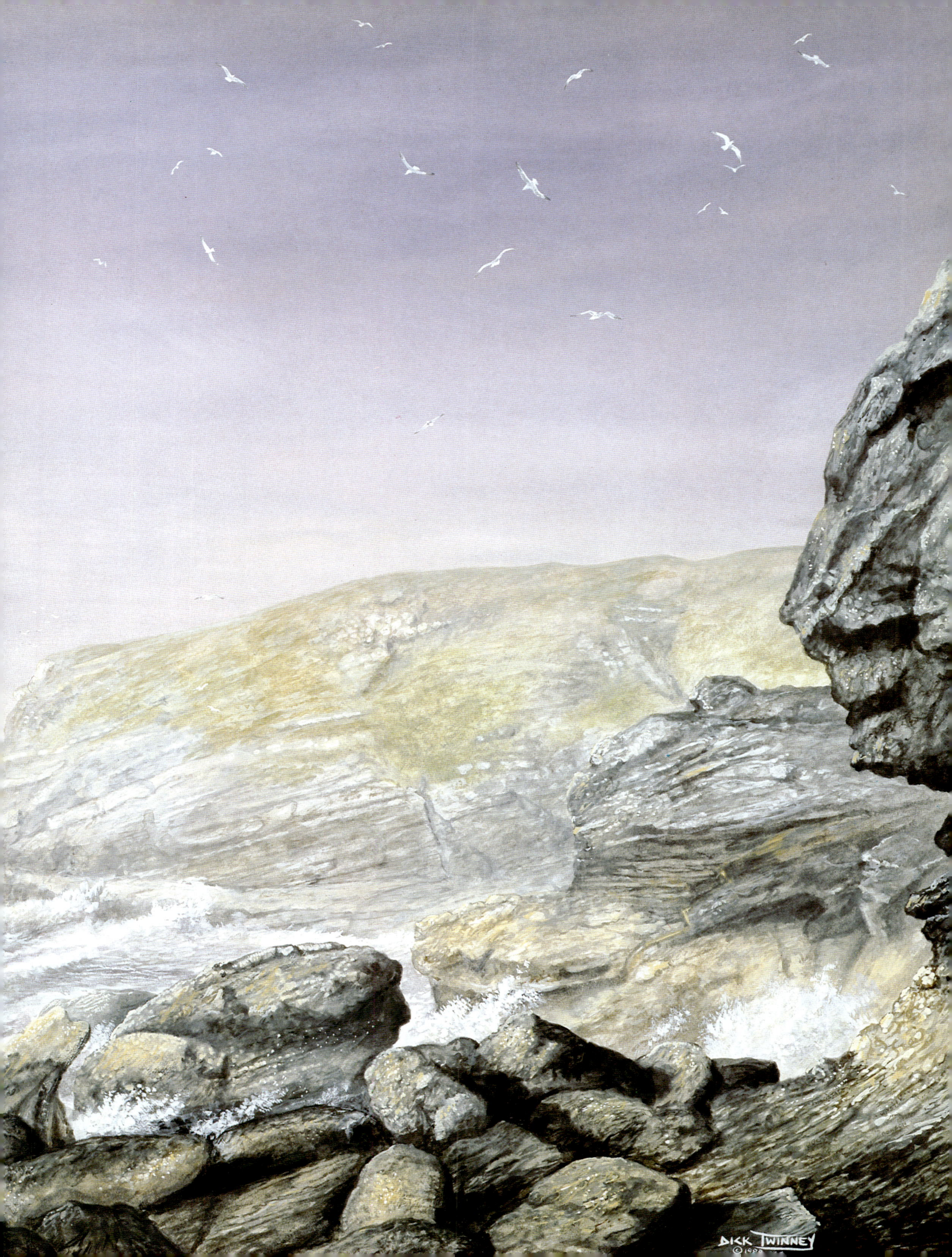
DICK TWINNEY

FIRST WEEK

BANK VOLES AND ROSE HIPS

One of the most important fruits of winter are rose hips, their vitamin-rich flesh sustaining a great variety of animals through the cold weather. One creature which makes good use of this valuable addition to nature's larder is the bank vole.

As its name implies, it is more often found in banks, hedges and woodlands, whereas the field vole prefers grassy areas. Bank voles have adapted to their chosen environment by developing quite considerable climbing skills and are frequently seen high in the hedgerows in pursuit of berries and seeds. In woodland areas they will eat acorns and hazelnuts and if this type of food is scarce they will also gnaw the bark of trees – something which makes the bank vole very unpopular with foresters.

In common with the field vole and other mouse-like mammals, the bank vole is heavily preyed upon, especially by predators which hunt in woodland such as the tawny owl, stoat and weasel. Bank voles combat this continuous depletion of their numbers by prolific breeding. There are usually four or five litters a year, each litter averaging four young. Occasionally if food is really plentiful, bank voles will continue breeding throughout the winter months, although it is unlikely that young voles born now would survive for long.

In this December picture I have included an interesting piece of elder. This particular tree grows into some amazing shapes in our hedgerows and always adds a new dimension to a painting. On my country walks I always take note of any bent and twisted fallen branches, odd logs and the like. Then, if I am stuck for inspiration, I know exactly what will fire my imagination.

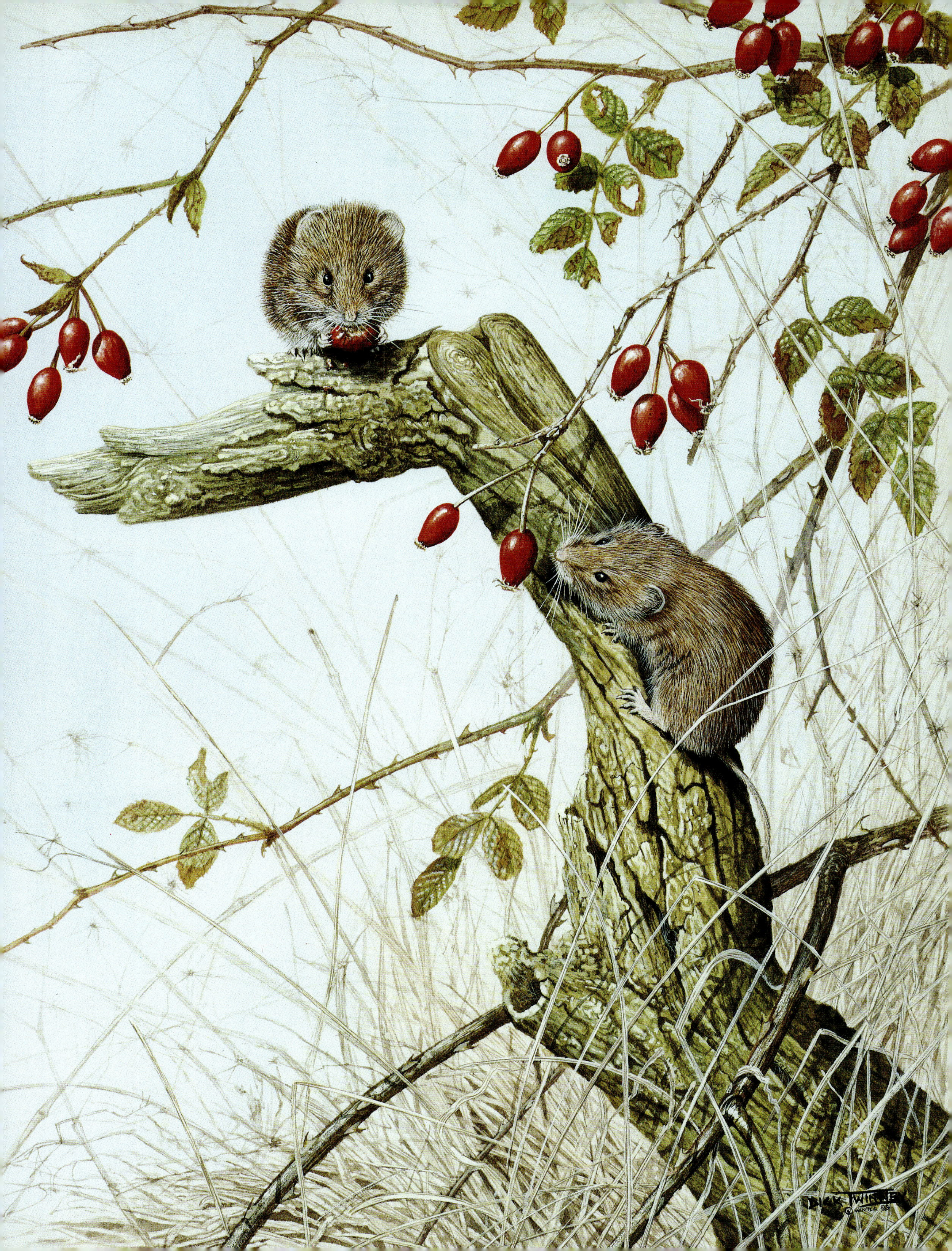

SECOND WEEK

GREY WAGTAIL

Wagtails are among the most attractive of British birds, particularly the beautiful grey wagtail. It is the most graceful and athletic of the species and a joy to watch when it is insect hunting among the roots and rocks of rivers and streams. Fast-moving rivers and streams are the grey wagtail's favourite habitat and, fortunately, most rivers are blessed with a regular pair of this water-loving bird.

The bird featured in the painting is a male, he is just losing the black bib he has sported all summer and soon his bright yellow breast will fade to buff, leaving only the rump a rich lemon yellow. The back remains grey throughout the seasons and is probably the best way to differentiate the grey wagtail from the summer visiting yellow wagtail whose plumage is characterized by a greenish yellow back and yellow underparts.

There has been a pair of grey wagtails on a small stream near my home for many years and I often come across them on my waterside walks. The area I have chosen for the painting is a slow-moving ditch which drains into the stream. I particularly like this area as it abounds with a multitude of mosses, lichens and rushes. It resembles a miniature Amazonian rain forest. The water-loving willow and alder trees are festooned with the moss-covered climbing stems of honeysuckle and ivy, all intertwining with fallen lichen-covered tree branches and exposed roots. A feast of material for the artist! Just the right tones of greenish yellow and grey in which to place the similarly coloured grey wagtail. I have brought the light in from low on the left and, diffused by the branches and creepers, it imparts to the painting a greenish glow.

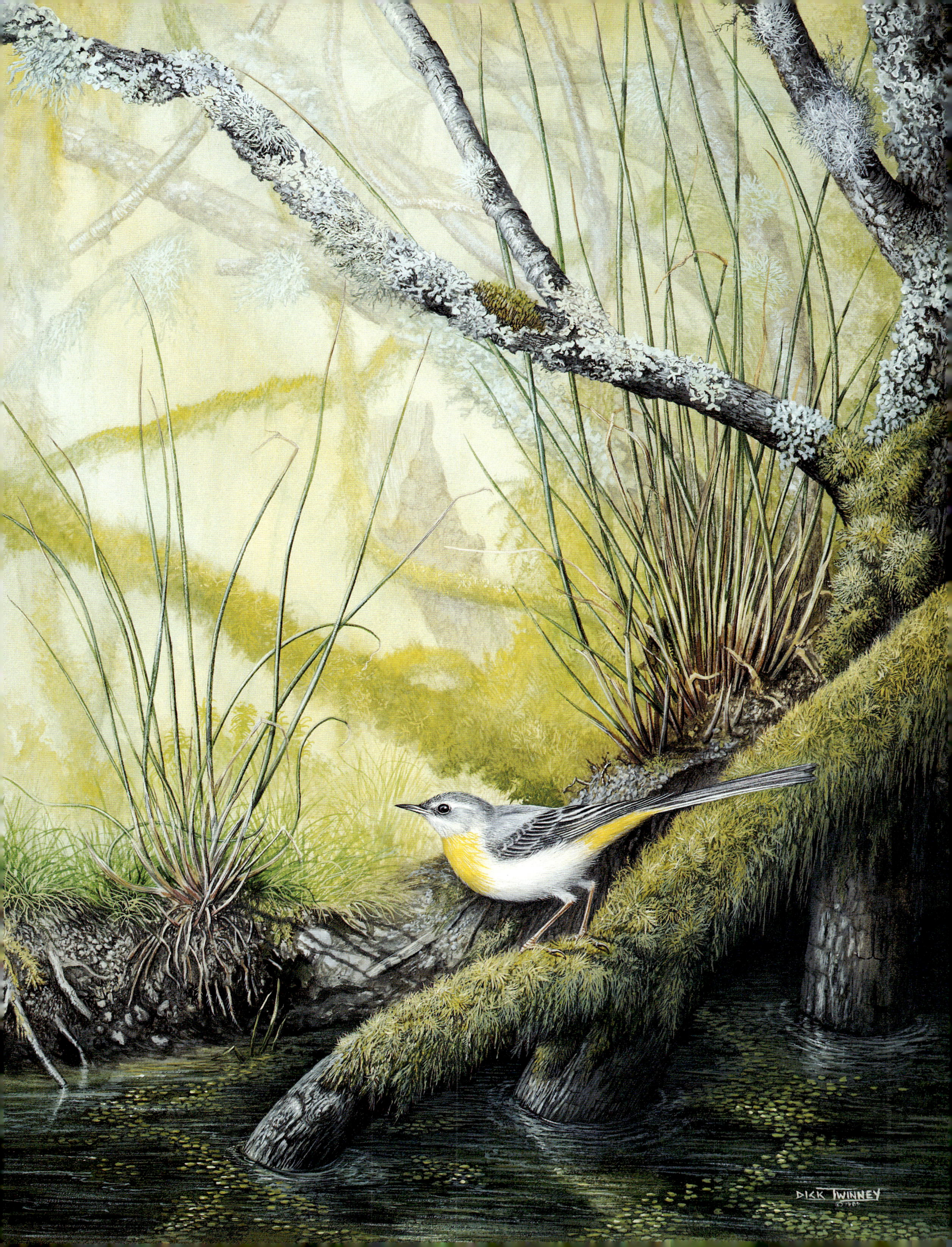
DICK TWINNEY

THIRD WEEK

STOAT

From the waterside greens of the previous painting we move to the more familiar colours of December which prevail in an overgrown hedge only a field away. Out of the hedge top grows a variety of deciduous trees whose fallen leaves provide a colourful carpet of russet, buff and brown, from which appear the rambling thorny stems of the blackberry.

I have twice spotted a stoat in this hedge. On one amusing occasion my attention was drawn to a slight movement in the hedge as I walked by. I glanced down and saw a small brown head with bright alert eyes looking at me from out of a little hole in the bank. At first I thought it was a vole, until I realized it was a larger animal: it was a stoat. I was very close to it, only about a metre away. I had all three dogs with me, although they were busy sniffing around further down the hedge. The stoat was obviously not very happy about my presence, perhaps the hole was a dead end and he felt trapped. He kept popping half out of the hole, watching me all the time, then shooting in backwards. He did this three or four times before plucking up the courage to leave and scurry away up the bank.

The stoat in the picture was painted from a dead specimen which unfortunately was a road casualty. Both this stoat and the weasel featured in the painting for the second week in May were painted to exact life size, showing clearly the size difference between the two mammals, which are often confused. Note also the distinctive black tip to the stoat's tail, a feature lacking in the weasel.

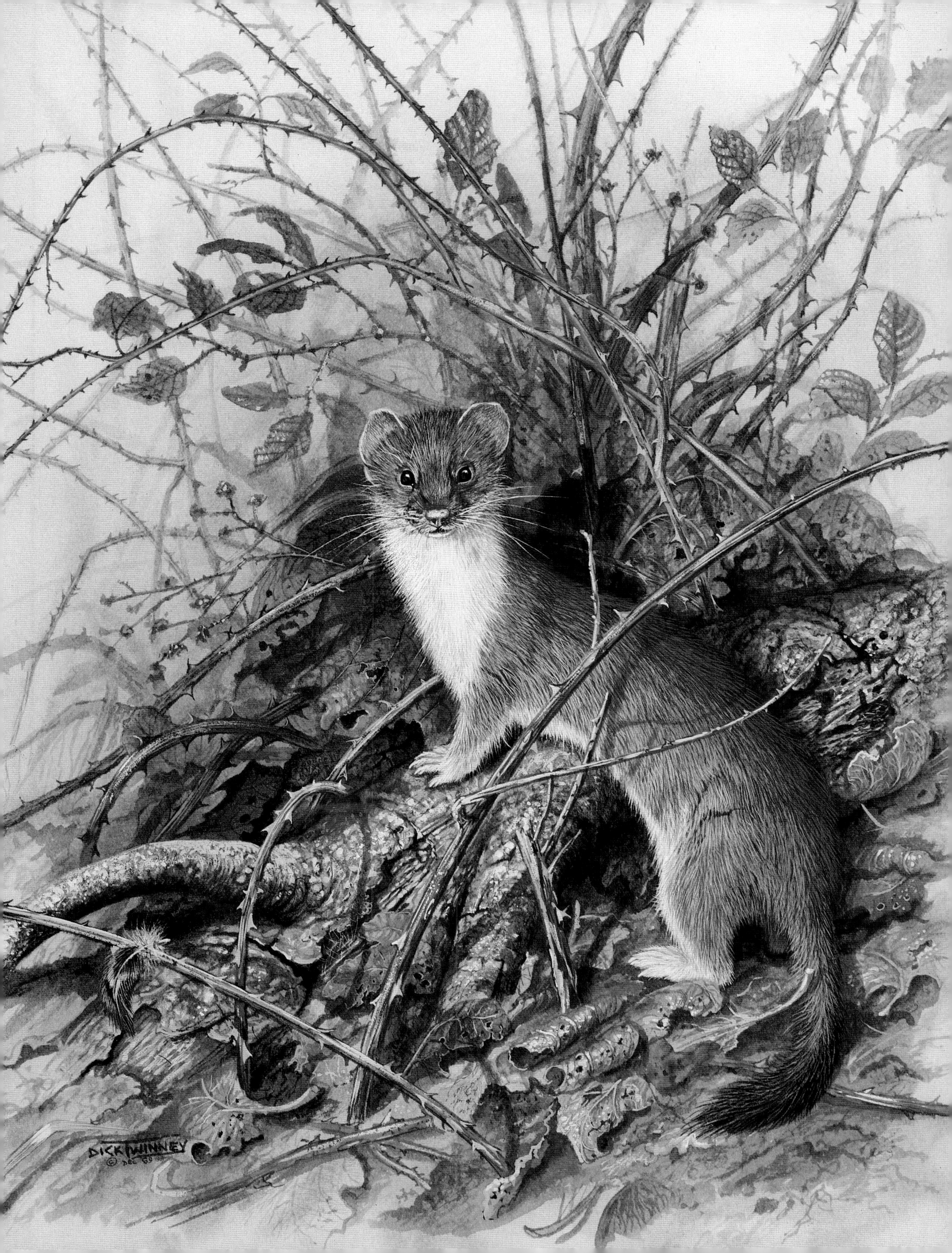
DICK TWINNEY
© DEC 89

FOURTH WEEK

ROBIN

There can be few gardens of any size which do not have their own resident robin. Our garden is no exception. I had always intended to finish the book with this friendly and popular garden visitor, as I could almost guarantee one would appear when needed.

Although it is Christmas week I wanted to avoid painting a typical robin/holly situation and this problem was easily solved. As everyone with a garden knows, start turning over soil and, as if by magic, the robin appears, usually totally unconcerned by your presence as he busily goes to work on the freshly exposed worms and grubs. So this is exactly what I did. Armed with spade and sketch-pad I chose a weedy grass-covered corner of the garden, turned over a few spadefulls and, before long, down he popped. Whether they see you or hear the sound of digging, if they are in the near vicinity they will always show up.

We had some new aviaries built which involved plenty of digging. This was much appreciated by 'our' robin, and as the work and summer progressed he became bolder and bolder. We had to be careful not to tread on him or accidentally strike him with the spade, so close did he come. This continual quest for food was very necessary to satisfy a nest full of young. In fact our robins successfully raised two broods during 1989.

It is particularly appropriate to close the book with a study of our national bird. The robin is a cherished resident of the garden. Its friendly disposition towards people and beautiful song ensure its special place in our hearts.

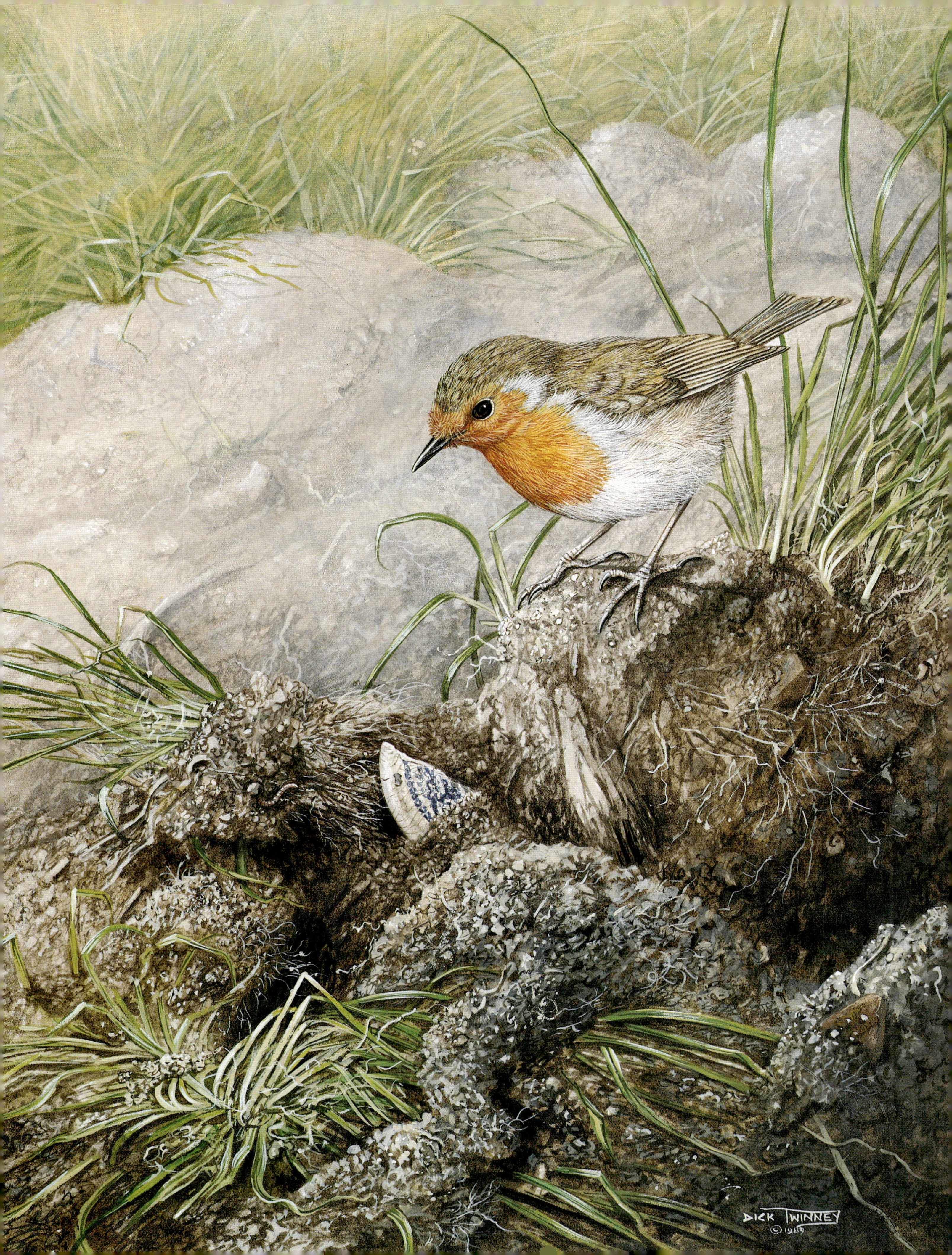
DICK TWINNEY
© 1989

ACKNOWLEDGEMENTS

I would like to thank the following people, without whom this book would not have been possible: Richard Webb and all at Webb & Bower for their interest, help and enthusiasm; Barrie Aughton for his superb photography; Alyson Gregory for her sympathetic editing. Vic Giolitto for his design work; Bernard Thornton, my agent and friend; all the farmers and landowners who allow me on their properties; all the people who have shown great interest and enthusiasm throughout this project; Ann, for just being there.
Lastly, many thanks to David Staff and Nicky Salter of Trevoyan for making this new reprint possible.

DICK TWINNEY
Wildlife and Countryside Artist

Dick Twinney has loved the Westcountry's wildlife and countryside for as long as he can remember. Originally from Devon, he has lived and worked in Cornwall for over 35 years.

Although his paintings, prints, collectors plates and giftware have spread worldwide and many of the books he has illustated are American, he still thinks of himself as a local artist, passionate about Cornwall, its scenery and its wildlife.

A real countryman, Dick always spends several hours each day in the 'field' walking with the family dogs over the moors, along the coast or in the local woods, observing wildlife in its natural habitat and seeking inspiration for his paintings.

He is always happy to discuss his work and will accept commissions for countryside subjects. Visitors are welcome to his home and studio by arrangement.

Phone: 01637 880606
E-mail: dicktwinney@btconnect.com
Web: www.dicktwinneyswildlifeart.co.uk

Printed in China